**THE SECRET OF THE KINGDOM SERIES** volume 3

# THE HIGHLIGHTS OF THE KINGDOM OF GOD

## IN THE OLD AND NEW TESTAMENTS

### The Main Bible Passages on the Kingdom

John Hatton

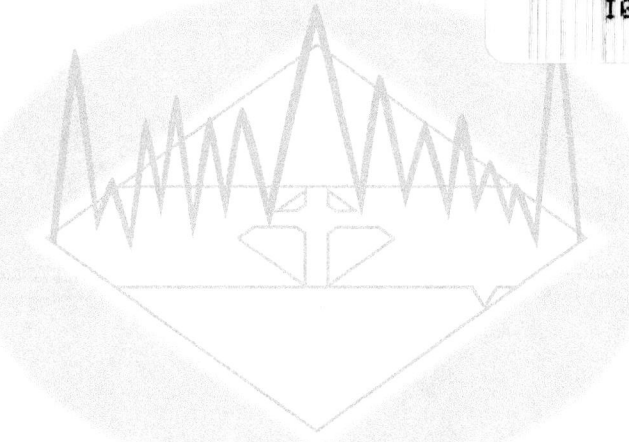

**A KINGDOM HANDBOOK**

*All he has made will give thanks to the LORD. Your loyal followers will praise you. They will proclaim the splendor of your kingdom; they will tell about your power, so that mankind might acknowledge your mighty acts, and the majestic splendor of your kingdom.*

Psalm 145:10-12 – NET Bible

Copyright © 2016 by John Hatton. All rights reserved.
Copyright Registration Number for text and artwork: TXu 2-005-989.

First published in March, 2020
ISBN 978-0-9994500-2-4

No part of this book may be reproduced or transmitted by any means without written permission of the author (jmhatton@pobox.com).

www.kingdomsecret.org

Cover, illustrations and book design by John Hatton.
Cover background adapted from NASA public domain photo.

# Bible versions used, abbreviations and copyright permissions

**AMP - Amplified** - Scripture quotations marked (AMP) are taken from the Amplified Bible, Copyright © 1954, 1958, 1962, 1964, 1965, 1987 by The Lockman Foundation. Used by permission.

**BLB - Berean Literal Bible** - The Holy Bible, Berean Literal Bible, BSB; Copyright ©2016 by Bible Hub; Used by Permission. All Rights Reserved Worldwide.

**BSB - Berean Study Bible** - The Holy Bible, Berean Study Bible, BSB; Copyright ©2016 by Bible Hub; Used by Permission. All Rights Reserved Worldwide.

**DBT - Darby Bible Translation** (the John Nelson Darby translation was first published in 1890. Public domain).

**DRV - Douay-Rheims Bible** (1582-16-10; Challoner Revision 1752. Public domain).

**ERV - English Revised Version** - A 1881-1894 British revision of the KJV of 1611. Public domain.

**ESV - English Standard Version** - Scripture quotations are from the ESV® Bible (The Holy Bible, English Standard Version®), copyright © 2001 by Crossway, a publishing ministry of Good News Publishers. Used by permission. All rights reserved.

**GW - GOD'S WORD® Translation** - Scripture is taken from GOD'S WORD®, © 1995 God's Word to the Nations. Used by permission of Baker Publishing Group.

**HCSB - Holman Christian Standard Bible** - Holman Christian Standard Bible®, Copyright © 1999, 2000, 2002, 2003, 2009 by Holman Bible Publishers. Reprinted and used by permission.

**ISV - International Standard Version** - Scripture taken from the Holy Bible: International Standard Version® Release 2.0. Copyright © 1996-2017 by the ISV Foundation. Used by permission of Davidson Press, LLC. ALL RIGHTS RESERVED INTERNATIONALLY.

**KJV - King James Bible** - Scripture taken from the New King James Version®. Copyright © 1982 by Thomas Nelson. Used by permission. All rights reserved.

**The Message** - Scripture quotations are taken from THE MESSAGE, copyright © 1993, 1994, 1995, 1996, 2000, 2001, 2002 by Eugene H. Peterson. Used by permission of NavPress. All rights reserved. Represented by Tyndale House Publishers, Inc.

**NASB - New American Standard Bible** - "Scripture taken from the NEW AMERICAN STANDARD BIBLE®, Copyright © 1960, 1962, 1963, 1968, 1971, 1972, 1973, 1975, 1977, 1995 by The Lockman Foundation. Used by permission."

**NCV - New Century Version** - Scripture taken from the New Century Version®. Copyright © 2005 by Thomas Nelson. Used by permission. All rights reserved.

**NET© - NET Bible®** - Scripture quoted by permission. Quotations designated (NET©) are from the NET Bible® copyright ©1996-2016 by Biblical Studies Press, L.L.C. http://netbible.com All rights reserved.
The names: THE NET BIBLE®, NEW ENGLISH TRANSLATION COPYRIGHT (c) 1996 BY BIBLICAL STUDIES PRESS, L.L.C. NET Bible® IS A REGISTERED TRADEMARK THE NET BIBLE® LOGO, SERVICE MARK COPYRIGHT (c) 1997 BY BIBLICAL STUDIES PRESS, L.L.C. ALL RIGHTS RESERVED

**NHEB - New Heart English Bible** - Public Domain.

**NIV - New International Version** - Scripture quotations marked (NIV) are taken from the Holy Bible, New International Version®, NIV®. Copyright © 1973, 1978, 1984, 2011 by Biblica, Inc.™ Used by permission of Zondervan. All rights reserved worldwide. www.zondervan.com The "NIV" and "New International Version" are trademarks registered in the United States Patent and Trademark Office by Biblica, Inc.™

**NKJV - New King James Version** - Scripture taken from the New King James Version®. Copyright © 1982 by Thomas Nelson, Inc. Used by permission. All rights reserved.

**NLT - New Living Translation** - Scripture quotations are taken from the Holy Bible, New Living Translation, copyright ©1996, 2004, 2007, 2013, 2015 by Tyndale House Foundation. Used by permission of Tyndale House Publishers, Inc., Carol Stream, Illinois 60188. All rights reserved.

**TLB - Living Bible** - Scripture quotations marked (TLB) are taken from The Living Bible copyright © 1971. Used by permission of Tyndale House Publishers, Inc., Carol Stream, Illinois 60188. All rights reserved.

**WEB - World English Bible** - Public domain.

**WNT - Weymouth New Testament** - From 1903. Public domain.

**YLT - Young's Literal Translation** - Public domain.

Note: Scripture references with words which appear in bold, italic or bold italic were highlighted by the author to help readers quickly identify the main terms being considered. Since this is a modern technique and obviously not part of the Biblical manuscript, there is no need to mention this fact next to each case, as is the custom of most publishers.

*To Lidia Dell, Bill and Sarah Janell*

Growing up with my sisters and brother was God's way of teaching me a bunch of life lessons. We had fun growing up together on the mission field in Rio de Janeiro, Brazil. Though we have grown geographically apart, we stay in touch and I still love each one of them.

**Lidia, Bill, Sarah, this book is dedicated to you.**

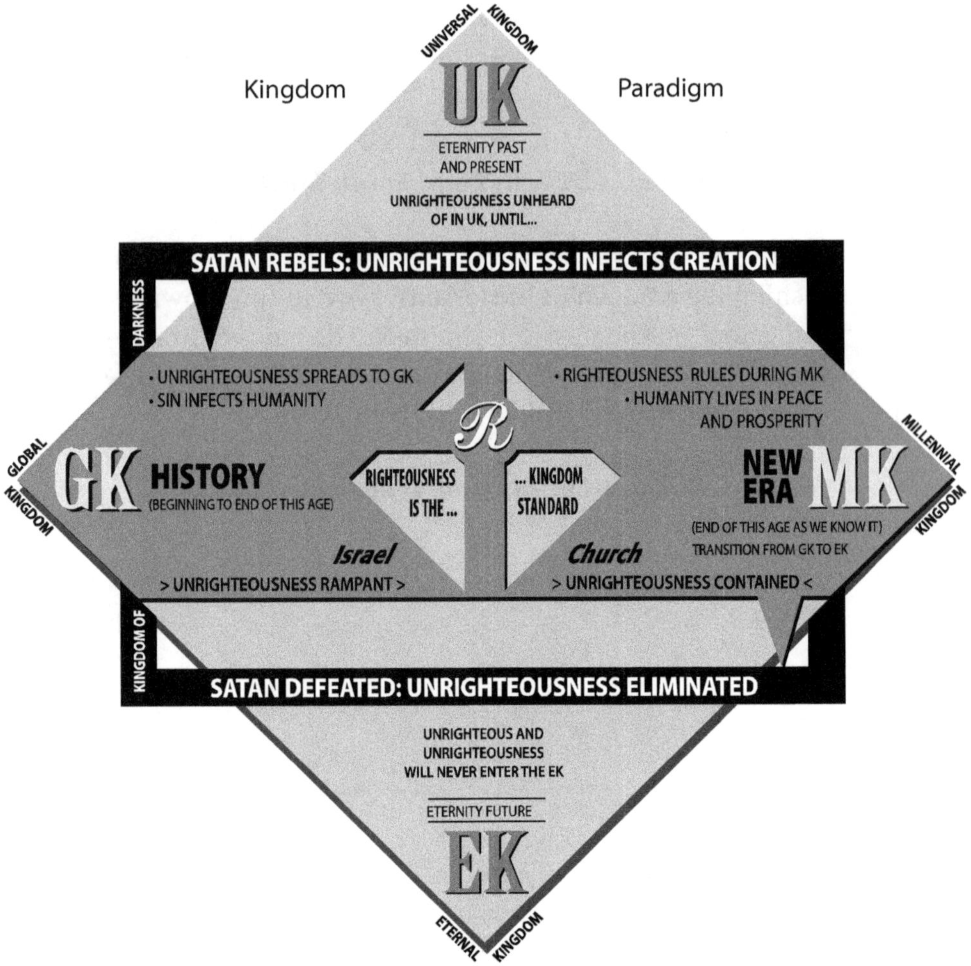
Kingdom
Paradigm
UNIVERSAL KINGDOM
UK
ETERNITY PAST AND PRESENT
UNRIGHTEOUSNESS UNHEARD OF IN UK, UNTIL...
SATAN REBELS: UNRIGHTEOUSNESS INFECTS CREATION
DARKNESS
KINGDOM OF
• UNRIGHTEOUSNESS SPREADS TO GK
• SIN INFECTS HUMANITY
• RIGHTEOUSNESS RULES DURING MK
• HUMANITY LIVES IN PEACE AND PROSPERITY
GLOBAL KINGDOM
GK
HISTORY
(BEGINNING TO END OF THIS AGE)
RIGHTEOUSNESS IS THE ...
... KINGDOM STANDARD
NEW ERA
MK
MILLENNIAL KINGDOM
(END OF THIS AGE AS WE KNOW IT)
TRANSITION FROM GK TO EK
Israel
Church
> UNRIGHTEOUSNESS RAMPANT >
> UNRIGHTEOUSNESS CONTAINED <
SATAN DEFEATED: UNRIGHTEOUSNESS ELIMINATED
UNRIGHTEOUS AND UNRIGHTEOUSNESS WILL NEVER ENTER THE EK
ETERNITY FUTURE
EK
ETERNAL KINGDOM

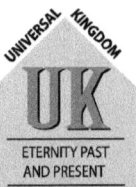

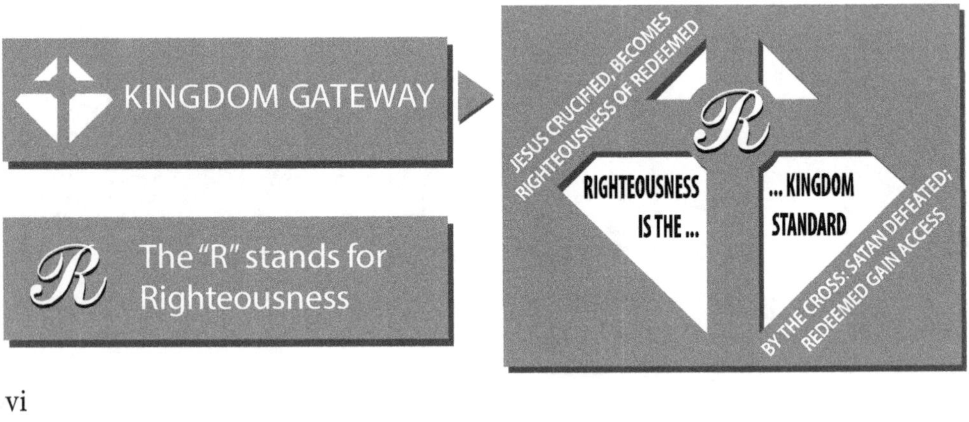
KINGDOM GATEWAY
The "R" stands for Righteousness
JESUS CRUCIFIED, BECOMES RIGHTEOUSNESS OF REDEEMED
RIGHTEOUSNESS IS THE ...
... KINGDOM STANDARD
BY THE CROSS: SATAN DEFEATED; REDEEMED GAIN ACCESS

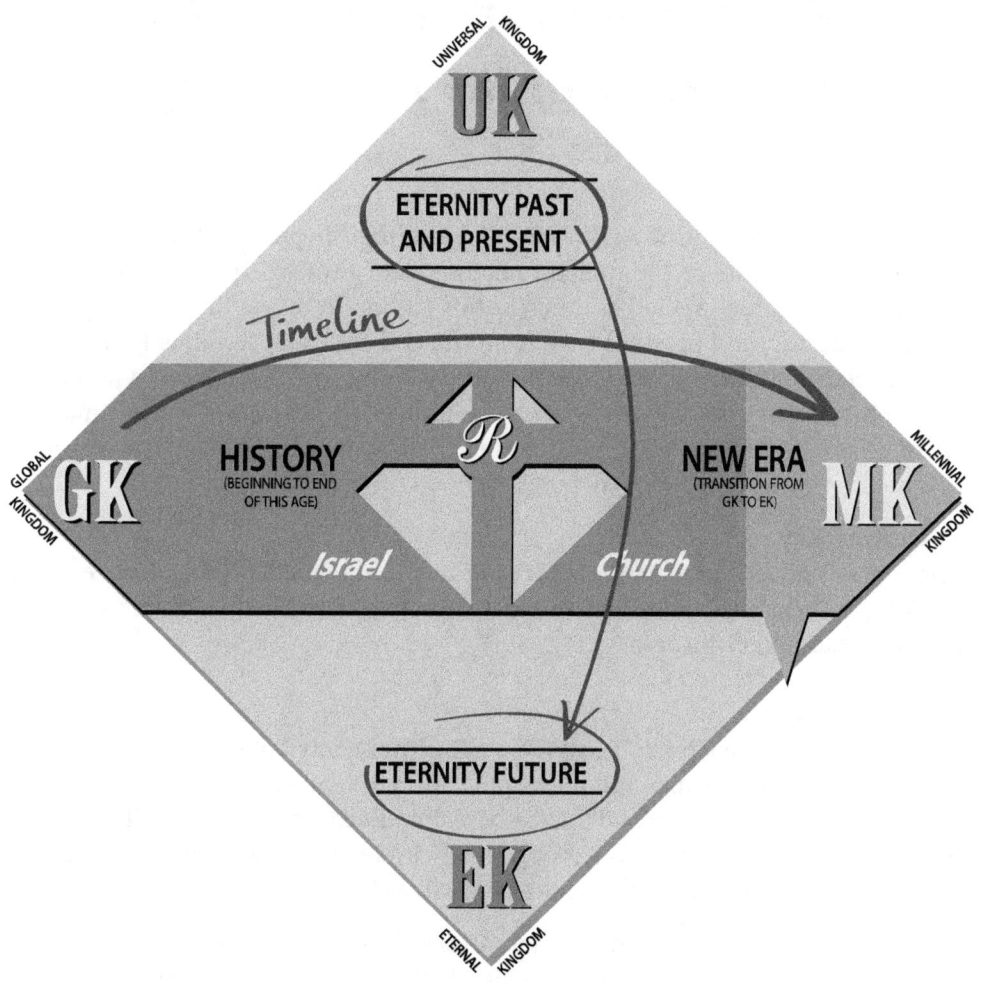

- **UK** to **EK** = **U**niversal **K**ingdom (eternity past to present) to **E**ternal **K**ingdom (present to eternity future).

- **GK** to **MK** = **G**lobal **K**ingdom to **M**illennial **K**ingdom timeline ("the beginning" to "the end of the age" and Millennium).

- **R** = **R**ighteousness as the core value of the Kingdom, gained for believers by **Jesus**, Who is the gateway to the Kingdom.

# What others are saying about *The Highlights of the Kingdom of God*

I highly recommend the book *The Highlights of the Kingdom of God* from author John Hatton as trustworthy and truthful. There are few Christians that have studied the Kingdom of God as much as this author. In this writing, he helps us understand scriptural passages both from the Old and New Testaments and the proper interpretations of these related to the Kingdom of God. This is a handbook of scriptural verses that I find to be very helpful in my own spiritual pilgrimage. All of us as Christians need to be more involved in the Kingdom enterprises, and this book will help us toward that end.

— **Dr. Guy Key**
Missionary with the International Mission Board of the SBC in Brazil since 1984, working in the area of church planting and mission mobilization. Studied in Arkansas, Texas and California.


The author of this fine book has made a significant contribution to evangelicals by exploring kingdom themes and their application to God's children and His world, both for the here-and-now and for the hereafter. Reading this book will raise fervor within your heart to pray (and actually understand the prayer) "Let your kingdom come and your will be done on earth as it is in heaven."

— **David Bledsoe, D.Min, Th.D**, International Mission Board missionary to Brazil in the area of training, and the Brazil-side Coordinator of the Master of Theological Studies (MTS) program for the Southeastern Baptist Theological Seminary (SEBTS). Author of articles and books in the area of missions.


John's writing is very clear, concise, understandable, and non-academic. John does an excellent job of supporting all his points with scripture and citing major authorities on the various topics he covers in his book. John also includes diagrams and charts that help to summarize and visualize his powerful content.

— **Dr. Dean R. Spitzer**
Award-winning author, management consultant, and Bible teacher

This is a very organized and extensive presentation. It also serves as a base or worldview concerning the things of God and His Kingdom. Should be required reading in seminaries, for pastors and other Christians. It does help make sense of the Kingdom.

— **Nancy Callis**, Emeritus International Mission Board missionary to Brazil. Nancy and her husband Danny served in Brazil from 1978 to 2015, with evangelism, church planting, teaching and discipleship.

John has provided a great service to followers of Jesus with this book. Some books are a quick scan, but you'll want to consider this a study course that is highly memorable. I personally have appreciated the definitions, organizational approach (with awesome graphic depiction), analogies using Scripture, and personal touches throughout.

— **Mark Snowden**, Director of Missional Leadership (DOM), Cincinnati Area Baptist Association, Cincinnati, Ohio. Owner of Snowden Ministries International, http://truthsticks.us.

I think this book will have a tremendous impact on all who embrace it and invest themselves in exploring the depth and breadth of its content. My hat is off to you, my friend. Thank you for sharing this with me.

— **Dr. David Garrison**, Executive Director of the Global Gates mission agency. Author of *Church Planting Movements* and *A Wind in the House of Islam: How God is Drawing Muslims to Faith in Jesus Christ Around the World*.

I have known author John Hatton for most of his life. I have followed his spiritual growth and am impressed with his practical writings on the Kingdom of God. The Bible is a map for our lives as we all prepare for eternity. Many Christians are confused about the subject of the Kingdom of God. Hatton writes a clear explanation of this subject.

— **Jerry Stanley Key, Ph.D.**
Former Professor at *Seminário Teológico Batista do Sul do Brasil* in Rio de Janeiro, Brazil, and at Southwestern Baptist Theological Seminary in Fort Worth, Texas. International Mission Board (IMB) Missionary to Brazil (1959-1997).

# Highlights

## As seen from the cover graphic

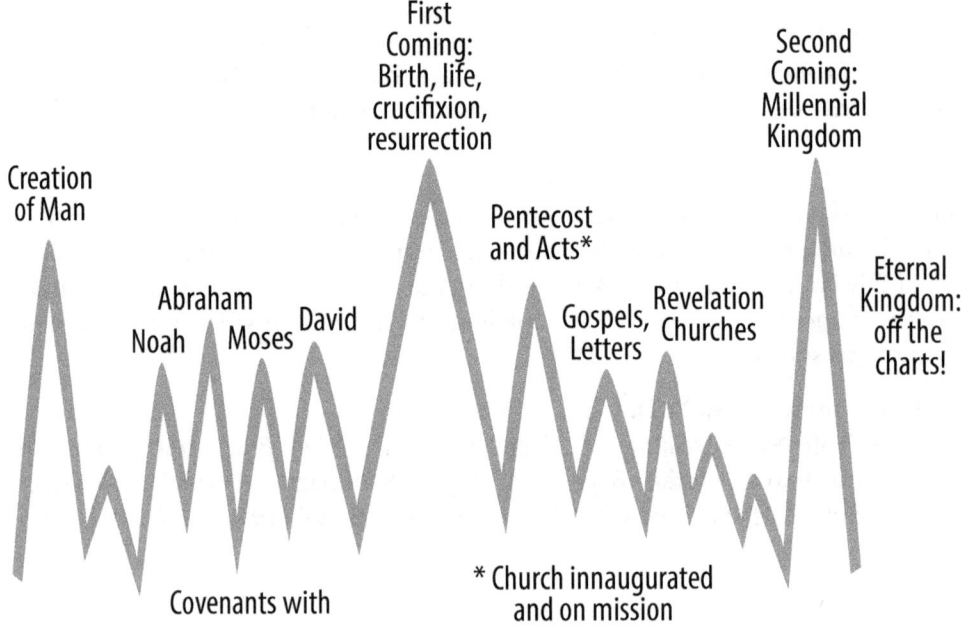

# Contents

## *The Highlights of the Kingdom of God*
### In the Old and New Testaments

- - Preface .................................................................................................. 3
- - Acknowledgments ............................................................................. 5
- - Introduction ...................................................................................... 7
- - Old Testament Books – Chart ......................................................... 8
- - New Testament Books – Chart ........................................................ 9

## FIRST DIVISION – Old Testament Kingdom Highlights

1 - Books of the Pentateuch ................................................................ 13
2 - Books of History ............................................................................. 31
3 - Books of Wisdom ........................................................................... 45
4 - Major Prophets ............................................................................... 67
5 - Minor Prophets ............................................................................... 99

## SECOND DIVISION – New Testament Kingdom Highlights

6 - Matthew: The Gospel of the Kingdom ....................................... 121
7 - The Gospels of Mark, Luke and John ......................................... 163
8 - History: Acts of the Apostles ....................................................... 197
9 - The Letters of Paul ........................................................................ 209
10 - The General Letters .................................................................... 235
11 - The Revelation of Jesus Christ .................................................. 247

*The Highlights of the Kingdom of God*

# Preface

## The Story of the Kingdom of God

I was so convinced the Kingdom was the central, unifying theme of the Bible that I made a wrap-around cover for my Bible with the above title and used it for over a year. When anyone at church asked about it, I shared my conviction that the whole Bible is all about the Kingdom.

I don't have that cover anymore, but I still believe the Kingdom is far from a mere backdrop in the history of the universe. It is the driving force and final purpose of God's activity, as described in the Old and New Testaments. He created humans to reign on Earth. When they fell, He sought and saved them, so they could enter and inherit His Kingdom. He promises to bring them eternal life so they could love, serve, worship and reign with Him forever.

Because the Bible is all about the Kingdom, it would not be practical or possible for a book like this to comment on every story, teaching or event in Scripture that somehow relates to God's Kingdom. Instead, the goal of this volume is to look at the direct references to: God the Father and God the Son as King; the Kingdom of God (or of Heaven, or of our Lord); and passages which speak of reigning or ruling—either by the Lord or by His servants—in the context of His Kingdom.

I hope this book will captivate and inspire you as you contemplate the wonderful reality of all God has prepared for those who love Him. Examine His **Kingdom Secrets** (there are close to 50 mentioned in this volume). Ponder His **Kingdom Principles** (close to 100 in these pages). Be motivated to go deeper as you study the main Bible passages on the Kingdom. Hang on to this book and refer back to it as a reference guide, a "Kingdom Handbook," to help you quickly find Bible passages that relate to the Kingdom. Then, share with others what you have learned.

If you will do so, then you will be part of the special group of people King David spoke of when he said: "They will speak of the glory of Your kingdom and will declare Your might, informing all people of Your mighty acts and of the glorious splendor of Your kingdom" (Psalm 145:11-12 - HCSB).

# Acknowledgments

## I am grateful ...

### To those who brought the Bible to us.
The Holy Land Experience, in Orlando, Florida, houses the largest private collection of historical Bibles in the world. The history of how we got the Bible unfolds at the Scriptorium museum, as tourists walk through "13 historical scenes beginning at Babylon's Ishtar Gate, circa 3,000 B.C., moving through third century Egypt's Library of Alexandria, to John Wycliffe's translations of the Old and New Testaments in the 1400s, and ending with biblical profiles that include Moses, David, Peter and Paul."[1]

What makes the tour so significant are the authentic and original items, such as "a section of Gutenberg's Bible from 1455" and "three William Tyndale Bibles, circa 1530,"[2] as well as other rare artifacts and copies of the Bible, having survived for hundreds of years. "The entire museum is a testament to, and a celebration of, those who struggled and died in the relentless battle to make the Bible available,"[3] epitomized by the blood-stained pages of a martyr's Bible.

Walking through the Scriptorium reminded me just how blessed we are today because several heroes of the faith offered their time, tears and blood in order to translate, copy, print, preserve, distribute and teach the Holy Scriptures to their generation.

Today, printed, electronic, and online Bibles are readily available and easily accessible. ***The Highlights of the Kingdom of God*** has made use of many versions of the English Bible, taken mainly from biblehub.com and biblegateway.com. This has made writing this book—and series—easier and more accurate, as copying and pasting is more reliable than trying to input verses manually. I am truly thankful for the service ministries such as these provide.

### To those who brought the Bible to me.
More specifically, my parents—William Alvin Hatton and Lydia Catherine Jordan Hatton—and my pastors: My father; James T. Draper, Sr.; Jerry Key; Robert Doyle; Bill Billingsley; José Maria de Souza; and Daniel Paixão.

# Introduction

## A Kingdom Handbook

This book is meant to be a reference guide, a handbook where you can quickly find the main Kingdom passages wherever they are found in the Bible. Each passage receives a quick commentary where I point out its importance and explain its meaning. The interested Bible student should then embark on his or her own journey to further understand and apply the truths presented in each passage.

"The best commentary on the Bible is the Bible." Because this is true, the more passages we can examine on a particular subject, the better. You know the rule: "don't base major doctrines on just one verse of the Bible." Check, cross-reference, compare and contrast. You will find the Bible to be extremely consistent, even though it was written by at least 40 authors during a time span of some 1,600 years.[1] The same holds true for the study on the Kingdom of God: the more we examine what different passages of Scripture have to say about it, the better we will grasp the concepts, aspects, principles, values and truths concerning God's rule through His Kingdom. *That* is the purpose of this book.

In this volume the length of each chapter varies according to the amount of direct and indirect references to the Kingdom of God in the books being covered. The more attention given to the Kingdom in the covered Bible passages, the longer the chapter in this volume will be. Psalms has 150 chapters and has much to say about the Kingdom, which is reflected in the "Books of Wisdom" chapter. Because Daniel is proportionally the most Kingdom-focused book in the Old Testament, it receives much attention as well. Matthew is known as "the Gospel of the Kingdom," and for this reason receives far more attention than all the other Gospels.

As you look at the bookshelves illustrated on the next two pages, you will notice a few books are missing. That's because those books do not have a more direct reference to the Kingdom of God or to God's kingship. For a quick reference to the books of the Bible covered in this volume, just glance back at those bookshelves.

I hope you will be inspired by God's holiness and righteousness, encouraged to never give up, and moved to action: serving God and others and producing much fruit for the Kingdom.

*The Highlights of the Kingdom of God*

# 1st Division: OLD TESTAMENT

## BOOKS OF THE PENTATEUCH

GENESIS | EXODUS | LEVITICUS | NUMBERS | DEUTERONOMY

## BOOKS OF HISTORY

JOSHUA | 1 SAMUEL | 2 SAMUEL | 1 KINGS | 1 CHRONICLES | 2 CHRONICLES | EZRA | NEHEMIAH

## BOOKS OF WISDOM

JOB | PSALMS | PROVERBS | ECLESIASTES

## MAJOR PROPHETS

ISAIAH | JEREMIAH | LAMENTATIONS | EZEKIEL | DANIEL

## MINOR PROPHETS

HOSEA | JOEL | AMOS | OBADIAH | MICAH | NAHUM | HABAKKUK | ZEPHANIAH | HAGGAI | ZECHARIAH | MALACHI

# 2nd Division: NEW TESTAMENT

## MATTHEW – KINGDOM GOSPEL

MATTHEW

## THE GOSPELS OF MARK, LUKE, JOHN

MARK | LUKE | JOHN

## HISTORY: ACTS OF THE APOSTLES

ACTS

## THE LETTERS OF PAUL

ROMANS | 1 CORINTHIANS | 2 CORINTHIANS | GALATIANS | EPHESIANS | PHILIPPIANS | COLOSSIANS | 1 THESSALONIANS | 2 THESSALONIANS | 1 TIMOTHY | 2 TIMOTHY

## THE GENERAL LETTERS

HEBREWS | JAMES | 1 PETER | 2 PETER | 1 JOHN | JUDE

## THE REVELATION OF JESUS CHRIST

REVELATION

# A Word of Explanation

## Identifying the Kingdom aspect in each Bible chapter

Beside each Bible chapter being considered you will find one or more of the following groups of letters: [L&K] [KiG] [UK] [GK] [MK] [EK]

This is what they stand for:

L&K = Lord and/or King
KiG = Kingdom in General
UK = Universal Kingdom
GK = Global Kingdom
MK = Millennial Kingdom
EK = Eternal Kingdom

The idea is to help you readily identify which aspects of the Kingdom are being discussed in the passages under investigation. (If you are unfamiliar with the concept of the Biblical Kingdom aspects, it would be helpful to read *The Secret of the Kingdom of God*, volume 1 in this series). When the Kingdom is referenced generically, without the mention of characteristics which belong to one or more of the four Kingdom aspects, then **KiG** is used. If the emphasis is on God or Jesus as King, sovereign, or Lord, and the focus is on His power, worthiness or majesty, then the letters **L&K** are used.

Identifying the main Kingdom aspects in each passage is not an exact science. There are subtleties and statements which have implications for the here and now (the Global Kingdom) *and* the hereafter (the Universal Kingdom, the Eternal Kingdom, or both). Or, passages which speak of our present circumstances yet also mention eternal consequences. In general, references to heaven and hell will fall under the Universal Kingdom, unless they have the future eternal state (Eternal Kingdom) in view. I identify the Rapture and the Second Coming (when the Millennial Kingdom is not mentioned) as belonging to the Global Kingdom (GK) aspect, since it will take place on Earth and in this present age.

The main reason for identifying the aspects is to help you in your own reading—in case you wish to concentrate on a particular aspect—or to aid in the preparation of Bible studies on the Kingdom which may be organized and presented one aspect at a time.

# *FIRST DIVISION*

# Old Testament Kingdom Highlights

# *Chapter* 1
# Books of the Pentateuch

**The Old Testament and the Kingdom**
The Kingdom is the overarching theme of the Bible, bringing both testaments together and creating the continuity seen from Genesis to Revelation.

Although the term "Kingdom of God" never appears in the Old Testament, the concept is not only present, it's center stage. Many times it's simply referred to as "the kingdom," and the term "kingdom of the Lord" is used in at least two different verses (1 Chronicles 28:5 and 2 Chronicles 13:8). God is referred to as "our King" (Psalm 47:6) and as "a great King above all gods" (Psalm 95:3 - BSB). Jerusalem, or "Mount Zion," is said to be "the city of the Great King" (Psalm 48:2).

# The Kingdom in Genesis

### [GK] Genesis 1 - The first reference to ruling

As early as Genesis chapter one we are told humans were created to rule. God made man and woman in His image, according to His likeness, with the stated purpose of ruling "all the earth," which specifically includes the fish, birds, livestock, the creatures that crawl, all the wildlife and every green plant. Although God created wonderful and powerful objects and beings, none were said to have been created in His image, except humans. In fact, the whole process of creation shown in Genesis 1 shows that Earth was being prepared for the arrival of the first humans, and that its purpose was to sustain human life, a fact attested to by science.

How could man (male and female) rule over the whole earth? Humans would have to multiply themselves, spread out and establish their authority. In order to do so, they would need God's help. That's why we are told "God **blessed** them, and God said to them, 'Be fruitful, multiply, fill the earth, and subdue it'" (Genesis 1:26-31 - HCSB).

While God is the ultimate ruler over all creation and all authority comes from Him (Romans 13:1), He chose to delegate authority to humans and have them rule over the Earth. While we usually emphasize the fact that humans were made to glorify God, we normally do not state that humans were made to rule. Yet those two things go together, because anything that fulfills its created purpose and design glorifies God, and one of the main ways we glorify Him is by reigning over this planet. Reigning means exerting authority and power. In God's Kingdom that is done by committed management and service. By taking care of each other, nature and being and industrious. Because of the fall, our control over nature was drastically reduced (Genesis 3:17-19), but in the Messianic Age full control will be restored (Romans 8:19-22).

God the Father and God the Son created everything in the beginning and the Holy Spirit worked with creation—especially human beings—in order to develop and perfect the divine creative work.[1] Although God is the "architect and builder" of the heavenly city (Hebrews 11:10), He chose not to directly build anything on Earth. He gave us the planet and its resources—a complete ecosystem—and endowed us with the insight and ability to survive and thrive, overcoming obstacles, establishing societies, creating culture, and advancing in knowledge. All of this for our benefit and for God's purposes and glory.

Much of this ability comes via the Holy Spirit, as He equips people to better use their brains, talents and hands (Exodus 35:30-34; 36:1-6; Deuteronomy 8:18). What a difference we see today when compared to the first days, when Adam and Eve strolled through the garden! Humans not only have multiplied and spread over the Earth, they have built empires, developed technology and put in place structures and infrastructure. Yes, most of what humans have built has also been used for evil, but the point here is that the population growth and development of human society since it's very simple and small inception has been phenomenal. And this can also be seen as the continued ministry of the Holy Spirit in creation.

"The heavens are the LORD's, but the earth He has given to the human race" (Psalm 115:16 - HCSB). From the onset we see God is interested in sharing the authority of His Kingdom with responsible and faithful humans, while setting a few limits and conditions (Genesis 2:16-17). "Then the Lord God took the man and put him into the garden of Eden to cultivate it and keep it" and "the man gave names to all the cattle, and to the birds of the sky, and to every beast of the field (Genesis 2:15, 20 - NASB).

There is a special relation between humanity and planet Earth. Earth was prepared as a wonderful, self and life-sustaining planet. Man was created from the earth: "Then the Lord God formed man of dust from the ground" (Genesis 2:7 - NASB). Man's first job was to cultivate the garden and name the animals (Genesis 2:15, 19-20). And we must remember what the ultimate destiny of the saved is: "You made them a kingdom [or, kings] and priests to our God, and they will reign on the earth" (Revelation 5:10 - HCSB). Christian urban specialist Ray Bakke, sees redeemed humanity moving from the Garden to the ultimate city: the New Jerusalem. Our special connection with planet Earth will continue, even after both we and the our planet have been redeemed (Romans 8:22-23; Revelation 21:1-2).

After evaluating each step of creation by seeing that what He had created was "good," when He creates man and woman, when He looks at all He had made as a whole, God finds everything to be "***very*** good" (Genesis 1:31). The Global Kingdom was off to a very good start.

## [GK] Genesis 2 - The details: the first couple

Genesis chapter two zooms in to show the first man, his first assignments, and the need for—and creation of—a companion. It also implies that, although Adam was created without sin, he and his wife would both need to be tested to prove their loyalty to God. God, we can deduce, wanted them to move from simply being "innocent" to being "holy." But holiness is a choice, a personal decision. And yet, if there are no rules to break, there can be no choice. So God provides one prohibition with a negative consequence: "you must not eat from the tree of the knowledge of good and evil; for in the day that you eat of it, you will surely die" (Genesis 2:17 - BSB).

Just as being made from the dust of the ground speaks of a vital connection with planet Earth, the fact that the first woman was taken from the man shows the intimate connection that exists between man and woman. The first man was given a mission—"be fruitful and multiply and fill the earth"—he could never complete alone. "Then the LORD God said, 'It is not good for the man to be alone. I will make a helper who is just right for him'" (Genesis 1:28; 2:18 - NLT). The Lord performed the first surgery with general anesthesia and took a rib from Adam, from which he made Eve. (Some still debate this issue as though genetically a missing rib should have passed on through generations. But if I have a gallbladder removed that does not affect my descendants in the least bit). That God took something from Adam is symbolic of the fact that now man was incomplete. That

God made woman from that part means that she had the same essence as the man and an intimate bond had been established with him. That woman was then presented to man as his wife allowed man to begin to fulfill the mission he had received from God.

Together, man and woman could now join God's creative activity and extend it by pro*creating*, by reproducing! This privilege carries the greatest of responsibilities because what is generated are human beings with souls and spirits. Precious lives that must be protected, loved, nurtured, and taught. This is one of the most wonderful Kingdom privileges given to humanity.

God delegated naming the animals to Adam "and whatever the man called a living creature, that was its name" (Genesis 2:19). God accepted all his decisions about what to name them, showing He had truly empowered humans over the tasks they were given. Of course this was before the fall, and Adam's mental capacity and spiritual connection with God were on a different level. Yet we get a clue as to how God not only delegates responsibility but the necessary authority to go with it.

But are humans really reigning over the Earth? As we think about God's calling and where we are today as the human race, we see a big gap between reigning over the Earth as God desired and the problems of pollution, the lack of clean water in many countries, poverty and hunger, the dangers of nuclear war and contamination, sickness, violence, crime, epidemics, immorality, sex slave trafficking, sexual abuse, abortion, high infant mortality rates, and so much pain, despair and increasing numbers of suicides. This discrepancy came about because of what happened in the next chapter of Genesis.

## [GK] Genesis 3 - Questions about the fall

So many questions surround this tragic event. We've seen the first couple had to undergo testing in order to exercise their free will and chose a life and state of holiness. But how did Eve fall for this seduction so easily? Why did her husband stand idly by, allowing his wife to be questioned like that, without offering any protection or resistance? When did Lucifer become Satan? At what point did he fall and bring rebellion and sin into God's Kingdom (for the first time ever, from what we can deduce)? Someone suggested that it could not have been before the process of creating the physical universe was concluded, as "God saw **everything** that he had made, and behold, it **was very good**" (Genesis 1:31a - ESV). Meaning, everything was suited for and accomplishing that for which it had been made. And Lucifer was definitely not originally made to be a devil.

There are many more questions. What would have happened had Adam and Eve not fallen? What would have happened if one of them had fallen but not the other? And, had they not fallen, would there be other attacks? Or would this suffice to confirm them in their state of holiness and faithfulness? Why would God even want to work with a fallen race of people? Was there not a way to start over, averting the tragedy of suffering and death that follow the fallen state of humanity? Avoiding the eternal damnation of so many souls down through the centuries? Dealing with spiteful, hateful, rebellious creatures who would use their now not-so-freewill to reject and blaspheme the Lord of lords and King of kings? Why would God subject Himself to this?

Many of these questions remain unanswered, as we are not given direct explanations for them. Mysteries remain, but there are a few principles which can help to guide us here. First, God is sovereign and nothing escapes His control. Second, He has chosen to reveal parts of our ancient history and is not afraid of our questions. If we understand His character and attributes, that He is love and truth (1 John 4:8; John 14:6), then we know we don't have to know everything we don't know.

Third, God seeks a genuine, voluntary relationship with those created in His image and likeness (us). He was willing to sacrifice so very much in order to create the right circumstances and situation that would allow for His special creation to learn to love Him back and worship Him from their own initiative and volition. To learn this, suffering would be a key factor. In fact, "it is necessary to go through many hardships to enter the kingdom of God" (Acts 14:22b - CSB). This raises other fundamental questions: Why is suffering so important? What does it accomplish that could not be accomplished without it? We know it has the potential to draw us closer to God, to remind us that we need God, to keep us humble. Or, to give others the opportunity to care for us and bless us in time of need, and to create a longing desire for the eternal state, to be in heaven with the Lord.

And fourth, we see over and over—in Scripture and in daily life—just how much God values our freewill. Some theologians say we really don't have freewill. This is not the place to enter into a theological debate over this, but notice how important people's choices are throughout the Bible. Spiritually, physically and emotionally, we could state that "you are what you choose." That you are defined by the choices you make. For instance, the Bible does not condemn the fact that there are evil desires within us. It condemns **choosing to follow** or give into them (Psalm 81:12; Jeremiah 3:17; 11:8; 13:10; 23:17; 2 Peter 2:10; 3:3; Jude 1:16, 18). Rebellion is a choice. Entering into a covenant relationship with the Lord is a choice. Being faithful to that covenant is a choice. Even believing—or not—in God is a choice. God provides opportunities to choose what is correct, good and righteous (Deuteronomy 30:19; Joshua 24:15). God does not choose for us: He gives us the opportunity to decide for ourselves. This principle is so important to God that

He was willing to "risk" creating beings with a free will, and face all the adverse consequences, because He deemed our freedom to choose to be of utmost importance.

The first reference to the coming Promised One is found in this context. God tells the serpent: "And I will put enmity between you and the woman, and between your seed and her seed; He shall bruise you on the head, and you shall bruise him on the heel" (Genesis 3:15 - NASB). God Himself began *spiritual warfare* by creating enmity between the serpent and its forces of darkness, and the woman and her Descendant, as well as His people. But God made it clear the Promised Seed or Descendant would be victorious (the blow on the serpent's head). The long preparation for the coming Messiah King was set in motion.

## [GK] [UK] Genesis 6-9 - Wickedness brings destruction, righteousness results in restoration

This passage does not directly reference the Kingdom of God, but contains critical information concerning an event which greatly influenced the antediluvian world. Because of the intrusion of fallen angels, the wickedness on Earth reached an unprecedented level and pervasiveness that God had to deal with radically. That influence was felt even after the flood and is believed by some to be the reason there has been so much violence and wickedness ever since. Another reason to cover this passage is the fact that God saved the human race because of the righteousness of a faithful person. This points to the high level of importance God attributes to righteousness in His Kingdom.

This most controversial passage tells us that "the sons of God saw that the daughters of mankind were beautiful, and they took any they chose as wives for themselves" (Genesis 6:2 - HCSB). With this, "mankind" became "corrupt" and "the Nephilim were on the earth both in those days and afterward, when the sons of God came to the daughters of mankind, who bore children to them. They were the powerful men of old, the famous men" (Genesis 6:3-4 - HCSB). The Nephilim are identified as being "giants," though probably not enormously tall. This led to evil becoming pervasive everywhere—it was all people thought about and engaged in (v. 5). God saw this, regretted having made human beings, and decided: "I will wipe off from the face of the earth mankind, whom I created, together with the animals" (Genesis 6:7a - HCSB). The flood came as God's solution to the corruption of humankind.

How should we interpret this passage? There are two main lines of thought: The first is that the "sons of God" refer to the godly descendants of Seth who were seduced by the beauty of the rebellious descendants of Cain, "the daughters of mankind." They intermarried and this corrupted even the righteous half of humanity which had been following God's will. The problem is this does not account for the appearance of the Nephilim and the offspring from this union which brought about "the powerful men of old, the famous men."

As strange as it may seem to conventional wisdom, Biblical scholars have seen evidence in 1 Enoch, from the Second Temple or Intertestamental period, and writings from Mesopotamia contemporary with the flood era, that shed light on this passage and give credence to the fact that it should be taken literally: the "sons of God" being celestial or angelic beings, referred to as Watchers (see Daniel 4:17 and mostly the first chapters of 1 Enoch), the daughters of mankind being human women, and their offspring being "giants."[2] One of the strongest arguments in favor of this interpretation comes from the fact that both Peter and Jude support it in their writings (Jude1:6; 14; 2 Peter 2:4-5).

While total depravity was dooming the world to utter destruction, a glimpse of hope: "Noah, however, found favor in the sight of the Lord" (Genesis 6:8 - HCSB). This favor came from the fact that "Noah was a righteous man, blameless among his contemporaries; Noah walked with God" (Genesis 6:9 - HCSB). The contrast could not be greater between the world at large and Noah and his family, who had chosen to serve the Lord and live according to the Kingdom standard of righteousness. God shared His plans with Noah and told him to build an ark and save his family and the animals. After the flood, God again gave the order: "Be fruitful and multiply and fill the earth," then told them they had authority over the animal kingdom and sternly warned them to refrain from violence (Genesis 9:1-7 - HCSB).

God also told Noah and his sons He was confirming His covenant with them, their descendants and the animals, to preserve them and to never again destroy humanity by flood. The sign of this covenant was the rainbow (Genesis 9:8-17). This event was crucial to the preservation of the human race and, therefore, to the continuity of God's Global Kingdom agenda, which could then proceed towards the preparation of the future appearing of Messiah. It is interesting to see how God operates: He began the human race with one couple: Adam and Eve. He restored the human race by starting over again with one family: Noah, his wife, his three sons and their wives. God's Kingdom also works through covenants. God told Noah: "But I will establish My covenant (promise, pledge) with you, and you shall come into the ark—you and your sons and your wife and your sons' wives with you" (Genesis 6:18 - AMPC).

## [L&K] [GK] Genesis 14 - The King of Righteousness

Otherwise known as Melchizedek, He was the king of Salem, or better, Jerusalem, and priest of the Most High God. He only appears in Genesis 14:18-20, being mentioned a few places elsewhere in Scripture (Psalm 110:4; Hebrews 5:6, 10; 6:20; 7:2-17). Since "his name means king of righteousness" and He was "king of Salem"—and Salem means peace—we can understand His title to be "king of peace" as well (Hebrews 7:2 - HCSB). Since He had no "father, mother, or genealogy" and no beginning or end (Hebrews 7:3), we may conclude He was either a foreshadowing of Jesus or Jesus Himself in a pre-incarnate state. Jesus' priesthood comes from this "order" of Melchizedek, as He was neither a descendant of Levi nor of Aaron, from which all regular priests had to be. In order to be the Messianic king, on the other hand, He had to be of the line of Judah (which is established later on and will be seen just below).

It is in this sense that God's promise pointed to the future Messiah, when He declared through the psalmist: "The LORD took an oath and will never recant: 'You are a priest forever, after the manner of Melchizedek'" (Psalm 110:4 - ISV). Early on, God was providing all the details for the coming Messiah and how this mysterious Melchizedek was already claiming Jerusalem as His city (Psalm 48:2; Matthew 5:35).

## [GK] Genesis 12 and 15 - The promises and covenant with Abraham

The covenants with Noah, Abraham, Moses and David are definitely highlights of the Global Kingdom. However, since these were covered in volume 1, we cannot again go in to their details here.[3] Enough to say God called Abraham and promised to make a great nation out of him, bless him, and that: "In you all the families of the earth will be blessed" (Genesis 12:1-3 - NASB). When Abraham moved to the land to which God had directed him, "The Lord appeared to Abram and said, 'To your descendants I will give this land'" (Genesis 12:7 - NASB).

After a profoundly spiritual experience, "On that day the Lord made a covenant with Abram, saying, 'To your descendants I have given this land, from the river of Egypt as far as the great river, the river Euphrates'" (Genesis 15:18 - NASB). The covenant with Noah secured humanity's future. By way of the promises and covenant with Abraham, God selected a Patriarch who would be the head of a great nation, and promised him the land which was before him. All of this was a vital Kingdom strategy, part of a much bigger plan.

Abraham, it must also be stated here, is the "father of faith" (Romans 4:3, 11, 16). He is the example of what it means to be made righteous by faith. Faith is a ***Kingdom Value*** by which we access and operate in the Kingdom. For this reason, we see faith throughout Scripture as a requirement, in our daily walk with God and as we live in this fallen world, where we must "live by faith, not by sight" (2 Corinthians 5:7 - NIV).

### [GK] Genesis 49 - The kingly line of Judah

"Then Jacob called his sons and said, 'Gather around, and I will tell you what will happen to you in the days to come. The scepter will not depart from Judah or the staff from between his feet until He whose right it is comes and the obedience of the peoples belongs to Him" (Genesis 49:1, 10 - HCSB). Although we are getting ahead of ourselves, it is important to establish a connection here by mentioning that the scepter of power and authority to rule was passed on to David, the second king of Israel and the first from the tribe of Judah (Saul was from the tribe of Benjamin; see 1 Samuel 9:21). The Messiah entered the scenario when God promised that one of David's descendants would rule forever on his throne (2 Chronicles 13:5).

We learn later in Scripture that the Messiah (the Anointed One) would hold the office of Priest, being from the order of Melchizedek (Hebrews 5:10); would hold the office of Prophet, being like Moses (Deuteronomy 18:15); and would hold the office of King, being from the lineage of David (Isaiah 9:7).

# The Kingdom in Exodus

### [GK] Exodus 14 - Moses' Kingdom hymn

Moses and the children of Israel had just crossed the Red Sea (Exodus 14), and were ecstatic with the victory the Lord had given them. Moses broke out in a psalm of praise, which ended with the following words: "You will bring [the people whom You purchased] in and plant them on the mountain of Your possession; Lord, You have prepared the place for Your dwelling; Lord, Your hands have established the sanctuary. The Lord will reign forever and ever" (Exodus 15:16-18 - HCSB).

From this we learn the Lord had been revealing to Moses some specific details of His plan for His people and Israel as a nation. He speaks of a mountain and a sanctuary. Apparently, Moses understood God's plans for filling the Temple with His glorious Presence on Mount Moriah. He ends by exclaiming that the Lord will reign forever, an inspired insight and first reference to the fact that His sovereign leadership would be without end. Although the word used here for eternal or everlasting (Hebrew *olam*) had been used before in relation to God's covenant, Abraham's descendant's possession of the land, and God and His name (Genesis 17:7, 8, 13, 19; 21:33; Exodus 3:15), this is the first time it is used in relation to God's reign and its duration.

Humanity's survival was guaranteed via the covenant with Noah. Israel's birth as a nation and the promise of land came through a covenant with Abraham (Leviticus 26:42). But this nation needed instructions as to how to live, relate with each other and worship God. This came through the covenant with Moses and the people he led. Moses was summoned to the top of Mount Sinai and "was there with the Lord forty days and forty nights; he ate no bread and drank no water. And he wrote upon the tables the words of the covenant, the Ten Commandments" (Exodus 34:28 - AMPC; see Exodus 32:15). The 10 Commandments are the summary of a covenant that covered an enormous amount of directives, including the moral, civil and ceremonial laws, which included the sacrificial system with its instructions. For Kingdom citizens today, the ceremonial laws no longer apply. The moral laws are to be carefully obeyed, especially as seen in the 10 Commandments.

## [GK] Exodus 19 - The first reference to the Kingdom

The first reference to the Kingdom of God in the Bible is found in Exodus 19:5-6, where God tells His people that "'if you obey me fully and keep my covenant, then out of all nations you will be my treasured possession. Although the whole earth is mine, **you will be for me a kingdom** of priests and a holy nation.' These are the words you are to speak to the Israelites."

This passage is so foundational because:
1. It is the first reference to the Kingdom ("you will be for me a kingdom");
2. It establishes God's general right to rule over the whole earth ("the whole earth is mine");
3. It expresses God's desire to relate to Israel in a special manner, ("out of all nations you will be my treasured possession");
4. It lays out the conditions for such a relationship ("if you obey me fully");
5. It defines God's Kingdom purpose for Israel ("you will be for me a kingdom of priests and a holy nation");
6. And, very importantly, it is made in the context of a covenant relationship ("if you ... keep my covenant").

This reference to the Kingdom—that of being "a kingdom of priests and a holy nation"—is of such importance that it was quoted by New Testament writers who also expounded some on the theme. John the Apostle addressed the seven churches of Asia with the fact that Jesus loves us, freed us by His blood, rules over the kings of the earth, "and He has made us to be a kingdom, priests to His God and Father—to Him be the glory and the dominion forever and ever. Amen" (Revelation 1:6 - NASB). Echoing this wonderful truth, the four living creatures and the twenty-four elders worshiped the Lamb by singing a hymn about His worthiness and sacrificial death in order to purchase people from every nation for God. They sang: "You have made them to be a kingdom and priests to our God; and they will reign upon the earth" (Revelation 5:10 - NASB).

Notice how the Apostle Peter refers to the "kingdom of priests and a holy nation" and being God's "treasured possession" in the following verse. He was making an earnest plea to his readers to realize their true heritage instead of giving in to the world's seduction. This is what he wanted Christians to remember: "But you are a chosen people, a royal priesthood, a holy nation, a people for God's own possession, to proclaim the virtues of Him who called you out of darkness into His marvelous light" (1 Peter 2:9 - BSB).

# The Kingdom in Leviticus

### [GK] Leviticus 23 - The Lord's Global Kingdom calendar: The Seven Feasts of the Lord

We find a complete list of the seven feasts of the Lord in one place: Leviticus 23, where they are mentioned in chronological order. The Lord told Moses he was to inform the people of Israel that "these are my appointed feasts" (Leviticus 23:2). They were not Israel's feasts, they were the Lord's. That is why they were to be taken seriously and observed consistently. God also declared they were to occur as "sacred assemblies." Being sacred meant they were to be set apart from other types of celebration, as these were special and entirely devoted to the Lord. Being assemblies, they were a means of bringing the whole nation together, a way in which whole communities could rejoice in the Lord corporately. Israel should also continue to observe a weekly "day of sacred assembly" which was "the seventh day" that is, "a Sabbath of rest" (Leviticus 23:3).

The list in Leviticus 23 simply mentions the name of the feasts and when they were to take place. Few instructions are given and no explanation concerning their meaning is provided (except for the Feast of Tabernacles). But the hidden meaning came to light during the Messiah's first coming: He fulfilled the prophetic meaning of the first four feasts and His second coming will fulfill the latter three.[4]

### 1) The Lord's Feast of Passover or *Pesach*, Nissan 14 (March / April), the first of the Spring Feasts *(Leviticus 23:4-5; Exodus 12)*

A complete description and detailed instructions concerning how the Hebrew households were to celebrate the first Passover are found in Exodus 12. The context was one of deliverance from bondage, not by fighting or fleeing, but by the hand of God. It was also a deliverance from God's judgment. The Lord said He would pass over those households (Exodus 12:13, 23) which had followed His instructions, sacrificed the lamb (or goat) and placed the blood on the sides over the door frames (Exodus 12:5-7). They would be spared the "destroyer" (Exodus 12:23). Their firstborn would not be slain (Exodus 12:27). And they would be free to leave their captivity and abandon a life of slavery (Exodus 12:31-36). God told them to celebrate the Passover as a lasting ordinance and to explain to their children what had happened and meaning of this ceremony (Exodus 12:24-27).

It is important to remember that the Jewish day begins at twilight, when the first two or three "lights" (stars) can be seen in the evening sky. Therefore, Passover begins in the evening of what for us would be the 13th day, yet what is the beginning of the 14th day of the "first month." The first month on the religious calender is Nissan (or Nisan, formerly called Abib).

**Original Meaning:** Deliverance by the blood of lambs (the Angel "passed over") and redemption from bondage as Egyptian slaves.
**Prophetic Meaning:** Christ, the Lamb of God, was slain (crucified) for our sins on the very day of Passover. We are delivered and redeemed (bought back) by His blood. The blood of the Lamb frees the believer from God's judgment on their sin.

### 2) The Lord's Feast of Unleavened Bread, Nissan 15-21 (March / April), Spring *(Leviticus 23:6-8)*

As this feast went on for seven days, and since it was attached to Passover (the day before) and to the Feast of Firstfruits (the day after Unleavened Bread began), these three feasts are sometimes seen as one great feast.

**Original Meaning:** Leaven represents decay, corruption, error, evil. Unleavened bread stands for sanctification, "sincerity and truth" (1 Corinthians 5:7-8; see Pharisee's leaven in Matthew 16:6).
**Prophetic Meaning:** 1) Jesus is the Bread of Life. 2) His body did not decay in the grave where it was placed that very day (Psalm 16:10). And 3) Jesus was without sin.

Are you seeing a pattern here? Although the original meaning of the Feast was largely tied to the agricultural cycle in the Spring and Fall, they point to God's redemptive and prophetic calendar.

### 3) The Lord's Feast of Firstfruits, Nissan 16 (March / April), Spring *(Leviticus 23:9-14)*

**Original Meaning:** The early or first fruits were offered to the Lord and were an indication of the harvest to follow.

**Prophetic Meaning:** "But now Christ has been raised from the dead, the firstfruits of those who have fallen asleep" (1 Corinthians 15:20 - HCSB). Jesus' resurrection took place this very day! And, just as there was an initial sample harvest, Jesus was the first to experience the resurrection, leading the way and setting the example we will one day follow.

### 4) The Lord's Feast of Weeks—Pentecost or *Shavuot*—50 days after Firstfruits (May / June), Spring *(Leviticus 23:15-22)*

**Original Meaning:** The summer harvest time, when all were to bake two cakes with leaven and present them at the Temple. Called the Feast of Weeks because the crops were ready to be fully harvested seven weeks plus one day after the Feast of Firstfruits.

**Prophetic Meaning:** The inauguration of the Church Age, marked by the outpouring of the Holy Spirit and the harvest of 3,000 souls, which happened 50 days after the Lord's resurrection. The Church was founded as a consequence of the Messiah's earthly ministry, shortly after the resurrected Jesus spent 40 days with His apostles and shortly after He returned to the Father (Acts 1:1-3).

Now, as we look at the Fall Feasts, it will be seen that they refer to the future.

### 5) The Lord's Feast of Trumpets—*Rosh Hashanah*—on Tishri 1, 2 (full moon) (September / October), Fall *(Leviticus 23:23-25)*

**Original Meaning:** A holy convocation, a day of sabbath-rest, of sacrifices and offerings unto the Lord, a memorial of blowing of trumpets (ram's horns).

**Prophetic Meaning:** The Rapture of the Church: "For the Lord himself will descend from heaven ... with the sound of the trumpet of God. And ... we ... will be caught up..." (1 Thessalonians 4:16-17 - ESV). A convocation is a calling of people to assemble—that is, a gathering. The Rapture of the Church will be a gathering of God's people as He calls out to them with the sound of the trumpet and brings them "to meet the Lord in the air, and so we will always be with the Lord" (1 Thessalonians 4:17b - ESV).

The sounding of the trumpet, Alfred Edersheim explains, was meant to summon Israel either to warfare or "days of public rejoicing, and feasts" (Numbers 10:10). It was, so to speak, the host of God assembled, waiting for their Leader; the people of God united to proclaim their King." And so, it "was a public acknowledgment of Jehovah as King," just as we see that "Christ is proclaimed King Universal" in

Revelations 11:15, "when the seventh angel is about to sound his trumpet."[5]

Although some discount the reality of the Rapture, claiming it is not literal, or that there is no mention in the Bible of two separate events: first, a Rapture, then the Second Coming proper. But *Rosh Hashanah* seems to indicate there is indeed a Rapture and, as seen below, the Feast of Tabernacles points to the physical return of the Lord.

## 6) The Lord's Feast of the Day of Atonement or *Yom Kippur*, Tishri 10 (September / October), Fall *(Leviticus 23:26-32; Leviticus 16)*

**Original Meaning:** A sabbath rest dedicated to confessing sins committed during the past year; the day the High Priest entered the Holy of holies to sacrifice for himself and the whole nation.

**Prophetic Meaning:** A day of confession and atonement for the survivors of the Day of the Lord—Jews and Gentiles alike—at the Lord's second coming. (See Matthew 25: 31-34).

*Yom Kippur* is still observed by faithful Jews today and is considered the most solemn day on the Jewish calendar. The day is dedicated to corporate and individual repentance for sins committed over the course of the previous year. This was a "cover all, catch all" solution in the Old Testament times: if there were sins that were unknown, unconfessed or which had not been covered by sacrifice, the Day of Atonement presented the opportunity for reflection and confession for these.

The ultimate fulfillment of the Day of Atonement for Israel as a nation will be when they finally recognize their true Messiah. "Then I will pour out a spirit of grace and prayer on the house of David and the residents of Jerusalem, and they will look at me whom they pierced. They will mourn for him as one mourns for an only child and weep bitterly for him as one weeps for a firstborn" (Zechariah 12:10 - CSB). The Feast of Trumpets—the Rapture of the Church—comes just before the Feast of the Day of Atonement, the recognition of Jesus as Israel's Messiah, which probably means the former will influence the latter.

## [MK] 7) The Lord's Feast of Tabernacles or *Sukkot*, Tishri 15-22 (September / October), Fall *(Leviticus 23:33-43)*

**Original Meaning:** Little booths were set up to remind Israel of God's provision as their forefathers wandered through the desert. Water was an important part of the feast.

**Prophetic Meaning:** The Lord Jesus Himself will tabernacle with (live among) His people in the Millennial Kingdom. He will provide for their every need. (For a preview, see Matthew 17:1-9).

After the Rapture (Feast of Trumpets) and the conversion of Israel (the Day of Atonement; Romans 11:26), the Lord comes back to establish His Millennial Kingdom. "The Lord will be king over the whole earth. On that day there will be one Lord, and his name the only name" (Zechariah 14:9 - NIV). The people from the nations that had attacked Jerusalem (Armageddon; Revelation 16:16; 19:19), "will go up year after year to worship the King, the Lord Almighty, and to celebrate the Festival of Tabernacles" (Zechariah 14:16 - NIV).

Although the Spring Feasts were fulfilled by Jesus in rapid succession, in a matter of days and weeks, it seems difficult to image how that would be possible with the Fall Feasts. Otherwise we would have the Rapture occurring one day and, nine days later, the conversion of Israel, and yet another five days after that, the physical return of the Messiah to establish His Millennial Kingdom. It would make more sense to see this in the context of Daniel's seventieth week, that is, the seven last years of history as we know it (see more on this under **"Daniel Chapter 9,"** in this volume). That these events will fall on the exact days of the Feasts seems probable, yet in different years: the Rapture at (or before) the beginning of the seventieth week, the triumphant return of Christ to reign over earth at the end of this period, and the conversion of Israel somewhere in-between.

Other passages on the Feasts of the Lord include Numbers 28, 29; Deuteronomy 16; and Nehemiah 8:10-18.

# The Kingdom in the Book of Numbers

### [GK] Numbers 22-31 - Balaam and the oracle about the star and Ruler that would come from Israel

Balak was the king of Moab, the land just west of the Jordan River, located in what today is the country of Jordan. When the Israelites reached this area on the final leg of their pilgrimage through the wilderness from Egypt to Canaan, the people of Moab were terrified. Balak figured the only way to defeat them, or at least survive them, was to call Balaam, a prophet or seer who lived in Pethor, near the Euphrates river, about 350 miles away (Numbers 22:1-5).

Balak sent for Balaam in hopes that he would curse the Israelites, weakening them so he could "defeat them and drive them out" (Numbers 22:6). Throughout this account, Balaam appears to be very loyal and obedient to God. And God clearly communicates His will to him on numerous occasions. There was, however, an important incident where the account indicates something was off and the Lord shows Balaam he has much to learn about the one true God, the God of Israel. God gives Balaam's donkey the ability to speak and Balaam, "the seer," the ability to see the Angel of the Lord with his sword drawn (Numbers 22:18-35).

Balaam first warned the emissaries of King Balak, then the king himself, that he would only utter what God told him to, no more and no less (Numbers 22:18, 38; 23:12, 13; 24:12). Balak wouldn't back down, giving Balaam several opportunities to curse the Israelites, but he always ended up blessing them instead (Numbers 23:8-11; 20-23; 24:5-10). In an outstanding oracle (Numbers 23:7-10), Balaam said, "No misfortune is in his plan for Jacob; no trouble is in store for Israel. For the Lord their God is with them; he has been proclaimed their king" (Numbers 23:21 - NLT). What incredible insight for a foreign prophet, to view God as the King of Israel!

Balak finally gave up and told Balaam to go home! Balaam agreed but warned Balak about "what this people will do to your people in days to come (Numbers 24:14 - NIV). And it was in this context that Balaam uttered his fourth oracle, a short but exceptional prophecy. And to think this somewhat unique prophecy only came about because Balak contracted Balaam's services to curse Israel!

Although Balaam was not a Hebrew and had no ties with Israel, we are told God spoke with him on several occasions, sent the Angel of the Lord to him, and, before he uttered his third oracle, "the Spirit of God came upon him" (Numbers 24:2 - ESV). Balaam introduces his prophecy by claiming this was "the oracle of the man whose eye is opened, the oracle of him who hears the words of God, and knows the knowledge of the Most High, who sees the vision of the Almighty, falling down with his eyes uncovered" (Numbers 24:15, 16 - ESV).

Then he declares: "I see him, but not now; I behold him, but not near: a star shall come out of Jacob, and a scepter shall rise out of Israel" (Numbers 24:17a - ESV).

"I see him" and "I behold him" indicates the prophecy concerns a person. "Not now" and "not near" indicate the fulfillment would be far in the future. "A star shall come out of Jacob" appears to be the only reference—if only a hint—of the star that would appear and guide the wise men to the house where the King of the Jews could be found. "A scepter shall rise out of Israel" refers to the same "ruler" mentioned two verses down. Looking back from our vantage point we can see this short but extraordinary vision pertains to the coming of the King in what for them was the distant future. A King welcomed by a star Who would arise out of Israel. The vision includes elements of the first and second coming, as Messiah's kingship must wait until He returns.

The fourth oracle of Balaam is without a doubt the most important and far-reaching prophecy he uttered. "The prophecy of the star out of Jacob and the scepter out of Israel is a specific prophecy of the coming messianic Ruler, the Lord Jesus Christ. Israel's future Deliverer will be like a star and a scepter in his royalty and will bring victory over the enemies of his people (see also v.19). That this prophecy was given through the improbable prophet Balaam is remarkable, reminding us of the unexpectedness of the thoughts of God (Isa 55:8)."[6]

The second part of this oracle states "he will smash the forehead of Moab," and "strike down all the Shethites," and that "Edom will become a possession... but Israel will be triumphant," while "One who comes from Jacob will rule" (Numbers 24:17b-19 - HCSB; see Jeremiah 48:42). This again seems to refer to the second coming of the King and finds its parallel in Revelation 19:15, which foretells that "from His mouth comes a sharp sword, so that with it He may strike down the nations, and He will rule them with a rod of iron; and He treads the wine press of the fierce wrath of God, the Almighty" (NASB).

Balaam never made it back to his home. He was killed by the Israelites as they fought against the Midianites. The reason given was that he tried to curse Israel and practiced divination (Numbers 31:8; Joshua 13:22). Yet it is possible that the main reason lies in one single verse. After Balaam's oracles, we are left with the impression that his overall performance was a good one. But the very next passage tells of the fall of Israel by way of Moabite women who invited men from Israel to go and sacrifice to Baal, which included sexual intercourse (Numbers 25:1-3). What a Machiavellian strategy to defeat this blessed nation with its mighty military power! And whose idea could this have been? Balaam's, no less (Numbers 31:16). This was referenced directly by our Lord, as He had John write to the church in Pergamum (Revelation 2:14). No wonder Bible references to Balaam are always negative (see Deuteronomy 23:3-6; Joshua 24:9-10; Nehemiah 13:1-3; Micah 6:5; 2 Peter 2:15-16; Jude 11).

# The Kingdom in Deuteronomy

### [GK] Deuteronomy 17 - Kings foretold and prior instructions given

Did God want Israel to have kings, or not? There is the widespread belief that God did not. It is easy to see how that can be inferred by the account in 1 Samuel 8 (see below), where the people demand a king from Samuel. Yet God had a problem with the *process* because the people of Israel were unwilling to wait for God's timing and refused to listen to Samuel (1 Samuel 8:19, 20). They also had the wrong motivation. They wanted to be like other nations; they sought a king who would serve ***them***. Their motivation should have been to serve God, to participate in His Kingdom program.

How can we know God wanted Israel to be governed by kings when the time was right? Because of God's promise to Abraham and instructions to Moses, as we will see below. When God reaffirmed His covenant with Abram, changed his name to Abraham, and instituted circumcision, He also promised: "I will make you extremely fruitful and will make nations and kings come from you" (Genesis 17:6 - HCSB). Although these "kings" may refer to the leaders of several tribes that were formed among his descendants (Genesis 25:1-4), they certainly also referred to the future kings of Israel and Judah.

There is even stronger and more direct proof God wanted Israel to have kings. Consider His instructions to Moses in Deuteronomy 17:14-20. God set down some guidelines as to how kings should be chosen in the future when they settled in the land. Instead of giving Moses a list of political qualifications, God told him how Israel's kings should behave and what kind of character traits they should possess:

**1. How a king should be chosen:** a) He should be of God's choosing; b) He must be chosen from among the Israelites (foreigners were out of the race) (Deuteronomy 17:14-15).

**2. How the king should behave:** a) The king "must not acquire great numbers of horses for himself;" b) "He must not take many wives, or his heart will be led astray;" c) He "must not accumulate large amounts of silver and gold;" and d) The king was to have his daily devotionals; that is, he was to have "a copy of this law" with him and "read it all the days of his life" (Deuteronomy 17:16-19 - NIV).

**3. What kind of character traits the king should possess:** a) Humility (he should "not consider himself better than his fellow Israelites"); and b) Faithfulness (he should never "turn from the law to the right or to the left"). Such a king could expect to "reign a long time over his kingdom in Israel" (Deuteronomy 17:20 - NIV).

This is great advice for any leader in God's Kingdom today: he or she should not be power-hungry or caught up with material possessions, but should be humble, faithful and a person of the Word. If only Israel had taken these instructions to heart, that nation's history would have been radically different.

# Chapter 2

# Books of History

## The Kingdom in Joshua

**[GK] Joshua 5 - The Commander of the Lord's army**

There is an insightful reference to the pre-incarnate Christ in the book of Joshua. The children of Israel had crossed the Jordan River and were set to conquer their first city in Canaan. "When Joshua was near Jericho, he looked up and saw a man standing in front of him with a drawn sword in His hand. Joshua approached Him and asked, 'Are You for us or for our enemies?' 'Neither,' He replied" (Joshua 5:13-14a - HCSB). Although Joshua must have been apprehensive and curious when he saw this imposing personality, he asked the wrong question. He should have started with, "Who are you?" Then he would have known He was transcendent over all, including over opposing sides. One on Whose side we must strive to always be, not the other way around.

This enigmatic Person identified Himself in this way: "I have now come as commander of the Lord's army." Joshua understood the implications and "bowed with his face to the ground in worship and asked Him, 'What does my Lord want to say to His servant?'" (Joshua 5:14 - HCSB). Joshua immediately recognized this Person as God Himself and worshiped Him. God (the Son) accepted his worship and told Joshua to "Remove the sandals from your feet, for the place where you are standing is holy." Joshua complied (Joshua 5:15 - HCSB). Just like his predecessor Moses (Exodus 3:5), Joshua was standing on holy ground because he was in the Presence of the Eternal King!

The importance of the conquest of Jericho cannot be overstated because this is the beginning of the resettlement and expansion of the theocratic kingdom of Israel in the Promised Land, which is a key element of the Global Kingdom, since Israel was the representative of God's Kingdom on Earth in the Old Testament times.

A further, striking link between the "Commander of the Lord's Army" and the incarnate Jesus can be found in the fact that Israel's Jordan crossing (which took place at an almost a straight parallel line across from Jericho), is very close to the traditional site of Jesus' baptism.[1]

# The Kingdom in 1st and 2nd Samuel

## [GK] 1 Samuel 8 - God is rejected as Israel's King

Samuel had been a great leader over Israel, but he was getting old and his sons were not following in his footsteps. Instead, they were taking bribes and perverting justice in their position as judges. Apparently, that was the excuse for demanding Samuel appoint a king for them. They wanted to be just like the surrounding nations. This didn't sit well with Samuel, who decided to seek the Lord's guidance. The Lord's answer was chilling. He told Samuel to give them what they wanted, because "they are doing the same thing to you that they have done to Me, since the day I brought them out of Egypt until this day, abandoning Me and worshiping other gods" (1 Samuel 8:1-8 - HCSB). Turning their backs on God as their King was a very dangerous move in the wrong direction.

So far, the Kingdom of Israel had been run as a theocracy, although God's leadership was largely ignored much of the time, during the period of the judges. It's not that the people had a vision of God's Kingdom and wanted to have an earthly king who would represent the King of kings over their land. No, they wanted to have a king like the other nations, one who would set himself up as the final authority.

The transition from being ruled by judges to being ruled by kings was not supposed to differ that much. "Both systems ought to have been theocratic in nature. Even when there was a human king, he was supposed to be only the representative of the divine King. The fact that the people had not understood this is reflected in the Lord's analysis that the people had rejected him, not Samuel."[2]

## [GK] 1 Samuel 9-2 Samuel 4 - David: becoming king of Israel

When Israel asked for a king, Samuel anointed Saul, following God's directions (1 Samuel 9). But soon it became clear Saul was not fully committed to God's will, and the prophet informed him he had been rejected by the Lord (1 Samuel 13 and 15). If it were not for his flagrant disobedience and lack of repentance, Saul's kingdom would have been established "over Israel for all time" (1 Samuel 13:13-14). As it was, Samuel told him his kingdom would not last very long and that another person had already been selected by the Lord.

God sent Samuel to anoint one of Jesse's sons as king and God showed him that David was the chosen one. Samuel anointed him and "the Spirit of the Lord took control of David from that day forward" (1 Samuel 16:13 - HCSB). When a priest, prophet or king was anointed it symbolized the Holy Spirit coming over them and equipping them for the exercise of their office.

Though he was anointed and was soon afforded a stunning victory over the nine foot tall Philistine warrior Goliath (1 Samuel 17:4), it would be years before David would be the *de facto* king over all of Israel. Soon after David's victory, King Saul's gratefulness quickly turned to jealousy, and he tried to kill David on several occasions (1 Samuel 18-19). But the Lord was with David and even Saul's daughter Michal fell in love with him and was given in marriage to him (1 Samuel 18:20, 26-29). Saul's son Jonathan became David's best friend (1 Samuel 20).

We come to the second book of Samuel. The Philistines kill Saul and his sons Jonathan, Abinadab and Malki-Shua (1 Samuel 31:1-2). After mourning their deaths, David inquired of the Lord if it was time for him to move towards becoming king. The Lord said "yes," and told him to move to Hebron where he became king over Judah for seven and a half years.

Dr. Brian Stephens teaches that "Hebron is the second holiest city of Israel, next only in importance to Jerusalem" and "is where Abraham, Sarah, Isaac, Rebecca, and Jacob are buried." Stephens says "there is great spiritual significance revealed in the Scripture in regard to the city of Hebron. The biblical word Hebron is derived from the Hebrew word meaning 'to join or unite.' The Bible teaches that Hebron is the place where Israel must be brought together in unity if Israel is to fulfill her divine calling."[3]

"Israel" (all the other 10 tribes, as opposed to Judah and Benjamin) took Ish-Bosheth, one of Saul's sons, to be their king. So there was a war between "the house of David and the house of Saul" until Ish-Bosheth's own people turned against him and he was murdered (2 Samuel 2-4).

## GK] 2 Samuel 5 - David becomes king over all Israel

David finally became the full-fledged and acknowledged king over the whole nation of Israel when "all the tribes of Israel came to David at Hebron" and "anointed David king over Israel." At that time "David was thirty years old" (2 Samuel 5:1, 3-4 - NIV; see 1 Chronicles 11:1-9). What followed in rapid succession was absolutely vital to God's Kingdom program and the covenant He would establish with the house of David.[4]

First, David conquered Jerusalem—"the fortress of Zion"—from the Jebusites, took up residence there, calling it "the City of David" (2 Samuel 5:6-12 - NIV). It became obvious to David that the Lord was exalting his kingdom, and He was doing so "for the sake of his people Israel."

Next, David defeated the Philistines (2 Samuel 5:17-25) and ordered the Ark of the Covenant be taken to Jerusalem. The ark was the single most important symbol of God's presence among the Israelites, the holiest of all the Tabernacle furnishings.

David's greatest achievements were to unify all tribes of Israel under his rule, creating a monarchy / theocracy with its capital in Jerusalem, centralizing the worship there by bringing to it the ark of the covenant and preparing the way for the construction of the Temple. All in all, "the days that David reigned over Israel were forty years: seven years he reigned in Hebron and thirty-three years he reigned in Jerusalem" (1 Kings 2:11 - NASB).

But before we move on, there are some very important declarations related to David's dynasty and God's Kingdom that we should examine.

## [GK] [EK] 2 Samuel 7 - David's kingdom established forever through an everlasting covenant

God promised David that after his death He would establish "the throne of his kingdom forever," through his descendant who would build the Temple (2 Samuel 7:13 - NASB). That descendant would be Solomon. And even when he sinned, God would not depart from him as He had with Saul. No, God made an unconditional promise to David that "your house and your kingdom shall endure before Me forever; your throne shall be established forever" (2 Samuel 7:16 - NASB).

David humbly and gratefully claimed God's promise. David realized this was one hundred percent God's choosing and doing. He was happy for his nation. He declared: "You have established for Yourself Your people Israel as Your own people forever." He was grateful that it involved his family line, saying: "May the house of Your servant be blessed forever." And he acknowledged it was all for God's glory: "That Your name may be magnified forever" (2 Samuel 7:19, 24, 29, 26 - NASB).

There is only one way God could keep this eternal and unconditional promise, and that would be through Messiah Jesus, the King. At the end of David's life he remembered God had "established an everlasting covenant" with him and his house (2 Samuel 23:2-5 - HCSB). David was keenly aware this would ensure that the future eternal King would reign on David's throne, as his Descendant. At that time, "the Lord will be king over the whole earth. On that day there will be one Lord, and his name the only name" (Zechariah 14:9 - NIV).

# The Kingdom in the 1ˢᵗ Book of Kings

Solomon's address and prayer for the dedication of the Temple, which appears in 1 Kings 8, is almost identical to the account in 2 Chronicles 6, so we will look at this special Kingdom passage under Chronicles, below.

## [GK] [EK] 1 Kings 9 - God's conditional Kingdom Promise to Solomon

As we will see in Chronicles, God promises unconditionally to bless David and his house, guaranteeing there will be someone reigning on his throne forever. Yet we must remember that the Lord also told David that a certain aspect of the promise was conditional on the faithfulness of his descendants. When King David was about to die and had finally declared Solomon to be his successor, he charged him with keeping the Lord's commandments in order for his plans to prosper. David told Solomon the Lord had warned him that "if your sons take heed to their way, to walk before Me in truth with all their heart and with all their soul... you shall not lack a man on the throne of Israel" (1 Kings 2:4 - NKJV). The Lord later told Solomon directly that the continuity of rulers on his throne, by himself and his descendants, was conditional to obedience, as was the permanence of the Temple which had just been inaugurated.

First, God tells Solomon He has heard his prayer and was willing to be present at the Temple perpetually (1 Kings 9:1-3). But the next phrase begins with the conditional *"now if..."* *If* Solomon walked "in integrity of heart and in uprightness" as his father David had, *then* God would "establish the throne of your kingdom over Israel forever," as promised to David his father.

What was not conditional, as seen above, was God's promise that there would be a King on David's throne, Someone from his house, one of his Descendants, ruling for all eternity. That promise was unconditional because it refers to King Messiah. And His Kingdom cannot and will not be determined or detained by man's failure and sin.

It must be emphasized that God did not guarantee there would be a Davidic or Solomonic descendant between the time of Solomon and the beginning of the Kingdom of the eternal King. In fact, quite the opposite is true. God told Solomon that if he or his sons turned away from His commands and worshiped other gods, He would remove Israel from the Promised Land and cast the Temple out of His sight, a clear reference to its destruction (1 Kings 9:6-9).

We know Solomon and his descendants did precisely what the Lord warned them to should avoid. The kingdom split after Solomon, the Northern Kingdom of Israel eventually being invaded by the Assyrians and the Southern Kingdom of Judah being led into captivity by the Babylonians, who also destroyed the Temple. With Jerusalem and the Temple destroyed, continuity on the throne became impossible.

But even after the Babylonian captivity, when Jerusalem had been restored and the Temple rebuilt, there still was no king to rule over Judah or Israel. Zedekiah (597-586 B.C.) was the last king of the line of David to sit on the throne in Jerusalem, and did so until the Babylonians destroyed the city, tore down the Temple, and killed his sons right in front of him (2 Kings 25). From the days of Zedekiah until now Israel has not had a king from the line of David ruling over the nation.

It has been said that with the destruction of Herod's Temple in 70 A.D., all family records were destroyed, making it impossible to trace someone's lineage back to David and thus to legitimize anyone's Messianic claims from that time onward. Therefore, the next descendant of David to lay hold of the throne will be Jesus, the Son of David, the Anointed and Righteous One! His lineage is on record and He has all the credentials to claim His rightful inheritance.

# The Kingdom in 1st and 2nd Chronicles

Chronicles begins by giving several genealogies and moves on to recount the stories of King Saul and the conquests of King David. After reigning over Hebron and taking Jerusalem from the Jebusites, "David knew that the Lord had established him as king over Israel" (1 Chronicles 14:2).

### [GK] 1 Chronicles 2 - The Lord's kingdom over Israel

David called his leaders and told them of his desire to build the Temple, "a house as a resting place for the ark of the Lord's covenant and as a footstool for our God" (1 Chronicles 2:2 - HCSB). Heaven was seen as God's throne and the Temple (as well as the Earth itself), as God's footstool (see Isaiah 66:1).

David had made preparations and floor plans for the Temple but the Lord told him he had too much blood on his hands and the job would fall to his son Solomon instead. Yes, God had chosen Judah, David's household, and then David himself. But now God was choosing "Solomon to sit on the throne of the Lord's kingdom over Israel" (1 Chronicles 2:5 - HCSB). The term "the Lord's kingdom" is as close as it gets to "the Kingdom of God" in the Old Testament (see also 1 Chronicles 28:5 and 2 Chronicles 13:8).

God told David He had chosen Solomon to "be My son, and I will be his father" (1 Chronicles 2:6 - HCSB), an affirmation very similar to the Messianic passage of Psalm 2 (especially verse 7). Not only did David prefigure the Messiah and His kingly rule but Solomon did as well. The prosperity and peace that Solomon's rule brought about is perhaps symbolic of the Messianic Age. As is the idea of establishing his kingdom forever, as promised conditionally in the next verse. The condition was that the king persevere in obedience.

The charge that went out to Solomon is the same that applies to us today: to know God and serve Him with integrity of heart and willingness of mind; to seek Him and never to forsake Him. David warned Solomon that "the Lord searches every heart and understands the intention of every thought" (1 Chronicles 2:9 - HCSB). Unfortunately, there was no follow-through. Solomon began well but did not end well, unlike his father David.

## [GK] 1 Chronicles 16 - Proclaim that the Lord reigns!

After his first, failed attempt to bring the Ark of the Covenant to Jerusalem, David is ecstatic when he succeeds the second time around. He bursts out in a psalm of praise where, among other things, he declares:

> Let the whole earth sing to the Lord! Each day proclaim the good news that he saves. Publish his glorious deeds among the nations. Tell everyone about the amazing things he does. Great is the Lord! He is most worthy of praise! O nations of the world, recognize the Lord, recognize that the Lord is glorious and strong. Give to the Lord the glory he deserves! Bring your offering and come into his presence. Worship the Lord in all his holy splendor. Let the heavens be glad, and the earth rejoice! Tell all the nations, "The Lord reigns!" (1 Chronicles 16:23-25a; 28, 29, 31 - NLT)

"Tell all the nations, 'The Lord reigns!'" Proclaiming the Good News to the nations so they will join together in worshiping and glorifying the Lord, the King, is the mission given to His people. Israel did so by preserving the Holy Scriptures. The Church must continue to do so by proclaiming and practicing them.

## [GK] 1 Chronicles 18 - A king of righteousness

In one sense, David prefigured Jesus. The Messiah was, after all, called "the Son of David." And, "so David reigned over all Israel, administering justice and righteousness for all his people" (1 Chronicles 18:14 - HCSB).[5]

## [GK] [UK] [EK] 1 Chronicles 29 - King David's Kingdom praise

One of the greatest Kingdom passages in the Old Testament is found in 1 Chronicles 29. The leaders and the people of Israel, led by King David, had wholeheartedly given of their personal treasures towards the building of the Temple of the Lord, which we call "Solomon's Temple." Overcome by joy, David utters this heartfelt praise to the King of kings:

> May You be praised, Lord God of our father Israel, from eternity to eternity. Yours, Lord, is the greatness and the power and the glory and the splendor and the majesty, for everything in the heavens and on earth belongs to You. Yours, Lord, is the kingdom, and You are exalted as head over all. Riches and honor come from You, and You are the ruler of everything. Power and might are in Your hand, and it is in Your hand to make great and to give strength to all. Now therefore, our God, we give You thanks and praise Your glorious name.
> 1 Chronicles 29:10b-13 - HCSB; (see also verses 14-19)

This passage is so rich with Kingdom information that it is worth emphasizing. If God is to be praised "from everlasting to everlasting," it is because He is eternal, without beginning or end. To Him belong all the power, glory and the Kingdom itself. His sovereignty is absolute: He rules over *everything*.

As covenants include sacrifices, it is to be expected that "the next day they made sacrifices to the Lord and presented burnt offerings to him: a thousand bulls, a thousand rams and a thousand male lambs, together with their drink offerings, and other sacrifices in abundance for all Israel. They ate and drank with great joy in the presence of the Lord that day (1 Chronicles. 29:20, 21a).

The understanding that "Yours, Lord, is the kingdom" is echoed by the Lord Jesus almost 1,000 years later in "the Lord's Prayer," when He said, "For Yours is the kingdom and the power and the glory forever. Amen" (Matthew 6:13 - NKJV).

## [UK] [GK] 2 Chronicles 1-4 - Solomon dedicates the Temple to the Lord

In 2 Chronicles chapters 1 and 2 the reader is informed that Solomon is made king, God speaks with him and grants him his wish of wisdom, and Solomon accumulates much wealth and prepares to build the Temple.

Once the Temple was built, with all its furnishings, on Mount Moriah, under Solomon's guidance and during his reign (2 Chronicles chapters 3 and 4), it was time to dedicate the structure to the Lord. This would be a holy place, inhabited by God Almighty Himself. Solomon knew God was bigger and greater and could not be confined to a small plot of land. He reflected: "but will God indeed dwell with men on the earth? Behold, heaven and the heaven of heavens cannot contain You. How much less this temple which I have built!" (2 Chronicles 6:18 - NKJV). God would later declare through the Prophet Isaiah: "Heaven is My throne, and earth is My footstool. What house could you possibly build for Me? And what place could be My home?" (Isaiah 66:1b - HCSB). All the same, God promised His Presence and His Name would be there gloriously.

## [GK] [MK] 2 Chronicles 5-7 - King Solomon dedicates the Temple

The Feast of Dedication of the Temple began when King Solomon summoned all the leaders of the tribes of Israel to take the ark of the covenant from the temporary Tabernacle David had built into the recently finished Temple. The Levites carried the ark as well as all the other furnishings from the dismantled Tabernacle. Once brought into the Temple court, where the king and his people were waiting, they sacrificed "so many sheep and cattle that they could not be recorded or counted." Then the priests took over and carried the ark into the Holy of Holies. After the Levites had played instruments and sung praises to the Lord, the Temple of the Lord was filled with a cloud and the priests who were inside had to come out (2 Chronicles 5:2-14).

Solomon stood before the altar, on a bronze platform he had made for the occasion, and addressed the people with a long and very meaningful speech. He declared the Temple to be a place for God to dwell forever and praised God for keeping His covenant of love and His promises to David (2 Chronicles 6:2, 12, 13, 14-17).

Solomon's speech, which was also a prayer, ended by welcoming God to His Temple. He said: "now arise, O Lord God, and come to your resting place, you and the ark of your might" (2 Chronicles 6:41). As soon as he had finished, fire rained down from heaven consuming the sacrifices on the bronze altar, and God's glory entered and filled the Temple (2 Chronicles 7:1-2). The people fell to their knees, worshiped and gave thanks to the Lord. Then they got up and offered the Lord 22,000 head of cattle and 120,000 sheep and goats in sacrifice!

The Festival of Dedication went on for seven days. The festivities were not yet over because it was time for the Festival of Tabernacles to begin. And this last festival of the year is also a seven-day event, going from the 15th through the 22nd of the month of *Tishri*. Only the next day, "on the twenty-third day of the seventh month," did Solomon send the people back to their homes (2 Chronicles 7:8-10).

Here is what is so significant about the Temple being inaugurated during the Feast of Tabernacles: the Millennial Kingdom, Scripture seems to indicate, will begin with the Day of Atonement (Zechariah 12:10) and lead up to the Feast of Tabernacles (Zechariah 14), when the Messiah will be with His people and they will be camped around the Temple area in Jerusalem. The main idea behind the Feast of Tabernacles is precisely camping around the Lord, being in His immediate Presence, enjoying sweet fellowship with Him. We see, then, that this Festival—especially as celebrated during the dedication of the first Temple—is a prophetic sign which points to a future event and reality.

After the dedication of the Temple, God appeared to King Solomon and told him He had chosen that site for Himself as "a temple for sacrifices" (2 Chronicles 7:12). It is highly significant that on that very site, a little over 1,000 years earlier, Abraham sacrificed a ram instead of his son (Genesis 22:12-13). It is even more significant that close to 1,000 years after God designated the Temple on mount Moriah to be a place for sacrifices, that Jesus Christ would be sacrificed on that very same mountain!

## [GK] 2 Chronicles 9 - The Queen of Sheba: *Solomon on God's throne as king for Him*

The Queen of Sheba heard of Solomon's fame and went to visit and closely observe his kingdom (2 Chronicles 9:1-12). She was pleasantly surprised to see his wisdom was even greater than she had been told. Her insight into God's influence and authority over the kingdom was extraordinary. She exclaimed: "may the Lord your God be praised! He delighted in you and put you on His throne as king for the Lord your God. Because Your God loved Israel enough to establish them forever, He has set you over them as king to carry out justice and righteousness" (2 Chronicles 9:8 - HCSB).

She understood Solomon had strategically been placed on God's "throne as king for the Lord your God." She clearly saw that Israel was part of something much larger, and perhaps even caught a glimpse of the fact that the kingdom of Israel was vitally connected to the Kingdom of God on earth. She concluded correctly that the purpose of this kingdom—and of Solomon as its king—was "to carry out justice and righteousness." It is clear that the Queen of Sheba was not only politically savvy, but spiritually wise enough to understand the central role of righteousness where God's government is concerned.

## [GK] 2 Chronicles 13 and 20 - King Abijah: *the "kingdom of the Lord"*

King Abijah used he term "kingdom of the Lord" (2 Chronicles 13:8, 12). But what exactly did he mean? Did he have a vision for the Kingdom of God? Or was he strictly referring to the kingdom of Judah?

The context of 2 Chronicles 13 is that of Jeroboam, the king of Israel, and his intention to go to war with Judah, the kingdom of the south; and Abijah, the king of Judah, trying to dissuade him. Abijah's argument is that God was with the kingdom of Judah because they had remained faithful to Him and were the legitimate continuation of the line of David, and so heirs of God's Kingdom covenant and promises. The Northern Kingdom of Israel, on the other hand, had fallen into idolatry. It was for this reason that King Abijah warned Jeroboam that by going to war he was resisting "the kingdom of the Lord, which is in the hands of David's descendants" (2 Chronicles 13:8 - NIV).

The term "Kingdom of God" never appears in the Old Testament, although the concept is certainly there. However, the term "kingdom of the Lord" is used in at least two separate verses (here in 2 Chronicles 13:8 and in 1 Chronicles 28:5; see also 1 Chronicles 2:5 for "the Lord's kingdom over Israel").

Abijah continued: "Don't you know that the Lord, the God of Israel, has given the kingship of Israel to David and his descendants forever by a covenant of salt?," he told Jeroboam. "God is with us; he is our leader," he declared. Abijah was a king with a Kingdom vision (quoted above are verses 8, 5, and 12 of 2 Chronicles 13).

Now, in this context, Abijah's use of "the kingdom of the Lord" may seem limited to the kingdom of Judah and appear not to include the broader view of the "Kingdom of God," as in God's rule over all. But let's remember that King Abijah was sandwiched between his great grandfather David and his grandson Jehoshaphat (Matthew 1:7-8), both of whom had a Kingdom vision that far surpassed the narrow view which might restrict it to the kingdom of Israel or Judah.

First, let's look at David. Although he had used the more limiting term "the throne of the Lord's kingdom over Israel" at one point (1 Chronicles 2:5 - HCSB), in his hymn of praise found in Psalm 145, David exalts the Lord as "my God the King" and states that those who belong to God will proclaim "the glory of Your kingdom" and "the glorious splendor of Your kingdom." He then reveals that "Your kingdom is an everlasting kingdom; Your rule is for all generations" (Psalm 145:1, 10-13 - HCSB).

Clearly David had a vision for God's Kingdom that well exceeded the idea of a limited, local kingdom. It was evident he understood it was *God's* ("Your")

Kingdom, not Israel's. And that God is the ultimate and eternal King. It is hard to imagine this was not common knowledge among his descendants who occupied his throne through the years.

Abijah's grandson, Jehoshaphat, also understood God's sovereignty was not limited to Judah, but extended over the whole world. "He prayed, 'O LORD, God of our ancestors, you alone are the God who is in heaven. You are ruler of all the kingdoms of the earth. You are powerful and mighty; no one can stand against you!'" (2 Chronicles 20:6 - NLT).

Although there is an understanding that the Kingdom belonged to God and included all of heaven and earth, there was the conviction that through a covenant relationship with Israel, this nation had been chosen to be the special representative of God's Kingdom on Earth. It was to be under God's sovereign leadership. Its king was to be God's representative, which made Israel a form of theocracy. "Theoretically, a theocracy would be a state over which God rules directly without human mediators or representatives. Israel was never a true theocracy in this sense. Although Israel always thought of herself as under the rule of God, that rule was always mediated through a judge, a king, or a priest."[6]

Back to King Jehoshaphat, his prayer, quoted above, was uttered during a time of crisis. He had learned of the eminent attack by enemies who had joined forces, was afraid and sought the Lord. He cried out to the Ruler over all kingdoms. "The Spirit of the Lord" used someone to tell him "do not be afraid or discouraged because of this vast number, for the battle is not yours, but God's."

Even before God gave them the victory, Jehoshaphat and the people demonstrated their faith in the Lord by falling down and worshiping Him (2 Chronicles 20:1-19). This is a practical illustration of how "the kingdom of the Lord over Israel" was supposed to work. Instead of resorting to alliances with pagan nations or striking out on their own, the king and people of Israel (or Judah) were to first consult the Lord, follow His lead, and leave the victory up to Him (see Psalm 108:12-13).

# The Kingdom in Ezra and Nehemiah

Much had happened since the time of Jehoshaphat. Close to 260 years and 16 kings had come and gone before the Babylonians struck Jerusalem and took most of its population captive for 70 years. In the mean time, the Persians had conquered the Babylonian kingdom.

## [GK] Ezra 1 and Nehemiah 1, 2 and 9 - Rebuilding Temple and walls

King Cyrus of Persia claimed "all the kingdoms of the earth have been given to me by the Lord God of heaven, and he has instructed me to build him a Temple in Jerusalem, in the land of Judah. All among you who are the Lord's people return to Israel for this task, and the Lord be with you" (2 Chronicles 36:23 - TLB; repeated in Ezra 1:1-2).

Nehemiah recognizes God as great, mighty and awesome, a "God who keeps his promises and is so loving and kind to those who love and obey him!" (Nehemiah 1:5 - NASB). Throughout his ministry he was confident that "the God of heaven will help us, and we, his servants, will rebuild this wall" (Nehemiah 2:20 - NASB). Nehemiah reminded the Lord He was a God "who keeps covenant and lovingkindness" (Nehemiah 9:32 - NASB).

Both the reconstruction of the Temple and the rebuilding of the walls around Jerusalem were instrumental in reestablishing Judah as God's Kingdom people, in preparation for the coming Messiah. After the Babylonian exile, the prophets Haggai (520 B.C.), Zechariah (520 B.C.), and Malachi (432 B.C.) ministered to the remnant that returned to the Promised Land. Then would come the 400 interbiblical years, before the birth of Messiah Jesus.

# Chapter 3
# Books of Wisdom

## The Kingdom in Job

We're going way back now, as Job is considered the earliest book in the Bible. There are some Kingdom gems in this narrative that are highlighted below.

**[UK] [GK] Job 15, 19, 38, 42 - God's Council, the resurrection, morning stars, and getting to know God personally**

One of Job's "friends" asked him: "do you listen in on God's council? Do you have a monopoly on wisdom?" (Job 15:8 - NIV). It is interesting that one of the oldest books of the Old Testament contains a reference to God's Heavenly Council. It may have been a generic or even poetic reference, or there may have been a deeper understanding of this council at that early date.

A surprisingly early understanding of the resurrection is also demonstrated as Job confesses, "I know that my redeemer lives, and that in the end he will stand on the earth." He then confidently declares that "after my skin has been destroyed, yet in my flesh I will see God; I myself will see him with my own eyes—I, and not another. How my heart yearns within me! (Job 19:25-27 - NIV).

God reveals exclusive information to Job when questioning him. I have found no other verse in the Bible that states celestial beings predate the creation of the physical universe. But here God tells Job that while He was laying the earth's foundation, marking off its dimensions, measuring it and putting it in place, "the morning stars sang together and all the sons of God shouted for joy" (Job 38:4-7 - HCSB). This information is important for a better understanding not only of

God's Universal Kingdom but of His Global Kingdom as well.

After all Job went through, when he responds to the Lord, it is evident that he has had a moving, personal experience as never before. He had heard of God, now He knew Him personally, and repented "in dust and ashes." His new understanding of God's sovereignty led him to say, "I know that You can do anything and no plan of Yours can be thwarted" (Job 42:2, 6 - HCSB).

# The Kingdom in the Psalms

Jesus gave His endorsement of the Psalms when He told His disciples that "everything written about me in the Law of Moses and the Prophets and the Psalms must be fulfilled" (Luke 24:44b - ESV). When quoting Psalm 110:1, Jesus asked "why does David, speaking under the inspiration of the Spirit, call the Messiah 'my Lord'?" (Matthew 22:43 - NLT). Jesus declared that the Psalms prophesy about Him and were written under the inspiration of the Holy Spirit.

The Psalms are full of Kingdom references! From them we learn so much about God's power and authority over heaven and Earth. Embedded in the psalms are prophecies which would be fulfilled during Jesus' first coming and others still to be fulfilled in the future. There are also, as in Proverbs, a great number of verses dealing with righteousness, the standard of the Kingdom. Yet, very few of those will be mentioned since there is not enough time or room here to cover them.

### [MK] Psalm 2 - God's Messiah reigns

The New King James has the following title for Psalm 2: "The Messiah's Triumph and Kingdom." This psalm speaks of God's Son (verses 7 and 12), His Anointed (verse 2), the One of Whom He says, "I have set My King on My holy hill of Zion" (verse 6 - NKJV). This King is God's choice, yet He is the One the kings of the Earth set themselves against to no avail. God tells Him to "ask of Me, and I will give You the nations for Your inheritance, and the ends of the earth for Your possession. You shall break them with a rod of iron; You shall dash them to pieces like a potter's vessel" (verses 8 and 9 - NKJV). The rod of iron—or iron scepter—are code words for Messiah's rule during the Millennial Kingdom (Revelation 2:27; 12:5; 19:15).

As early as Genesis 49:10 Jacob prophesied that "the scepter will not depart from Judah, nor the ruler's staff from between his feet, until he to whom it belongs shall come and the obedience of the nations shall be his" (NIV). Jesus is from the tribe of Judah, and to Him belongs the Kingdom authority over all nations, which He will exercise vigorously during the Millennium Kingdom.

## [GK] Psalm 5 - God is King

While in Psalm 4:1 David calls on "my righteous God," here he cries out to "my King and my God," and understands He is against wickedness, evil, the boastful, evildoers, liars, and those who shed blood and are treacherous (verses 2, 4-6). With this in mind, David asks the Lord to "lead me in Your righteousness" and to "make Your way straight before me" (verse 8 - HCSB)

## [GK] Psalm 7 - God judges righteously

Although there is no direct mention of the Kingdom, David speaks of God's office as judge, His righteous character and His demand for repentance. David says "the Lord judges the peoples" (v. 8), he asks Him to "establish the righteous," declares He "is a righteous God" (v. 9), as well as "a righteous judge" (v. 11), and warns that "if anyone does not repent" they can be sure God's judgment will find them (v. 12). He ends by saying, "I will thank the Lord for His righteousness" (v. 17). (HCSB).

## [UK] [GK] Psalm 9 - God is enthroned as a righteous judge

David sings of God's wonderful works and proclaims, "You are seated on Your throne as a righteous judge" (v. 4) over the nations. "The Lord sits enthroned forever; He has established His throne for judgment. He judges the world with righteousness; He executes judgment on the nations with fairness" (v.v. 7-8). David sees the Lord dwelling in Zion, that is, in Jerusalem (v. 11). (HCSB)

## [EK] Psalm 10 - God is an eternal King

The psalmist writes: "the Lord is King forever and ever" (v. 16 - HCSB). Just as Daniel would later proclaim, not only is God eternal, but He is eternally the sovereign King, which means His Kingdom is also eternal.

## [UK] [GK] Psalm 11 - God controls everything from heaven

David asks, "when the foundations are destroyed, what can the righteous do?" (v. 3). Apparently not much, because the next verse puts all the focus on God. As we watch the foundations of our nation collapse, our hope does not have to erode with it. Because "the Lord is in His holy temple; the Lord's throne is in heaven. His eyes watch; He examines everyone. The Lord examines the righteous and the wicked" (v. v. 4, 5). God is still in control. He will punish the wicked and reward the upright (they "will see His face"), "for the Lord is righteous; He loves righteous deeds" (v. 7). God is not taken by surprise, neither can the forces of darkness subvert or sabotage the plans of His Kingdom. (HCSB)

## [GK] Psalm 15 - Righteous behavior

This is a great chapter on righteousness, spelling out in practical terms what righteousness "looks like" in everyday life. (See "What does living righteously look like?" on page 21 of *The Values of the Kingdom*, volume 2 in this series).

## [GK] Psalm 22 - Messiah sacrificed; kingship belongs to the Lord

David was more than a good writer. He was a prophet. And in this psalm, under divine inspiration, he writes about Messiah's suffering and describes the pain and suffering experienced by one who is crucified. But it was all worth it, because "all the ends of the earth will remember and turn to the Lord. All the families of the nations will bow down before You" (v. 27). And they will do so because they will recognize that "kingship belongs to the Lord; He rules over the nations" (v. 28). And this would extend from generation to generation, as "they will come and tell a people yet to be born about His righteousness—what He has done" (v. 31). (HCSB)

## [GK] Psalm 24 - God owns the Earth; He's the King of glory

King David informs us just how much of planet earth and its population belong to the Lord: all of it! "The earth is the Lord's, and everything in it. The world and all its people belong to him" (Psalm 24:1 - NLT). It is all His domain. It is His Global Kingdom. That is why He is Lord of lords and King of kings (Revelation 17:14; 19:1).

In a poetic portion, David exalts the Lord as the King of glory:

> Lift up your heads, O you gates; and be lifted up, you age-abiding doors, that the King of glory may come in. Who is the King of glory? The Lord strong and mighty, the Lord mighty in battle. Lift up your heads, O you gates; yes, lift them up, you age-abiding doors, that the King of glory may come in. Who is [He then] this King of glory? The Lord of hosts, He is the King of glory. Selah [pause, and think of that]! (Psalm 24:7-10 - AMP).

## [UK] [GK] Psalm 29 - Worshiped by heavenly beings; King forever

The psalmists regularly call on us mortals to exalt and worship the Lord. But here David calls on the heavenly beings to do so as well. "Ascribe to Yahweh, you heavenly beings, ascribe to the LORD glory and strength. Ascribe to Yahweh the glory due His name; worship Yahweh in the splendor of His holiness" (Psalm 29:1,

2 - HCSB). It is clear that only God, our King, is worthy of adoration—by humans and celestial beings alike.

One of the most catastrophic events of human history did not escape God's control. And it is good to know that our benevolent King is still in control now, and will be for all eternity. "The LORD sat as King at the flood; Yes, the LORD sits as King forever" (Psalm 29:10 - NASB).

## [GK] Psalm 33 - God loves righteousness; observes all on Earth

This psalm doesn't mention God as King, but mentions a couple of attributes that are essential to His reign. First, the Lord "loves righteousness and justice; the earth is full of the LORD's unfailing love" (Psalm 33:5 -HCSB). And the knowledge that "the LORD looks down from heaven and sees the whole human race. From his throne he observes all who live on the earth. He made their hearts, so he understands everything they do" (Psalm 33:13-15 - NLT). God is a righteous, just, loving, all-seeing, all-knowing, and all-understanding King.

## [MK] Psalm 37 - Meek to inherit the Earth

Quoted by our Lord in His sermon on the mount (Matthew 5:5), this portion of this psalm promises "the meek shall inherit the earth; and shall delight themselves in the abundance of peace" (Psalm 37:11 - KJB). It will not necessarily be the rich and famous or the politically powerful, but the meek who will inherit the (new) Earth as their eternal abode. Meekness is an important **Kingdom Value** (see **Kingdom Value** #3 in *The Values of the Kingdom of God*, the second volume in this series). We are to reflect and imitate our King and His character and being meek is an essential way of doing so.

## [GK] Psalm 44 - God is our King

The Sons of Korah had heard the stories of the Lord's great achievements in the days of their forefathers. This led them to profess, "You are my King, O God; Command victories for Jacob" (Psalm 44:4 - NASB). They asked Him to act again as they also faced battles and difficulties. Knowing our King's track record encourages us to believe He Who did marvelous things in the past can do them again for us!

## [UK] [GK] [EK] Psalm 45 - "God, your God, has anointed you"

The Psalmists, the Sons of Korah, provide precious information about God's Kingdom: it is eternal and based on justice and righteousness. They declare: "Your throne, God, is forever and ever; the scepter of Your kingdom is a scepter of justice. You love righteousness and hate wickedness; therefore God, your God, has anointed you with the oil of joy more than your companions" (Psalm 45:6-7 - HCSB).

The last portion of this psalm is quoted in Hebrews 1:8-9, where the author says it refers to "the Son." God's Son is God the Son. God the Father anointed Him as Messiah with the oil of joy. This passage seems to convey that the Son was delighted to take on the mission given Him by the Father, because it would lead to establishing the Kingdom with righteousness on this Earth which had lost its way.

The Jewish community should examine and answer the question this chapter raises: how could God have a God? How could God have a Son? This is not a purely Christian idea. The fact God has a Son appears in Proverbs 30:4: "Who has gone up to heaven and come down? Who has gathered the wind in His hands? Who has bound up the waters in a cloak? Who has established all the ends of the earth? What is His name, and what is the name of His Son– if you know?" (HCSB). This is not a mistranslation. The same truth is found in the Tanakh, the Hebrew Bible.

## [GK] [MK] Psalm 46 - the river and presence of God; exalted over all

A description of the earth trembling, mountains toppling into the seas, waters roaring, and mountains quaking (verses 2 and 3) is contrasted with the next vision: "There is a river— its streams delight the city of God, the holy dwelling place of the Most High. God is within her; she will not be toppled. God will help her when the morning dawns" (Psalm 46:4-5 - HCSB).

Do you see a correlation with the life-giving river in Ezekiel 47:1-12, which flows from the Temple and speaks of a time or restoration and renewal in the Holy Land? When will this take place? The prophet Zechariah tells us that "on that day living water will flow out from Jerusalem (...) On that day Yahweh will become King over all the earth—Yahweh alone, and His name alone" (Zechariah 14:8-9 - HCSB). The context of this whole chapter in Zechariah is the Lord's triumphant return when He will set up His Millennial Kingdom. Notice, back to Psalm 46, that "God is within ... the city of God," which we know to be Jerusalem.

Further proof this speaks of the Messianic Age is that it says "the earth melts when He lifts His voice," that "He makes wars cease throughout the earth. He shatters bows and cuts spears to pieces; He burns up the chariots," and He orders, "stop your fighting—and know that I am God, exalted among the nations, exalted on the earth" (Psalm 46:6b, 9, 10 - HCSB).[1]

## [GK] [MK] Psalm 47 - God is King of all the Earth

The New American Standard Bible has included the title "God the King of the

Earth," for this chapter. When the Lord comes to set up His Millennial Kingdom, it will be time to celebrate!

> O clap your hands, all peoples; Shout to God with the voice of joy.
> For the Lord Most High is to be feared, A great King over all the earth.
> God has ascended with a shout, The Lord, with the sound of a trumpet.
> Sing praises to God, sing praises; Sing praises to our King, sing praises.
> For God is the King of all the earth; Sing praises with a skillful psalm.
> God reigns over the nations, God sits on His holy throne.
> (Psalm 47:1, 2; 5-8 - NASB)

Joy is a ***Kingdom Value***. It is present when the Lord manifests His Presence and love. There will be so much of it when He comes back to establish a Kingdom of justice, fairness, understanding and peace, all qualities notoriously missing in the world today.

One could make the case that this psalm—and others like it—are simply declaring God's ownership and sovereignty over the world in this present age. And there is certainly a degree of this, as God is sovereign over His Global Kingdom, here and now. But there are descriptions that are more than merely poetic or ideal: they definitely point to the Messianic Era when peace and righteousness will reign because God will personally rule over the whole Earth.

## [GK] Psalm 48 - the greatness of the Lord on Mount Zion

The description of the Messianic Age continues. "Great is the Lord, and greatly to be praised, in the city of our God, His holy mountain. Beautiful in elevation, the joy of the whole earth, is Mount Zion *in* the far north, the city of the great King" (Psalm 48:1, 2 - NASB). Mount Zion will put the moon and sun to shame (these will be darkened on the Great Day of the Lord), "because the LORD of Hosts will reign as king on Mount Zion in Jerusalem, and He will display His glory in the presence of His elders" (Isaiah 24:23 - HCSB; see also Psalm 68:16; 99:2 and Micah 4:7).

The psalmists further proclaim the city of God will be established forever. They recall God's lovingkindness, declare His "right hand is full of righteousness," and tell us Zion and Judah rejoice because of His judgments—a sign they are just and fair.

## [GK] Psalm 50 - Mighty God owns it all

Asaph, the author of this psalm, presents God as "the Mighty One, God, the Lord" who is getting ready to judge His covenant people. While it seems His people thought they could placate His wrath by "feeding" Him animal sacrifices, God tells them "I do not need the bulls from your barns or the goats from your pens. For all the animals of the forest are mine, and I own the cattle on a thousand hills. I know every bird on the mountains, and all the animals of the field are mine" (Psalm 50:9-11 - NLT). Furthermore, even if God were hungry, He wouldn't tell them about it, "for all the world is mine and everything in it" (Psalm 50:12b - NLT).

God is the rightful owner of the whole world and sovereign over the entire Global Kingdom. What He desires is genuine commitment and fellowship, to rescue us and to receive glory (verses 12-15).

## [GK] Psalm 63 - David confesses deep thirst for God and His love

David exemplifies precisely the attitude God is looking for in us. Jesus said blessed are those who hunger and thirst for righteousness. David, who was in the wilderness when he wrote this psalm, confessed, "O God, you are my God; I earnestly search for you. My soul thirsts for you; my whole body longs for you in this parched and weary land where there is no water" (Psalm 63:1 - NLT).

David had genuinely experienced God in his life. And God had shown him amazing things about Himself, His Kingdom, and the coming Messiah. "I have seen you in your sanctuary," he said, "and gazed upon your power and glory" (Psalm 63:2 - NLT). It is easy to get so involved with describing the Kingdom that we forget to adore the King. David not only knew God as a powerful and glorious King, he longed to be in deep fellowship with Him. We see a similar attitude in Mary, Martha's sister, in the Gospel of John.

## [GK] Psalm 67 - God rules fairly; may nations praise Him

The psalmist asks that God's favor be shown so that His ways "will be known on earth" and "all nations will see that you have the power to save." His desire is to see the peoples of all the nations on earth praising the Lord (Psalm 67:1-3). God ruling over the whole earth is a good thing and brings true fulfillment. So the psalmists prays, "May the nations be glad and sing with joy. You rule the people of the earth fairly. You guide the nations of the earth" (Psalm 67:4 - NIRV). We should join in and pray the same. Jesus did. He asked, "our Father in heaven, may your name be kept holy. May your Kingdom come soon. May your will be done on earth, as it is in heaven" (Matthew 6:9, 10 - NLT).

## [MK] Psalm 68 - God will dwell on Mount Zion forever

Mount Zion is going to be a very special place (see comments on Psalm chapter 48, above). Look! "You mountains of many peaks, why do you watch with envy the mountain in which God has chosen to dwell? Indeed, the LORD will live there forever" (Psalm 68:16 - ISV). Isaiah, too, had a vision of Jerusalem, which sits atop of Mount Zion. He got a glimpse of the Millennial Kingdom and describes what he saw in Isaiah 2:1-4 (see more below, under "The Kingdom in Isaiah").

## [UK] [GK] [MK] [EK] Psalm 89 - the Royal, Davidic Covenant

This is a prophetic, Messianic covenant in which God promised King David that one of His descendants would occupy his throne forever. Jesus first came as Isaiah's Suffering Servant, but will return as the Glorious King of the Millennial Kingdom (Isaiah 42:1; Psalm 2). The prophecy is clearly stated here: "The Lord said, 'I have made a covenant with My chosen one; I have sworn an oath to David My servant: 'I will establish your offspring forever and build up your throne for all generations'" (Psalm 89:3-4; see also 2 Samuel 23:5; 2 Chronicles 13:5; 21:7; Jeremiah 33:20-21).[2]

"Offspring" translates the Hebrew word for "seed," first used to refer to the promised Messiah in Genesis 3:15. It simply means "descendant" but takes on a special meaning when referring to "the Promised One." God told Isaac: "And I will make your descendants multiply as the stars of heaven; I will give to your descendants all these lands; and in your seed all the nations of the earth shall be blessed" (Genesis 26:4 - NKJV). The "descendants" were the future generations of Israelites; the seed was to be the Messiah, Who blesses all nations through His life, death and resurrection.

The Davidic covenant assures "David's dynasty of glory, divine support, and continuity." The covenant is, in part, conditional, because "the responsibility lies on each king of David's dynasty to fulfill his role as a representative of God's rule on earth." "The Davidic king 'administers' the kingdom of God as a vassal. He rules 'in the name' of Yahweh."[3] The Messianic portion of the covenant is unconditional, as verses 30 through 35 make abundantly clear.

As we examine other sections of this psalm, we read that "righteousness and justice are the foundation of Your throne" (Psalm 89a:14 - HCSB). We see the Lord is called "the Holy One of Israel" (Psalm 89:18). David is referred to as "our king" in relation to Israel, and "My servant" in relation to God, Who anointed him with "sacred oil" (Psalm 89:20). God promised to "always be with him" and "strengthen him" (Psalm 89:21). Some of what this psalm says is directed at David, some at the coming Messiah, and some to both, in the same breath. God declares, concerning the Messiah:

- **He will have God's support and power:** "My faithfulness and love will be with him, and through My name his horn will be exalted" (Psalm 89:24). "I will extend his power to the sea and his right hand to the rivers" (Psalm 89:25).

• **He is God's Son:** "He will call to Me, 'You are my Father, my God, the rock of my salvation'" (Psalm 89:26).

• **He will be the greatest King the world has ever known:** "I will also make him My firstborn, greatest of the kings of the earth" (Psalm 89:27 - HCSB).

God promised: "My covenant with him will endure" (Psalm 89:28), and that, "I will establish his line forever, his throne as long as heaven lasts" (Psalm 89:29). God reaffirms His commitment to the Messianic covenant by promising not to betray His faithfulness (v. 33) and that, "I will not violate My covenant or change what My lips have said" (Psalm 89:34). In the strongest terms, God states: "Once and for all I have sworn an oath by My holiness; I will not lie to David" (Psalm 89:35).

The intended goal and promise of the Messianic or Royal covenant is that of an eternal Ruler in an Eternal Kingdom. "His offspring will continue forever, his throne like the sun before Me" (Psalm 89:36) (HCSB).

Psalm 89 also speaks of "the assembly of the holy ones" (v. 5), "heavenly beings" (v. 6) who cannot be compared to the Lord, and "the council of the holy ones" (v. 7), where God is greatly feared. All of this tells the story of an all-powerful God and His highly organized Universal Kingdom. Yet we know God never abuses His power, instead acting righteously, lovingly and faithfully towards all He has created.[4]

## [UK]-[EK] Psalm 93 - the Lord reigns

The Holman Christian Standard Bible titles this chapter as "God's Eternal Reign." While Psalms 90-106 belong to a new division in the collection of psalms (Book IV), "this psalm belongs to a group of psalms (47; 93-100) that affirm Yahweh's rule over the earth."[5]

The psalmist shares important insights into God's Kingdom and mentions some of God's attributes. God is acknowledged as an eternal Being and eternal King; His glory is admired and His holy character celebrated. He declares that "the Lord reigns!," His "throne has been established from the beginning." This tells us the Kingdom of God is eternal. We may assume God has always been King. The psalmist describes God as being "from eternity" and as "robed in majesty" and strength. He states that God's "testimonies are completely reliable," and that "holiness is the beauty of Your house for all the days to come" (v.v. 1, 2, 5) (NKJV).

## [GK] Psalm 94 - God is Judge over the Earth

We are the present, active participants of the Global Kingdom, God's Kingdom on Earth. But how can we reconcile God's righteousness with the prevailing injustice seen in our society? This is a message about the unrighteous world system, a system we can readily identify with today. It is also a message of hope because of God's sovereignty.

The psalmist refers to God as the "Judge of the earth" (v. 2), and questions why the proud and the wicked have gone unpunished for so long. This is a question that often comes to mind as we observe our world today. If God is a fair Judge and King over all the earth, why are people, governments and systems so unfair?

In the difficult times that lay ahead for God's people, it is good to be reminded that "the Lord will not forsake His people or abandon His heritage," and that we can look forward to the day when "justice will again be righteous" (v.v. 14-15). As King, God has a vested interest in His people. He is their helper, refuge and rock of protection (verses 17 and 22).

The psalmist then asks: "can a corrupt throne—one that creates trouble by law—become Your ally?" (v. 20). We might contextualize the question by asking: "can God bless America if it turns away from God's law?" Then, as if reading from today's headlines, the psalmist declares: "They band together against the life of the righteous and condemn the innocent to death" (v. 21). But God "will pay them back for their sins and destroy them for their evil. The Lord our God will destroy them" (v. 23) (HCSB). There is a high price to pay for those who ignore God's laws and His ***Kingdom Values***.

## [GK] Psalm 95 - God is the Great King

While the previous psalm speaks of God as Judge and Lord, here the psalmist, perhaps the same writer, in an attitude of joyful worship, refers to the Lord as "the great God, and the great King above all gods" (v. 3). He also sees Him as having control over the whole earth because He is the Creator, our Maker, Whom we should worship, "for He is our God, and we are the people of His pasture" (v.v. 4-7) (NKJV).

## [GK] Psalm 96 - the King of the Earth

The message is that we should exalt and worship the Lord. To "declare His glory among the nations" (v. 3a) because "the Lord is great" (v. 4), and He "made the heavens" (v. 5). God is described with expressions such as "splendor and majesty," "strength and beauty" (v. 6) and "holiness" (v. 9).

We are to "say among the nations: 'The Lord reigns'" and "He judges the peoples fairly" (v. 10). Paradoxically, *life isn't fair* but God is! The exclamation "let the heavens be glad and the earth rejoice" (v.11), shows how both are linked with a special bond. Messiah Jesus would teach His disciples to pray "your kingdom come, your will be done, on earth as in heaven (Matthew 6:10 - NABRE). God's ideal is that the world become *heaven on earth*. At the end, when this comes to fruition, there will be fellowship between God's heavenly sons and God's earthly sons, celestial beings and redeemed human beings, in one big, joyful family (Ephesians 3:14-15).

Earth can rejoice because understanding and embracing God's sovereignty leads to true joy (happiness is the result of righteous living).

Lastly, we are clued in that "He is coming to judge the earth. He will judge the world with righteousness" (v. 13) (HCSB). What a scary thought for the wicked: they will be measured against God's **Kingdom Values**, the very values they ignored and ridiculed their whole life. But what a relief and comfort for the righteous to know that God is going to judge with impartial justice, with perfect knowledge of motivations and actions alike, and set everything right. Thankfully, God's righteous judgment applies His grace to those who believe and repent.

## [GK] Psalm 97 - the Majestic King

The fact that "the Lord reigns" is cause for celebration. "Let the earth rejoice," the psalmist says (v. 1). We are again told—this time very directly—that "righteousness and justice are the foundation of His throne" (v. 2). We are reminded that God is "the Lord of all the earth" (v. 5), and "the Most High over all the earth" (v. 9). Zion is glad and Judah rejoices because of the Lord's judgments (v. 8) (HCSB). It is refreshing to know that, although most powerful earthly rulers continue to be corrupt, God's standard of righteousness and values of honesty, integrity and fairness continue to be the way He runs our world and His universe.

## [GK] Psalm 98 - the Victorious King

"Sing a new song to the Lord, for He has performed wonders; His right hand and holy arm have won Him victory" (Psalm 98:1 - HCSB).

It was 3:15 AM on February 27, 2010, when my wife Monica, daughter Melissa and I were awakened in Santiago, Chile, with a violent shake, then another one, followed by continuous shaking, rattling and a deep, eerie moan rising up from the earth below. The floor started jumping up at us and the walls began cracking and swaying all around us. It lasted one minute and forty seconds of what seemed like a very long time. We had just experienced an 8.8 magnitude earthquake!

After it was over and we were sitting in the living room, I had the feeling God was telling me, "you feel my power?" Although I was having a very hard time processing what had just happened, there was one thing I was sure of: God *is* mighty and powerful.

The psalmist was reminiscing about unforgettable wonders and victories God had won for the nation of Israel. Perhaps it was the exodus from Egypt and the way He led them through the desert. The nations in the area heard about what had happened and had to concede God was giving Israel victory after victory. Through this story and others registered in the Old Testament, "the Lord has made His victory known; He has revealed His righteousness in the sight of the nations" (Psalm 9:2 - HCSB).

God's victories should cause His people to "shout triumphantly in the presence of the Lord, our King" (Psalm 9:6 - HCSB). Even nature rejoices because the Lord, the King, "is coming to judge the earth. He will judge the world righteously and the peoples fairly" (Psalm 9:9 - HCSB; see 96:13).

## [GK] Psalm 99 - an invitation to worship the King

"The Lord, the Fair and Holy King" is the title the Expanded Bible provides for this chapter. The psalm begins affirming "the Lord reigns" and "sits [enthroned] above the cherubim" (Psalm 99:1 - AMP). The ark of the covenant with the cherubim on the lid (the mercy seat), as well as the large cherubim towering above, in the holy of holies in the Temple, were a picture of this reality. The invitation to "extol the Lord our God and worship at His footstool!" (Psalm 99:5 - AMP) is an invitation to worship at the Temple in Jerusalem.

The psalmist enumerates some of God's attributes as a ruler: He is "great" and "high above all the peoples" (v. 2). He has a "great name," that is "awesome and reverence inspiring," and He and His name are holy (v. 3). He executes "justice and righteousness" (v. 4), is a "forgiving God" but avenges "evildoing and wicked practices" (v. 8). For a third time, God is declared to be holy (v. 9).

## [UK] [GK] [MK] [EK] Psalm 102 - the Sovereign King

The author of this psalm cries out to the Lord for help in the midst of suffering, grief, and depression. Although he is faced with a crisis and Jerusalem must be in dire straits, he can be sure of this: "but, Lord, you rule [are enthroned] forever, and your fame [memory] goes on and on [throughout the generations]" (Psalm 102:12 - EXB). The fact God, the King, is on His throne and is ruling forever without change, brings stability, strength and comfort when everything else feels like it is out of control.

Notice how all four aspects of the Kingdom are mentioned in this psalm.
**The Universal Kingdom (UK):** "The Lord looked down from his sanctuary on high, from heaven he viewed the earth" (v. 19).
**The Global Kingdom (GK):** "In the beginning you laid the foundations of the earth ... the work of your hands" (v. 25).
**The Millennial Kingdom (or Messianic Age) (MK):** "For the Lord will rebuild Zion and appear in his glory. So the name of the Lord will be declared in Zion and his praise in Jerusalem when the peoples and the kingdoms assemble to worship the Lord" (v.v. 16, 21-22).
**The Eternal Kingdom (EK):** "But you remain the same, and your years will never end" (v. 27). (All verses in Psalm 102, except v. 12, from the NIV).

## [GK] Psalm 103 - the Compassionate King

This is an uplifting chapter which speaks of God's grace and forgiveness. Although the Lord is ready and willing to forgive our shortcomings, He always "does what is fair (righteous), and executes justice for all the oppressed" (v. 6).

Who has ever heard of a king who has so much power and authority and yet is willing to erase from his records what would amount to treason? And yet "the Lord is compassionate and merciful; he is patient and demonstrates great loyal love" (v. 8). What a King we serve! For "he does not deal with us as our sins deserve; he does not repay us as our misdeeds deserve" (v. 10). To the extent that "as far as the eastern horizon is from the west, so he removes the guilt of our rebellious actions from us" (v. 12).

The psalmist goes on to say how the Lord is compassionate like a father because He knows our makeup, that we are fragile as clay, our earthly life ephemeral as grass. The Lord takes that into consideration and keeps on loving His "faithful followers" and "those who keep his covenant" and really seek to obey Him (v.v. 17, 18).

David, the author of this psalm, first dwells on how God positively affects our daily lives and relationship with Himself. He then focuses on the Universal aspect of the Kingdom, by declaring that "the Lord has established his throne in heaven; his kingdom extends over everything" (v. 19). In order to understand the Kingdom of God we must first understand He rules from heaven over every*thing*, and every*body*, every*where* (see chapter 4, "The Universal Kingdom," of ***The Secret of the Kingdom of God***, the first volume in this series).

David then spells out what God expects and desires from His created beings, in this case, the celestial ones: "praise the Lord, you angels of his, you powerful warriors who carry out his decrees and obey his orders!" Angels are God's "warriors" and "servants." They "obey his orders" and "carry out his desires" (v. 21).

Angels are not the only created beings God has brought to life. And so, the psalmist brings this charge to all: "praise the Lord, all that he has made, in all the regions of his kingdom! Praise the Lord, O my soul!" (v. 22). The King of kings is worthy of our devotion, praise and worship. We were created for this!
(Psalm 103 from the NET Bible).

## [GK] [MK] Psalm 110 - "The Lord said to my Lord"

Inspired by the Holy Spirit, David tells of the time when "the Lord (God) says to my Lord (the Messiah), Sit at My right hand, until I make Your adversaries Your footstool" (Psalm 110:1 - AMP).

This verse is so central to the Messiah's identity that it is quoted in Matthew (22:44); Mark (12:36), Luke (20:42) and Acts (2:34-36; Peter's sermon during Pentecost, applying the psalm to Jesus Who is both "Lord and Messiah").

Jesus refers to this psalm because the Sadducees and Pharisees had been trying to trip Him up with trick questions and mind games. A scribe noticed the commotion and asked Jesus which was the greatest commandment. After answering him and seeing his positive reaction, Jesus told him "you are not far from the kingdom of God" (Mark 12:34 - HCSB). We can infer Jesus meant his understanding and attitude towards God was such that he was well on his way to salvation.

Jesus then took the lead and questioned the Pharisees about the identity of Messiah. "Whose Son is He?"—Jesus asked. "David's"—they answered. Jesus quotes this portion of Psalm 110, reminding them David wrote under the inspiration of the Holy Spirit. He then asks them, "if David calls Him 'Lord,' how then can the Messiah be [David's] Son?" (Matthew 22:45 - HCSB). They were stumped. That was the last time they attempted to outsmart the Lord with their traps.

As to the meaning of "sit at My right hand, until I make Your adversaries Your footstool," the verse indicates a joint government of the Son with the Father during a period which will come to a close once the Son's enemies are permanently defeated. This process will be completed at the end of the Millennial Kingdom.

This means the Millennial Kingdom will be both a time of prosperity, justice, and peace, but also a time of eliminating the remaining rebellious people and kingdoms of the earth. To this purpose "the Lord will extend [His] mighty scepter from Zion" and Messiah will "rule over [His] surrounding enemies" (v. 2; see Isaiah 2:3-4).

The following description may well relate to the period right before the establishment of the Millennial Kingdom, since it claims the Lord "will crush kings on the day of His anger" (v. 5), and "He will judge the nations, heaping up corpses; He will crush leaders over the entire world" (v. 6). The time of His wrath speaks of the Day of the Lord. The portion about judging the nations may relate to the judgment of the sheep and the goats in Matthew 25:31-46.

Supporting this idea is a passage that undeniably has to do with Jesus' return to earth with His saints to set up His Millennial Kingdom. It was revealed to John that "coming out of his mouth is a sharp sword with which to strike down the nations. 'He will rule them with an iron scepter.' He treads the winepress of the fury of the wrath of God Almighty" (Revelation 19:15 - NIV; see Psalm 2:9 and Revelation 2:27; 12:5 for more on the iron scepter or rod).

The Holman Christian Standard Bible titles this Davidic psalm "The Priestly King" because of verse 4: "the Lord has sworn an oath and will not take it back: 'Forever, You are a priest like Melchizedek.'" Messiah is an eternal priest, not from the tribe of Levi, as all other Jewish priests, but in the order of Melchizedek, the King of [Jeru]Salem (meaning Peace) and the King of Righteousness. (Psalm 110:2-6 from HCSB).

## [UK]-[GK] Psalm 113 - the Merciful King

A tribute to the merciful King, Whose servants should praise Him "both now and forever," and "from the rising of the sun to its setting" (v.v. 2, 3). Praise is something the King desires to receive from His people, as seen above in Psalms 103 (verses 19-22).

A strong connection between heaven and Earth—between the Universal Kingdom and the Global Kingdom—can again be seen in this passage: "Yahweh is exalted above all the nations, His glory above the heavens" and that "the One enthroned on high ... stoops down to look on the heavens and the earth" (v. v. 4-6) (Psalm 113 from HCSB).

## [UK] [GK] Psalm 115 - Global Kingdom shared with human beings

"May you be blessed by the Lord, who made the heavens and the earth. The highest heavens belong to the Lord, but he gave the earth to human beings" (115:15-16 - ISV). Here is a central passage for the Global Kingdom. The Lord created the heavens (literally "heaven of heaven") and the earth. Heaven is His special domain, His headquarters as it were, but He has delegated authority to human beings when it comes to planet earth. This is not *laissez faire*. To delegate implies supervision and accountability.

Paul explained this concept to Timothy by saying God is the "only Sovereign, the King of kings and Lord of lords" (1 Timothy 6:15b - NASB). Humans are destined to become kings (small "k") and lords (small "l"), but they still answer to God, the King and Lord (capitals "K" and "L"). This truth is brought home by another psalm, which states "the Lord does whatever pleases him in heaven and on earth" (Psalm 135:6 - ISV). That would be a good definition of "sovereign."

But we must not imagine God a tyrannical power player, a politician or corporate tycoon in the sky. David's psalms regularly speak of our King as interested in the plight of the poor and needy. David once said that "though the Lord is on high, yet He regards the lowly; but the proud He knows from afar" (Psalm 138:6 - NKJV). Although all-powerful, God loves His people and has their best at heart.

## [GK] Psalm 132 - David's Descendant to rule on his throne

We have seen in Chronicles and Kings that God chose one of David's descendants to reign forever. Here this prophecy is referenced again. To avoid confusion, we must read verses 11 and 12 carefully, because there is a critical difference between the two which must be taken into account. Verse 11 says "the Lord swore an oath to David, a promise He will not abandon: 'I will set one of your descendants on your throne.'" This is a prophecy which pertains to the future rule of Messiah. This promise is not conditional and involves an oath.

But verse 12 is conditional, and says that if one of David's "sons keep My covenant and My decrees that I will teach them, their sons will also sit on your throne forever." The Messiah descends from David and rules forever. If David's son, grandson, and their descendants had remained faithful to the Lord as David had, their lineage would have been in place without interruption. But David's son Solomon forfeited that privilege when he turned his back on the Lord and went after the idols his many wives convinced him to pursue. (For a more detailed discussion, see "God's conditional **Kingdom Promise** to Solomon," under "The Kingdom in the Book of Kings," above).

The following verses are about Messiah's rule from Zion, the place He has chosen as "His home," His "resting place forever." From there, David's powerful Descendant ("a horn ... for David"), God's Anointed One, will put His enemies to shame; there He will wear a glorious crown (v.v. 13-18). (Psalm 132 from HCSB).

## [GK] [EK] Psalm 145 - the Kingdom Psalm: The glorious splendor of God's Kingdom

We close the Kingdom emphasis in the Book of Psalms with one of the most beautiful and complete hymns about the Kingdom of God. And how fitting that it was written by King David.

David calls the Lord "my God the King" and promises to praise Him every day and forever (v.v. 1-2). When he promises to "honor Your name forever and ever" (v. 2), one is reminded of what our Lord Jesus said: "You should pray like this: Our Father in heaven, Your name be honored as holy" (Matthew 6:9-10 - HCSB).

Once exposed to the reality of the Kingdom and the greatness and compassionate nature of the King, one should spontaneously share this experience and information with others everywhere. Therein lies the basis for every missionary effort, the foundation from which we witness, teach and proclaim the Good News. It is, or have we forgotten, the Good News *of the Kingdom* (Matthew 24:14; Mark 1:14, 15; Luke 8:1; Acts 8:12). The King Himself said, "I must preach the Good News of the Kingdom of God ... because that is why I was sent" (Luke 4:4 - NLT).

David says "one generation will declare Your works to the next and will proclaim Your mighty acts" (v. 4). He promises: "I will speak of Your splendor and glorious majesty and Your wonderful works" (v. 5). Which is precisely what he was doing with this psalm, an important portion of the Holy Bible, now found in the over six billion copies which have been printed worldwide, in 451 languages, with 1,300 translations into new languages currently in progress.[6]

As for each generation, they will also "proclaim the power of Your awe-inspiring acts" and "give a testimony of Your great goodness" (v.v. 6-7). The psalmist will join in and "joyfully sing of Your righteousness" (v. 7), one of the King's main attributes and the foundational principle and standard on which God's Kingdom is built. From righteousness flow the **Kingdom Values**.[7] David enumerates some the Lord manifests: "The Lord is gracious and compassionate, slow to anger and great in faithful love. The Lord is good to everyone; His compassion rests on all He has made" (v.v. 8, 9). The response to God's grace, compassion, patience, faithfulness, love, and goodness should be that "all You have made will thank You, Lord; the godly will praise You" (v. 10).

Before expressing more virtues of the King, David tells of the qualities of the Kingdom, and that each generation "will speak of the glory of Your kingdom ... informing all people of Your mighty acts and of the glorious splendor of Your kingdom" (v.v. 11-12). One of the most impressive qualities is that "Your kingdom is an everlasting kingdom; Your rule is for all generations" (v. 13). David did not fear that future generations would see the demise of God's Kingdom. He knew that, unlike earthly kingdoms, this King and Kingdom would be around forever.

David returns to his list of ***Kingdom Values*** that God demonstrates in His dealings with those He has created. Our King is truthful—"faithful in all His words," and yet full of grace—"gracious in all His actions" (v. 13b). Like when our Lord spoke to the Samaritan woman at the well (John 4). He told her to call her husband and come back. She said she had no husband. Jesus validated her honesty and told her about her past without shaming her. By her reaction it is clear she did not feel put down or humiliated. The story shows Jesus was there to save her, not to condemn or alienate her. Jesus spoke the truth to her in love (Ephesians 4:15).

David claims "the Lord helps all who fall; He raises up all who are oppressed" (v. 14). God is a King Who takes special interest in each individual. Those who love Him and seek to follow Him will be helped along the way. Even if they fall and fail, He will be there to help them up again.

As a benevolent King, He is the ultimate provider. We provide what we can glean from God's world. But it is God Who originates everything, from the forces and laws that rule the universe to our planet's ecosystem. It all starts with God and is sustained by Him. Therefore, "all eyes look to You, and You give them their food at the proper time. You open Your hand and satisfy the desire of every living thing" (v.v. 15, 16).

The perfectly consistent practice of the ***Kingdom Values*** of truth, grace, service, mercy, and provision prove "the Lord is righteous in all His ways and gracious in all His acts" (v. 17). Furthermore, He is near to all who call on Him, hears them when they cry for help, gives them what they want, and protects them—that is, those who show integrity, who fear Him and who love Him (v.v. 18-20a). As for the wicked, He is on a mission to destroy them (v. 20b).

God is delighted to receive our worship and praise (see Psalm 103), and we have just seen once more, why He more than deserves them. The fact that it is important to Him to receive praise from us is like the biggest compliment we could ever receive. Because while He is worthy to receive our praise, we are not even worthy of giving it! Let me explain. I imagine it would be easy for Picasso to dismiss praise for his art coming from an uneducated beggar. He might have thought: "poor fellow, he knows nothing about art or aesthetics, so his compliment really means nothing to me." Yet, that would all change if the compliment came from his three-year-old grandson. As a grandfather myself, I value what Heidi, Derek and Asher say, not because of their "worthiness" or expertise, but because of who they are to me.

So let us rejoice in this wonderful privilege and, with David, let us say, "my mouth will declare Yahweh's praise; let every living thing praise His holy name forever and ever" (v. 21). Amen! (Psalm 145 from the HCSB).

# Kingdom Principles in Proverbs

**[GK] The whole book of Proverbs is about life in the Global Kingdom**

Proverbs speaks of practical aspects of life within the Kingdom, setting forth principles and values based on righteousness. If I were to give Proverbs a title, it would probably be, *A Handy Guide to Practicing Kingdom Values—how to apply them to everyday circumstances.* On the back cover I would mention, "lively explanations and concrete examples provided on every subject."

This marvelous collection of words of wisdom addresses the difference between the wise and the foolish, the righteous and the wicked, the upright and the sinner. The word "righteousness" appears 20 times in Proverbs and "righteous" 65 times (see especially chapters 10 and 11; while "righteousness" is found 55 times in Isaiah, Proverbs holds the Biblical record for the word "righteous"). Among the stated goals of the book, in 1:2-6, is: "To receive instruction in wise behavior, righteousness, justice and equity" (Proverbs 1:3 - NASB; see 2:9). The term "The Righteous One" appears in 21:12 and, by all indications, refers to God (see Exodus 9:27; Isaiah 24:16; 53:11; Job 34:17; Acts 3:14; 7:52; 22:14; 1 John 2:1 for other references to God as "The Righteous One").

Proverbs teaches us the best ethical practices, guides us with sound advice, and is overflowing with good, old fashioned common sense. This book of wisdom is a great companion to other portions of Scripture that teach **Kingdom Values**.

Since there is no direct mention of the Kingdom in Proverbs and there would not be enough space here to comment on all the verses that cover righteousness, we will move on. But first, there is a very important—yet mostly ignored—verse which really should be considered before "leaving" Proverbs.

**[GK] Proverbs 30 - A verse about the Son of God**

Jerry Young, a Messianic Jew and Bible scholar in his own right, told me he once shared the Gospel with a non-believing Jewish friend. His friend asked him: "if Jesus is so important, why does He not appear in the Tanakh?" (The Tanakh is the Jewish Bible, our Old Testament). "But He does!" Jerry told him and proceeded to read Proverbs 30:4 to him in a "Christian Bible:" "Who has ascended into heaven and descended? Who has gathered the wind in His fists? Who has wrapped the waters in His garment? Who has established all the ends of the earth? What is His name or His son's name? Surely you know!" (Proverbs 30:4 - NASB). This passage speaks of attributes only God possesses and then asks about His name and His Son's name. Still skeptical, Jerry's friend went home and consulted his Tanakh, only to see the reference to God's Son there as well and just as clearly. Soon afterwards he gave his life to Jesus.

# *Kingdom Principles* in Ecclesiastes

### [GK] Ecclesiastes: the paradoxes of life in the Global Kingdom

By the time he wrote Ecclesiastes, it seems King Solomon had become somewhat cynical about life. It had become clear to him that life makes no sense—that is, if God is left out of the equation. There are interesting principles to keep in mind as we move through life in the Global Kingdom, such as "there is an occasion for everything, and a time for every activity under heaven" (Ecclesiastes 3:1 - HCSB). Another principle in this chapter is that "all God does will last forever; there is no adding to it or taking from it. God works so that people will be in awe of Him" (Ecclesiastes 3:14 - HCSB).

Even the wisest man on earth had a hard time figuring God out. But after philosophizing about life, Solomon comes back around to the importance of remembering our Creator before it's too late. "When all has been heard, the conclusion of the matter is: fear God and keep His commands, because this is for all humanity. For God will bring every act to judgment, including every hidden thing, whether good or evil" (Ecclesiastes 12:1, 13, 14 - HCSB).

As in Proverbs, there are no direct references to God's Kingdom in Ecclesiastes.

# Chapter 4
# Major Prophets

## The Kingdom in Isaiah

The Book of Isaiah—along with the Psalms and the Book of Daniel—is one of the richest sections of the Old Testament concerning the Kingdom of God. Because of its great relevance it is often quoted in the New Testament, especially by Paul.

**[MK] Isaiah 2 - The Millennial Kingdom and The Day of the Lord**

> In the last days, the mountain of the Lord's house will be the highest of all—the most important place on earth. It will be raised above the other hills, and people from all over the world will stream there to worship. People from many nations will come and say, "Come, let us go up to the mountain of the Lord, to the house of Jacob's God. There he will teach us his ways, and we will walk in his paths." For the Lord's teaching will go out from Zion; his word will go out from Jerusalem. The Lord will mediate between nations and will settle international disputes. They will hammer their swords into plowshares and their spears into pruning hooks. Nation will no longer fight against nation, nor train for war anymore. (Isaiah 2:1-4 - NLT)

The New Living Translation places the title "The Lord's Future Reign" over the portion of Isaiah 2:1-4. This passage describes the Millennial Kingdom and envisions the time when people from all over the world will stream to the Lord's house in Jerusalem to worship Him. The Lord Himself will teach people His ways, for "the Lord's teaching will go out from Zion; his word will go out from Jerusalem" (v. 3; see Isaiah 11:9b; Isaiah 1:26-27 speaks of the city's status during that time). He "will mediate between nations and will settle international disputes," which will result in global peace, as all military equipment will be converted into farming utensils and "nation will no longer fight against nation, nor train for war anymore" (v. 4). Jerusalem will be the Kingdom's headquarters during the Messianic Age. From Jerusalem Messiah's "direction, instruction, or law" will be sent out to the whole world. This will probably not be limited to the moral law, but may include scientific, medical, engineering, economic, and architectural information as well.

From the glorious golden age, the text backs up to what happens prior to the Millennial Kingdom: the Day of the Lord. "The Lord Almighty has a day in store for all the proud" (Isaiah 2:12 - NIV), when the unrepentant population left over from the time of the tribulation will face the full extent of God's fury. It will be a time when "the arrogance of man will be brought low and human pride humbled" and "the Lord alone will be exalted in that day" (v. 17 - NIV). "The splendor of his majesty, when he rises to shake the earth" (v. 19 - NIV) will be so frightening that they will run and hide in caves and holes in the ground (v.v. 10, 19, 21).

## [MK] Isaiah 4 - The Millennial Kingdom

Isaiah 4:2-6 describes Zion's future glorious condition when "the Branch of the Lord," a Messianic term, "will be beautiful and glorious" and "the Lord will create a cloud of smoke by day and a glowing flame of fire by night over the entire site of Mount Zion and over its assemblies" (v.v.2, 5 - HCSB).

## [GK] Isaiah 5 - Woe to those distorting *Kingdom Values*!

The International Standard Version (ISV) has the subtitle "Judgment on Mockers" over Isaiah 5:18, which states: "How terrible it will be for those who parade iniquity with cords of falsehood, who draw sin along as with a cart rope." Next, over verse 20, the subtitle "Judgment on Moral Relativists" is used: "How terrible it will be for those who call evil good and good evil, who substitute darkness for light and light for darkness, who substitute what is bitter for what is sweet and what is sweet for what is bitter!"(Isaiah 5:20 - ISV). Never in our lifetime have we seen such a value reversal as we see today! Not only are traditional values being abandoned, but those who continue to hold them dear, if outspoken, are being harassed, sometimes to the point of receiving death threats. We must remember that God's **Kingdom Values** do not change with the times.[1]

## [UK] Isaiah 6 - Isaiah's calling; his vision of the King

Isaiah "saw the Lord seated on a high and lofty throne, and His robe filled the temple" (v. 1 - HCSB). In his commission vision he also saw seraphim—exalted celestial beings, probably akin to cherubim—who continuously called to each other with a chorus of "holy, holy, holy is the Lord of Hosts" (v. 3 - HCSB; see

Revelation 4:8). But it was his vision of God that led him to exclaim in fear, "my eyes have seen the King, the Lord of Hosts" (v. 5 - HCSB). What an extraordinary privilege the prophet was given! To gaze upon the King of the universe, in His throne room, being worshiped by celestial beings, and being invited to join Him in Kingdom ministry.

## [GK] Isaiah 7 - The promise of the virgin birth of Immanuel

The Lord promised King Ahaz: "Therefore the Lord Himself will give you a sign: Behold, a virgin will be with child and bear a son, and she will call His name Immanuel" (Isaiah 7:14 - NASB), which means "God with us." When this came to pass, when God was with them in the Person of Jesus (Immanuel), He told them "the Kingdom is near" (Mark 1:15). The Kingdom manifests itself when God is present. This prophecy had a double fulfillment: the first seen in Isaiah 8:3-4, and the other in Matthew 1:18-23, with the birth of Jesus.

## [GK] Isaiah 8 - Stumbling over the Rock

The Lord told Isaiah that only He was to be considered holy and only He should be feared, "but for the two houses of Israel, He will be a stone to stumble over and a rock to trip over, and a trap and a snare to the inhabitants of Jerusalem" (v.v. 13, 14 - HCSB; see verses 15-18). Quoting Psalm 118:22 and the passage above (Isaiah 8:14), the Apostle Peter calls Jesus "the stone that the builders rejected—this One has become the cornerstone and a stone to stumble over, and a rock to trip over" (1 Peter 2:7-8 - HCSB). The prophecy reveals the Messiah would be rejected but that He would be foundational to the *building,* anyway.

## [GK] Isaiah 9 - Reigning from David's throne

God would, in the future, "bring honor to ... Galilee..." and people who were in darkness would see "a great light" (verses 1-2).

> For a child will be born for us, a son will be given to us, and the government will be on his shoulders. He will be named Wonderful Counselor, Mighty God, Eternal Father, Prince of Peace. The dominion will be vast, and its prosperity will never end. He will reign on the throne of David and over his kingdom, to establish and sustain it with justice and righteousness from now on and forever. The zeal of the LORD of Armies will accomplish this. (Isaiah 9:6-7 - CSB)

This prophecy is among the most revealing concerning the coming King. He would be born as a human child, He will one day be the One in charge of ruling, and He has been given honorary names like "Mighty God" and "Prince of Peace," because that is Who He is. He will rule over a vast domain forever, on David's throne (as promised), and will rule over Israel, upholding it with justice and righteousness forever.

Although speaking of God the Son, the title "Eternal Father" is used. This can be a little confusing until we understand that the literal translation of the Hebrew here is "Father of Eternity" (Young's Literal Translation).

## [GK] Isaiah 10 - Unjust and oppressive lawmakers will be judged

"How terrible it will be for the one who enacts unjust decrees, for those who write oppressive laws that they have prescribed to deprive the needy of justice and to rob the poor of my people of their rights, so that widows may become their spoil and so that they may plunder orphans!" (Isaiah 10:1-2 - ISV). **Kingdom Values** are to be upheld by those in authority on all levels—from the international to the local. When God's laws are thrown out and man's rules prevail, corruption, the abuse of power, and the concentration of wealth are usually the norm.

## [GK] Isaiah 11 - David's Descendant filled with the Spirit, clothed with righteousness

The Holman Christian Standard Bible's title for this section (v.v. 1-9) is "Reign of the Davidic King." The mentioned shoot of the stump of Jesse (v. 1) and the "Root of Jesse" (v. 10), both refer to the Descendant of King David, as Jesse was David's father (Ruth 4:22; Matthew 1:6). The Descendant both came after David ("a shoot") and was before him ("root"). The reference is messianic and applies to Jesus.

Jesus was full of the Holy Spirit of God "without limit" (John 3:34). Isaiah speaks of Him as One on Whom "the Spirit of the Lord will rest;" the Spirit being a Spirit of wisdom, understanding, counsel, strength, and knowledge (v. 2 - HCSB). He is described as a righteous judge Who will "execute justice for the oppressed of the land" (v.v. 3-4 - HCSB). In a clear reference to the Messianic Age, Isaiah says "He will strike the land with discipline from His mouth, and He will kill the wicked with a command from His lips" (v. 4 - HCSB).

The standard of the Kingdom is righteousness. And "righteousness will be a belt around His loins" (v. 5 - HCSB).

The Messianic Age (Millennial Kingdom) is again foretold by describing what it will be like to have the curse on the natural world lifted (see also Isaiah 65:25). It will be a period when what we now know as wild and dangerous animals (wolves, leopards, lions, bears, snakes) and domesticated farm animals (lambs, goats, calves, cows, oxen) will live side-by-side, as an infant plays beside them in total safety. The promise is that "none will harm or destroy another on My entire holy mountain" because, just as humans will be flocking there to learn from the King, "the land will be as full of the knowledge of the Lord as the sea is filled with water" (v. 9 - HCSB).

## [GK] Isaiah 13 - The Day of the Lord described

This chapter contains one of the most complete descriptions of the Day of the Lord in Scripture. Although the passage begins as a prophecy against Babylon, it meshes into a list of events that will happen during The Day of the Lord, mentioned by name in verses 6 and 9. God calls on His own warriors to carry out His wrath, while nations come together for war. They come to destroy. What is about to be announced is terrifying. "Wail, for the day of the Lord is near" bringing "destruction from the Almighty" (Isaiah 13:6 - NIV). The effect will that "all hands will go limp, every heart will melt with fear. Terror will seize them, pain and anguish will grip them; they will writhe like a woman in labor. They will look aghast at each other, their faces aflame" (Isaiah 13:7-8 - NIV).

Again, the warning: "See, the day of the Lord is coming—a cruel day, with wrath and fierce anger;" and an explanation as to why this will be brought about: "to make the land desolate and destroy the sinners within it" (Isaiah 13:9 - NIV). Since The Day of the Lord precedes the establishment of the Millennial Kingdom, it is only logical to assume this desolation and destruction happen to prepare the way for the earth to undergo a makeover and rid the planet of rebellious sinners who do not belong in the new world order Messiah will bring about.

In most passages about The Day of the Lord, the same cosmic disturbances are mentioned, such as "the sun and the moon will turn dark. The stars will no longer shine" (Joel 3:15 - GWT; see also Joel 2:1, 10; Matthew 24:29; Revelation 6:12-17). Here it is no different, as "the stars of heaven and their constellations will not show their light. The rising sun will be darkened and the moon will not give its light" (Isaiah 13:10 - NIV). If that were not terrifying enough, this and other passages also foretell God "will make the heavens tremble; and the earth will shake from its place" as part of "the wrath of the Lord Almighty, in the day of his burning anger" (Isaiah 13:13 - NIV).

God "will punish the world for its evil" and in the process "will put an end to the arrogance of the haughty and will humble the pride of the ruthless," resulting in making "people scarcer than pure gold" (Isaiah 13:11-12 - NIV; see Isaiah 23:9).

## [UK]-[GK] Isaiah 14 - A quick reminder of God's sovereignty

As God exerts His prerogatives as King and Judge, it is important to remember He is sovereign, detaining full authority and control. There is nothing that can deter Him or frustrate His plans. Here is what He declares:

> I have a plan for the whole earth, a hand of judgment upon all the nations. The Lord of Heaven's Armies has spoken—who can change his plans? When his hand is raised, who can stop him? (Isaiah 14:26-27 - NLT)

## [GK] [MK] Isaiah 16 - Reining from David's throne

One day "the oppressor will come to an end, and destruction will cease; the aggressor will vanish from the land" (Isaiah 13:4b - NIV). And when that happens, "in love a throne will be established; in faithfulness a man will sit on it—one from the house of David—one who in judging seeks justice and speeds the cause of righteousness" (Isaiah 13:5 - NIV). We understand this will be the Messiah. We know His name is Jesus, the Righteous One. And many believe the Millennial Kingdom will fulfill this prophecy.

## [GK] Isaiah 24 - God will destroy the earth

This chapter picks up where chapter 13 left off, with news of the horrors to come. "Look! The Lord is about to destroy the earth and make it a vast wasteland. He devastates the surface of the earth and scatters the people" and great and small will be affected, "none will be spared" as "the earth will be completely emptied and looted" (Isaiah 24:1-3 - NLT). Why is this going to happen? "Its people must pay the price for their sin" (Isaiah 24:6 - NLT). Specific sins that brought on God's wrath are mentioned, such as chaos and mobs in the cities, homes having to be locked because of intruders, the prevalence of deceit and treachery (v.v. 10-11, 16).

How many will survive? "Throughout the earth the story is the same—only a remnant is left" (Isaiah 24:13 - NLT). But, surprisingly, we are told those who do survive shout for joy, praise the Lord and sing "songs that give glory to the Righteous One!" (Isaiah 24:16 - NLT; see verses 13-16).

The unimaginable will occur. The prophecy states the earth will break up, collapse, be violently shaken then stagger like a drunk, not to rise again (v.v. 19-20). We must remember that hyperbole is used in prophetic language. Yet it is clear that catastrophe of global proportions awaits our planet at the end of times.

God will not only punish "the proud rulers of the nations on earth," He will also "punish the gods in the heavens," who will all "be rounded up and put in prison" (Isaiah 24:21-22 - NLT). These "gods" are probably fallen celestial beings and authorities. Remember that as the Millennial Kingdom begins, "an angel coming down from heaven, holding the key of the abyss and a great chain in his hand," captures "the dragon, the serpent of old, who is the devil and Satan, and bound him for a thousand years" (Revelation 20:1-2 - NASB). If the Messianic Age is to be the golden age, not only Satan will need to be locked up, but all his demons will too.

The identifier of this time period as The Day of the Lord comes at the end of the chapter, when it is said that "then the glory of the moon will wane, and the brightness of the sun will fade, for the Lord of Heaven's Armies will rule on Mount Zion. He will rule in great glory in Jerusalem, in the sight of all the leaders of his people" (Isaiah 24:23 - NLT). Notice that sunshine will no longer be needed because the Lord will be ruling in great glory in Jerusalem (see Zechariah 14:6-7).

## [MK] Isaiah 25 - A banquet prepared

Some cutting-edge business nowadays are rewarding their employees in ingenious ways. One of them offers the privilege of dinning with the CEO, in his home, with a meal prepared by the host himself, to employees who have accumulated a certain amount of "points." I would think those would be "job-well-done" and loyalty points. This is the principle behind the banquet God is going to offer His people.

"The Lord of hosts will prepare a lavish banquet for all peoples on this mountain" (Isaiah 25:6a - NASB). The mountain is "Mount Zion," the one mentioned in the last verse of the previous chapter where "the Lord of hosts will reign" (Isaiah 24:23 - NASB). Although there are differing interpretations, it seems clear this banquet is offered at the beginning of the Millennial Kingdom on the earthly Mount Zion, in or around Jerusalem. Would this banquet be the same as "the wedding feast of the Lamb," mentioned in Revelation 19:7-9?

The Revelation passage is a hymn about the supper, not the supper itself. The invitation is made in heaven and, immediately after the announcement, Jesus leaves on a white horse to put an end to the reign of the beast and the kings of the world under his control. In chapter 20, Jesus establishes His millennial reign. No wonder "a man sitting at the table with Jesus exclaimed, 'what a blessing it will be to attend a banquet in the Kingdom of God!'" (Luke 14:15 - NLT). This is also what the angel would tell John, years later: "blessed are those who are invited to the wedding feast of the Lamb" (Revelation 19:9 - NLT).

The prophecy continues, and Isaiah reveals that "on this mountain He will swallow up the covering which is over all peoples, even the veil which is stretched over all nations" (v. 7 - NASB). Although some commentaries believe this is linked with the next verse and refers to the elimination of death, others (like *The Pulpit Commentary*), understand this to refer to the elimination of prejudice and ignorance so prevalent in human relations in this age. The result would be harmony and peace among the different peoples of the earth.

The reason some feel this banquet refers to the eternal state and not the Millennial Kingdom, is because the next verse promises God "will swallow up death for all time, and the Lord God will wipe tears away from all faces" (v. 8a - NASB; see Revelation 7:17 and 21:4). But prophecies jump around a lot: different eras and realities are sometimes interspersed in prophetic passages (as in Isaiah 9:6). And this seems to be the case here. The Millennial Kingdom is the first step in that direction, but it is a transitional Kingdom and the full realization of God's ideal for redeemed humanity will only occur in the Eternal Kingdom.

At that same time, or "in that day," those present will say "behold, this is our God for whom we have waited that He might save us. This is the Lord for whom we have waited; Let us rejoice and be glad in His salvation" (Isaiah 9:9 - NASB). Life can seem long and dreary. Waiting for God's ultimate salvation takes patience and perseverance. But on that day it will all have been worth it. And I suspect it will have felt like a blink of the eye compared to eternity with the King.

## [GK] Isaiah 28 - A Stone in Zion

"So this is what the Lord GOD says: 'See, I lay a stone in Zion, a tested stone, a precious cornerstone, a sure foundation; the one who believes will never be shaken" (Isaiah 28:16 - BSB). "Zion," or better, "Jerusalem," here relates to Jesus' first coming. Isaiah is quoted by Peter (1 Peter 2:6), who also refers to Jesus as "the living Stone," "the capstone," and "a stone that causes people to stumble and a rock that makes them fall" (1 Peter 2:4, 7, and 8 - NASB, where he again quotes Isaiah, this time chapter 8:14; see Mark 12:10; Acts 4:11).

Poetically, God says "I will test you with the measuring line of justice and the plumb line of righteousness" (Isaiah 28:17a - NLT). The standard by which this Stone will measure everything is both justice and righteousness, in keeping with all we have seen about the Kingdom.

## [GK] Isaiah 32 - Righteousness at the helm

"Behold, a king will reign in righteousness, and princes will rule with justice" (Isaiah 32:1 - NKJV). John MacArthur, commenting on this verse, says: "in contrast to bad leaders... the prophet turned to the messianic king and His governmental assistants during the future day of righteousness. These will be the apostles (Luke 22:30) and the saints (1 Cor. 6:2; 2 Tim. 2:12; Rev. 2:26, 27; 3:21)."[2]

## [UK]-[GK] Isaiah 33 - Judge, Lawgiver, King, and Savior

"For the Lord is our judge, the Lord is our lawgiver, the Lord is our king; it is he who will save us" (Isaiah 33:22 - NIV). The Lord is head over the Judicial branch (He is "Judge"), Legislative branch (He is the "Lawgiver"), and Executive branch (He is the "King") of His Kingdom. Because the Lord is a holy and righteous King, He needs no checks and balances (there would be nobody more trustworthy than Himself). He makes the law, He judges according to the law, He governs—plans, decides and executes—in harmony with the law. Like the Sheriffs back in the Wild Wild West, He *is* the law. But God is also full of grace and mercy, and He does everything in His power to save us.

## [UK]-[GK] Isaiah 37 - A Kingdom prayer

King Hezekiah received some disturbing news. The king of Assyria was taunting him, telling him not to believe his God could deliver him from his hand. He headed up to the Temple and prayed a strong prayer of faith to the King of the universe:

> Lord Almighty, the God of Israel, enthroned between the cherubim, you alone are God over all the kingdoms of the earth. You have made heaven and earth. Give ear, Lord, and hear; open your eyes, Lord, and see; listen to all the words Sennacherib has sent to ridicule the living God. Now, Lord our God, deliver us from his hand, so that all the kingdoms of the earth may know that you, Lord, are the only God. *(Isaiah 37:16-17, 20 - NIV)*

God heard Hezekiah's prayer and delivered Jerusalem.

## [GK] Isaiah 40 - The King's herald foretold

We've seen so many prophecies about the future Kingdom that it would be good to see how these are fulfilled. Are they literal? Word-for-word? We have the perfect example in Isaiah 40:3-4, with the fulfillment being referred to in Matthew 3:1-3:

> In those days John the Baptist came, preaching in the Wilderness of Judea and saying, 'Repent, because the kingdom of heaven has come near!' For he is the one spoken of through the prophet Isaiah, who said: A voice of one crying out in the wilderness: Prepare the way for the Lord; make His paths straight!" (Matthew 3:1-3 - HCSB)

A few verses down, there is a description of God's greatness as He relates to the Global Kingdom (and notice the description of the circular form of the earth):

> Have you not known? Have you not heard? Has it not been told you from the beginning? Have you not understood from the foundations of the

earth? It is He who sits above the circle of the earth, And its inhabitants are like grasshoppers, Who stretches out the heavens like a curtain, And spreads them out like a tent to dwell in. (Isaiah 40:21-22 - NKJV)

## [GK] Isaiah 41 - Jacob's King

God calls Israel "My servant, Jacob, whom I have chosen… and not rejected;" He promises to help, strengthen and "hold on to you with My righteous right hand." God then identifies Himself as "Jacob's King" (Isaiah 41:8-10, 21 - HCSB).

## [GK] Isaiah 42 - God's Servant

"Behold my Servant, Whom I uphold, My elect in Whom My soul delights! I have put My Spirit upon Him; He will bring forth justice and right and reveal truth to the nations" (Isaiah 42:1 - AMP). This verse identifies Jesus as God's Suffering Servant. It is one of the two verses God the Father quoted at Jesus' baptism and then again at the moment of Jesus' transfiguration (the other being Psalm 2:7). How appropriate that the verse mentions that God's Spirit was placed on Him, as Jesus' anointing as Prophet, Priest and King was not with oil—the type—but with the Spirit Himself, and occurred at His baptism. The kingly aspect of Jesus' role and mission, emphasized in Psalm 2, was seen at His transfiguration, and was reason enough to repeat the declaration that, "This is My beloved Son, in whom I am well pleased. Listen to Him!" (Matthew 17:5 - BSB).

The next few verses speak of a gentle Man Who "will bring forth justice in truth," and will not give up "till He has established justice in the earth" (v.v. 3-4 - AMP).

## [UK]-[GK] Isaiah 43 - No other God, Savior, King

God reaffirms His identity and speaks of how we should relate to Him. We are to be His witnesses, just as His chosen Servant. We are to know Him, believe Him, and understand that "before Me there was no God formed, neither shall there be after Me" (v. 10 - AMP), a truth some cults ignore or deny. God declares He is the Lord and "besides Me there is no Savior" (v. 11 - AMP). He is "your Holy One, the Creator of Israel, your King" (v. 15 - AMP).

## [UK]-[GK] Isaiah 44 - God, the one and only

"God, King of Israel, your Redeemer, God-of-the-Angel-Armies, says: 'I'm first, I'm last, and everything in between. I'm the only God there is'" (Isaiah 44:6 - MSG). He is the only one Who knows the future and tells it in advance. He asks, "Have you ever come across a God, a real God, other than me?" (Isaiah 44:8 - MSG). And answers, "There's no Rock like me that I know of" (Isaiah 44:8 - MSG; see also Isaiah 46:9-10).

## [GK] Isaiah 52 - Proclaiming that God reigns!

> How beautiful upon the mountains
> Are the feet of him who brings good news,
> Who proclaims peace,
> Who brings glad tidings of good things,
> Who proclaims salvation,
> Who says to Zion,
> "Your God reigns!"
> (Isaiah 52:7 - NKJV)

This verse has been used by preachers and teachers to emphasize the importance of sharing the Good News. It is a great reference for witnessing and missions, but let's not stop there. This is a positive message (*good things*) of peace, joy (*glad tidings*), forgiveness, hope and acceptance (*salvation*)—and that the basis for all of this is the fact that "Your God reigns!"

## [GK] Isaiah 53 - God's Servant's vicarious sacrifice

The importance and messianic value of this chapter cannot be overstated. The description fits Jesus' trial and crucifixion so closely that upon hearing its content and being unaware of its location in Scripture, one could easily believe it belongs in the New Testament. Yet, Isaiah was written some 700 years before Christ.

We cannot do justice here to what is one of the greatest prophecies concerning Messiah's coming trial and vicarious death. We must limit ourselves to mentioning the substitutionary death God's "man of suffering" or "righteous Servant," the Messiah, would suffer to secure our salvation and entrance into His Kingdom.

He "bore our sicknesses, and He carried our pains" (v. 4); He "was pierced because of our transgressions, crushed because of our iniquities; punishment for our peace" (v. 5); "the Lord has punished Him for the iniquity of us all" (v. 6); He "was struck because of my people's rebellion" (v. 8); The Lord made Him a sin, guilt, or "restitution offering" (v. 10); God's "righteous Servant will justify many, and He will carry their iniquities" (v. 11); and "He submitted Himself to death" and "bore the sin of many" (v. 12; all verses HCSB).

This is a messianic prophecy and the predictions are too similar to reality to be coincidental. There's the prediction that He would not answer His accusers but would be silent like a sheep while being sheared; that He would be pierced (the Hebrew *chalal* means "wounded" or "pierced") for our transgressions, indicating the kind of death He would suffer; that His grave would have to do with a rich man in His death, a death He would voluntarily submit Himself to; and that He would be someone Who "had done no violence and had not spoken deceitfully."

There is no doubt that Jesus fulfilled these prophecies to the last detail.

## [GK] [MK] Isaiah 57 - Inheriting the land, possessing the holy mountain

Isaiah has emphasized the nation of Israel over and over. But when God denounces idol worship, he makes a promise to *everyone* who would be faithful to Him. He says, "but *whoever* takes refuge in Me will inherit the land and possess My holy mountain" (Isaiah 57:13b - HCSB). The language is the same used in many passages covering the Messianic Age and refers to inheriting the earth (Isaiah 60:21; Psalm 37:9, 11; Matthew 5:5), and possessing the Lord's holy mountain (Isaiah 11:9; Isaiah 56:7; Isaiah 66:20; Joel 3:17; Psalm 2:6; 15:1).

This is not a privilege limited to the faithful remnant of Israel. Just a couple of chapters back, an open invitation was also extended to "*everyone* who is thirsty," with the offer of water, wine and milk—God's provision and His best for those who will put their trust in Him (Isaiah 55:1 - HCSB).

## [MK] Isaiah 60 - The Earth's riches taken to Israel

The scene opens with the Lord's light shining where there had been darkness covering the whole earth. This attracts the nations and their leaders. "You" (v. 5), probably meaning Israel, will become radiant and filled with excitement and joy. The wealth of the seas and riches of the nations will "come" to God's chosen nation. The Lord will receive them as offerings and they will decorate His Temple. The islands will look to the Lord and ships will bring silver and gold to honor the Holy One of Israel, Who "has endowed you with splendor" (Isaiah 60:9 - NIV).

The narrative leads us to understand that what is being described here is the Messianic Age. What had happened earlier was the destruction of a large portion of Jerusalem. Now, foreigners are rebuilding its walls and their kings are serving the population of this holy city, the gates of which will always be open, day and night, so people "may bring you the wealth of nations" (Isaiah 60:11 - NIV). Those nations which choose not to serve Israel will end in ruin. Even the sons of their former oppressors will "come bowing before you" and "call you The City of the Lord, Zion of the Holy One of Israel" (Isaiah 60:14 - NIV). This will totally reverse the world's attitude towards Israel, which had been forsaken and hated for so long. Now God will make them the everlasting pride of the earth, with violence and destruction being a thing of the past. Now there will only be salvation and praise within its gates (v.v. 15-18). And there will also be light!

The lights had gone out in the world. After the Tribulation and The Day of the

Lord, the sun, moon and stars were no longer shining. That is why it is foretold that "No longer will the sun be your light by day, nor the brightness of the moon shine on your night; for the LORD will be your everlasting light, and your God will be your splendor" (Isaiah 60:19 - BSB; see Zechariah 14:6-7).

All the inhabitants of Jerusalem will be righteous and take possession of the land forever, with even the least multiplying and the smallest becoming a mighty nation. This will all happen quickly, when the time comes (v. 22).

## [GK] [MK] Isaiah 61 - The Spirit on Messiah; priests of the Lord

When Jesus went to His hometown of Nazareth, He entered the synagogue and read Isaiah 61:1-2a from the scroll of this prophet which had been handed to Him. He stopped in the middle of verse two, in mid sentence. He was signaling He had come "to proclaim the year of the LORD's favor," not "the day of vengeance of our God"—the latter a constant theme in Isaiah's book (Isaiah 61:2 - ISV). This passage describes Messiah's earthly ministry, His first coming. Jesus stunned His audience when He told them "today as you listen, this Scripture has been fulfilled" (Luke 4:21 - HCSB). Jesus was fulfilling this prophecy in their presence while declaring to them God's favor, and all they wanted to do was reject His message and throw Him off a cliff!

But Jesus said "God blesses those who do not turn away because of me" (Matthew 11:6 - NLT). This He said after telling John the Baptist's disciples to "go back to John and tell him what you have heard and seen— the blind see, the lame walk, the lepers are cured, the deaf hear, the dead are raised to life, and the Good News is being preached to the poor" (Matthew 11:4-5 - NLT). To reassure John that He was indeed the expected Messiah, Jesus quotes Isaiah 61:1. It was Jesus' way of helping John realize His first coming would be very different from His second coming. He first came as Isaiah's Suffering Servant (Isaiah 42 and 53). He will return as a conquering King, setting up His Kingdom, sitting on the throne of David, ruling from Jerusalem over the whole world.

Isaiah 61 also mentions the Millennial Kingdom. While verses 3-5 and 7-11 all have aspects which point to the Messianic Age, I would like to focus on verse 6: "you will be called priests of the LORD, ministers of our God. You will feed on the treasures of the nations and boast in their riches" (Isaiah 61:6 - NLT). This promise refers back to the first mention of the Kingdom of God in the Bible, where God promises the faithful in Israel that "'if you will obey me and keep my covenant, you will be my own special treasure from among all the peoples on earth; for all the earth belongs to me. And you will be my kingdom of priests, my holy nation.' This is the message you must give to the people of Israel." (Exodus 19:5-6 - NLT).

## [GK] Isaiah 62 - Your Savior is coming with His reward!

Isaiah proclaims the coming righteousness (*tsedeq*) which all the nations will see in its shining glory. He tells of the time when Israel will be the praise of the Earth (comparable to a "glorious crown" and a "royal diadem" in God's hands). It will be a time when those who produce will not have to relinquish their goods to foreign enemies.

Then he says "the LORD has made proclamation to the ends of the earth: "Say to Daughter Zion, 'See, your Savior comes! See, his reward is with him, and his recompense accompanies him'" (Isaiah 62:11 - NIV). This same Savior repeated His promise elsewhere, when He said, "look, I am coming soon! My reward is with me, and I will give to each person according to what they have done" (Revelation 22:12 - NIV).

Those who belong to the Lord will be called "the Holy People, the Redeemed of the LORD," while Jerusalem will be called "Sought After, the City No Longer Deserted" Isaiah 62:12 - NIV).

## [MK] [EK] Isaiah 65 - The Millennial Kingdom described

Isaiah speaks of the New Heaven and New Earth first, then describes what almost certainly is the Millennial—not the Eternal—Kingdom. We can assume this because Jesus said that "when the dead rise, they will neither marry nor be given in marriage. In this respect they will be like the angels in heaven" (Mark 12:25 - NLT). Yet in the passage that follows there are references to infants and people aging and dying.

We start this section with God's promise to "create a new heaven and a new earth," where "past events will not be remembered or come to mind," and people will "be glad and rejoice forever" and Jerusalem will be a joy (Isaiah 65:17-18 - HCSB). Remember: We will spend eternity on the New Earth, not in heaven; and the New Jerusalem will have come down from heaven to the New Earth.

The prophecy switches to the Millennial Kingdom. Perhaps because, after all, it is all one Kingdom. (During His earthly ministry, Jesus would speak of the different aspects of the Kingdom without naming them).

Jerusalem is still central to God's plans. God will rejoice in that city, where "the voice of weeping shall no longer be heard in her, nor the voice of crying" (Isaiah 65:19 - NKJV), infant mortality will be minimal or nonexistent, the old will live long lives, and not reaching 100 years of age will be a curse (v. 20). People will reap the benefits of their work instead of building or planting solely for others (v.v. 21-22). People will be guaranteed success in their workplace and can expect a bright future for their kids (v. 23). Prayers will be answered instantaneously—or even before—because God promises that "even before they call, I will answer; while they are still speaking, I will hear" (v. 24 - HCSB). The curse of nature will have been revoked, since "the wolf and the lamb will feed together, and the lion will eat straw like the ox, but the serpent's food will be dust!" (v. 25 - HCSB).

What people have always dreamed of, what deep down we all wish the world were like, will become reality when Jesus is reigning from Jerusalem and sin will have been dealt a mortal blow.

## [UK] [GK] [MK] [EK] Isaiah 66 - The Lord judges, reigns, brings peace to Israel

God declares that "Heaven is My throne, and earth is My footstool" and that "My hand made all these things, and so they all came into being" (Isaiah 66:1 - HCSB). He is the King over the Universal and Global aspects of His Kingdom because He created both. Which means there is an intimate link between heaven and Earth, which will only grow stronger as we rush towards the end of history as we know it.

God asks: "Shall a land be born in one day? Or shall a nation be brought forth in a moment?" (Isaiah 66:7-8 - AMP). History answers with a resounding *Yes!* "On 14 May 1948, David Ben-Gurion, the Executive Head of the World Zionist Organization and president of the Jewish Agency for Palestine, declared 'the establishment of a Jewish state in Eretz Israel, to be known as the State of Israel.'"[3]

Concerning Jerusalem, the Lord announces that "I will make peace flow to her like a river, and the wealth of nations like a flood" (v. 12), signaling a time of peace and prosperity (v.v. 12-14). Isaiah sees the Lord coming to execute judgment on everyone and slaying many (v.v. 15-16). The Millennial Kingdom, then the Day of the Lord, then back to the Millennium when some who survive will proclaim God's glory to the nations. "All your brothers [will be taken] from all the nations as a gift to the Lord ... to My holy mountain Jerusalem" (v. 20 - HCSB), along with the Israelites who take their offering to the Lord.

Not only will the New Heavens and New Earth be eternal, so will its inhabitants (v. 22). And the original purpose and final goal of humanity will be realized in those inhabitants, as "'all mankind will come to worship me from one New Moon to another and from one Sabbath to another,' says the Lord" (v. 23 - CSB).

# The Kingdom in Jeremiah

### [GK] Jeremiah chapter 4 - No idea how to practice *Kingdom Values*

Most of the book of Jeremiah concerns his prophesying against a sinful, rebellious, unrepentant, and hard-headed people who had turned their backs on God. It had come to the point where God's people did not know Him and had become foolish and without understanding. "They are clever enough at doing wrong, but they have no idea how to do right!" (Jeremiah 4:22- NLT).

### [GK] Jeremiah 10 - Only God is the King of nations

God tells His people to stop trying to imitate other nations and picking up their useless customs, like idol-making. They should, on the other hand, understand that there is no one like Yahweh. "Who should not fear You, King of the nations? It is what You deserve. For among all the wise people of the nations and among all their kingdoms, there is no one like You." He is "the living God and the everlasting king" (Jeremiah 10:6-7, 10a - ISV). He has all the right to be King since "it is he who made the earth by his power, who established the world by his wisdom, and by his understanding stretched out the heavens" (Jeremiah 10:12 - ESV).

### [GK] Jeremiah 23 - The Righteous Branch

The Lord announces that He will raise up a Righteous Branch from David Who "shall reign as king and deal wisely, and shall execute justice and righteousness in the land." He will save and will be called "The Lord is our righteousness" (Jeremiah 23:5-6 - ESV). The description and title are Messianic. It is no coincidence that the emphasized characteristic of this King is righteousness, as this quality is strongly connected to the Kingdom of God. The description is clearly that of the coming Messiah, as no fallible human would be characterized in this manner.

### [GK] Jeremiah 25, 27 - Terrible wrath; God is the owner

Jeremiah 25:15-38 speaks of God's terrible wrath that is coming over the whole earth, the extent and intensity of which leads to the conclusion that this is a reference to The Day of the Lord.

God is the owner of all human and animal life because He created everything and has the right to do with it what He wishes (Jeremiah 27:4-8).

### [GK] [MK] Jeremiah 30 - The future King David

The time of Jacob's trouble, the Tribulation, is mentioned as a time of terror like no other in all of history. "Yet God will rescue" His people, break their yoke, snap their chains and set them free from foreign masters. They will "serve the Lord their God, and David their King, whom I will raise up for them, says the Lord" (Jeremiah 30:7-9 - TLB). The Messiah is both called the Son of David and, as in this verse, David himself. We know that the then future David is Jesus, Who is of the tribe of Judah and the line of David, both from His father's and mother's side.

## [GK] Jeremiah 31 - The New Covenant

When all seemed lost, God called Noah and saved humanity. The situation also seemed hopeless in Judah in the days of Jeremiah. But God promised there would come a day when He would establish a New Covenant with His people, unlike the ones that had come before. This time, God said, "I will put My teaching within them and write it on their hearts. I will be their God, and they will be My people," and "I will forgive their wrongdoing and never again remember their sin" (Jeremiah 31:31-34 - HCSB).

## [GK] Jeremiah 32 - No limits to God's power

God spoke to Jeremiah and told him "behold, I am the Lord, the God of all flesh; is there anything too hard for Me?" (Jeremiah 32:27 - AMP). God is Lord over all and there are no limits to His power.

## [GK] [MK] Jeremiah 33 - Jerusalem restored; the Righteous Branch

God points to the future, restored Jerusalem to bring hope to a hopeless situation. In that future the people's guilt and rebellion will be forgiven and there will be peace and prosperity that the Lord will provide (Jeremiah 33:6-9).

The Lord promises to send the Righteous Branch (the Messiah). He will descend from David and bring justice and righteousness to the land, save Judah and provide safety to Jerusalem. His title will be "The Lord is Our Righteousness." As David's "son" and the fulfillment of the covenant established with David, He will sit on the throne over Israel, be called "David My Servant", and "be ruler over the descendants of Abraham, Isaac, and Jacob" (Jeremiah 33:26; see v.v. 14-26 - AMP).

## [UK]-[GK] Jeremiah 46 - The King is the Lord of Hosts

The Lord swears by His name, saying: "as I live, says the King, Whose name is the Lord of hosts" (Jeremiah 46:18 - AMP). God, the Lord of the Heavenly Armies, is King over all creation!

# The Kingdom in Lamentations

[UK]-[GK] **Lamentations of Jeremiah 5 - The Lord reigns forever**

Even in the face of God's fierce judgment on Judah, the prophet Jeremiah, though feeling forgotten and alone, confessed to the One Who had called Him: "You, Lord, reign forever; your throne endures from generation to generation" (Lamentations 5:19 - NIV). Even in the midst of such a bewildering and desperate time, Jeremiah recognized God's sovereign leadership and lordship.

# The Kingdom in Ezekiel

Although Ezekiel is called "son of man" throughout the book, it is not from the term as it is used here that Jesus took the title He applied to Himself (see the comment in Daniel, below, under 7:13-14).

[UK] [GK] **Ezekiel 1-10 - Ezekiel is shown God's glory**

After describing four living creatures (Ezekiel 1:4-25; compare to Revelation 4:6b-8), Ezekiel reported on "what the glory of the Lord looked like to me" (Ezekiel 1:28 - NLT). Like Daniel and the Apostle John, Ezekiel was given the privilege of peering into eternity. He received end-time revelations, witnessed the activity of celestial beings and contemplated God in His glory. The curtains were pulled back, and he was able to see the Kingdom of God manifest right before his eyes.

Ezekiel chapter seven declares "the end" will be well on its way when "an unheard of disaster is coming," matching other passages which speak of The Day of the Lord's vengeance against the unrepentant rebellion and arrogance of the wicked.

In Ezekiel chapters nine and 10 the prophet understands the four living creatures he had seen are cherubim. The cherubim (mentioned 19 times in chapter 10) are closely tied to the glory of the Lord, which usually hovered above them (see 9:3 and 10:4, 18-19).

[UK] [GK] **Ezekiel 28 - The fallen cherub**

Ezekiel devotes many chapters to the problem of Israel's sin and rebellion. Then, in chapter 28, verses 11-19, there is a portion about a fallen cherub. "An anointed guardian cherub" (28:14), created in splendor and beauty, covered with precious stones, and dressed with crafted gold. He had been appointed by God to minister on His holy mountain (probably in proximity to God's throne) and was blameless until he wasn't. When wickedness was found in him he was filled with violence and pride took over his heart. God then banished him and cast him down to Earth. Who else could this be but Satan himself? The leader of all who oppose the Kingdom of God.

## [GK] Ezekiel 30, 32 - The Day of the Lord

Ezekiel 30 refers to The Day of the Lord in passing. The theme is taken up again in chapter 32 and the usual description appears as God warns He will "darken their stars. I will cover the sun with a cloud, and the moon will not give its light" (Ezekiel 23:7 - HCSB). The threat here is made to Egypt but has implications for many peoples and nations.

## [GK] Ezekiel 36 - The New Covenant described

"And I will give you a new heart, and a new spirit I will put within you. And I will remove the heart of stone from your flesh and give you a heart of flesh. And I will put my Spirit within you, and cause you to walk in my statutes and be careful to obey my rules" (Ezekiel 36:26, 27 - ESV). This is similar to Jeremiah 31:31-34 (see above), and describes the New Covenant, established by Jesus (Luke 22:20; 2 Corinthians 3:6; Hebrews 9:15). Before receiving a new spirit, a heart of flesh and God's Holy Spirit, living in close fellowship with the Lord, Scripture seems to show, was reserved for a few heroes of the faith in the Old Covenant times. With the coming of the Lord Jesus and the outpouring of the Holy Spirit, all of that changed. Before, a select few received the Holy Spirit on a temporary basis (1 Samuel 19:20-21). Others, even kings like David, ran the risk of losing the indwelling of the Holy Spirit due to sin (Psalm 51:11). God's description of the New Covenant describes what happens at the moment of salvation, when a person enters the new life in Christ (Acts 10:44-48; 11:15-18).

## [GK] Ezekiel 37 - The Valley of Dry Bones

Ezekiel 37:1-14 speaks of the Valley of Dry Bones, which is modern Israel, or Israel revived! (37:9-14; especially v. 11). This prophecy began to take place on May 15, 1948, when the modern state of Israel was re-established and recognized by many countries. When in Israel, our group's tourist guide took us to Masada and showed us where there had been a synagogue. At that location a scroll containing Ezekiel 37 had been buried and then excavated shortly after Israel had re-emerged as a nation. Finding this chapter that predicted the resurgence of Israel after being as good as dead for a long period, was confirmation that God was the One bringing this about. The latter part of this chapter (Ezekiel 37:15-28) prophesies that Israel would be reunified and never again have a problem with idols. With the modern state of Israel in place, the stage is set for the King's Second Coming.

## [GK] Ezekiel 38, 39 - Gog from the land of Magog to attack Israel

Ezekiel 38 and 39 announce the coming of Gog, the "prince of Rosh, Meshech, and Tubal ... of the land of Magog" (Ezekiel 38:2 - ASV). The prophecy declares that "a long time from now you will be called into action. In the distant future you will swoop down on the land of Israel, which will be enjoying peace after recovering from war and after its people have returned from many lands to the mountains of Israel. You and all your allies—a vast and awesome army—will roll down on them like a storm and cover the land like a cloud" (Ezekiel 38:9, 9 - NLT). Of Rosh, Meshech, and Tubal, author Joel C. Rosenberg states that "a study of ancient Hebrew, ancient history, and modern-day geography points us to Russia, Moscow and Tobolsk (in Siberia), respectively."[4]

The allies that will be joining Gog, the leader of the Northern power and multinational coalition, will be Persia (modern day Iran), Ethiopia, Libya, Gomer, Beth-togarmah "and many others" (Ezekiel 38:5-6). God, "the Sovereign Lord," tells Ezekiel to deliver this message to him: "Gog, I am your enemy!" (Ezekiel 38:3; 39:1 - NLT). God goes on to inform Gog that he, his whole army and the allies that joined him will be left helpless and die on the mountains of Israel. Magog and the populations of the allies will receive a shower of fire, and all will know the Lord is the Holy One of Israel (Ezekiel 39:2-8). Some believe these events will take place close to the time of the Rapture of the Church.

## [MK] Ezekiel 40-42 - The Millennial Temple

Ezekiel 40, 41 and 42 cover the New Temple plans for what would have to be the Messianic Age. The revelation was made to the prophet through a special vision. "The vision has four basic segments that are primarily noted by the differences of subject matter: (1) the description of the millennial temple (40:5-42:20); (2) the return of God's glory to the temple (43:1-9); (3) the temple regulations (43:10-46:24); and (4) the topographical aspects of the Millennium (47:1-48:35)."[5]

If Ezekiel's Temple belongs to the Millennial period, why would there still be sacrifices performed at that venue? King Jesus will be reigning in glory from the new Temple in Jerusalem and the fact that He had died an excruciating death on the cross so many years before could easily be forgotten. Just as the Israelites needed concrete prophetic symbolism pointing to the future Messianic sacrifice, the world population of the Messianic Age will need a visual and dramatic reminder of the suffering, sacrifice and death Jesus endured in order to make salvation and the new order of things possible. "The sacrifices in Ezekiel are memorials of Christ's work even as the Mosaic sacrifices were picture lessons and types of the work he would do. Neither is efficacious."[6]

## [MK] [EK] Ezekiel 43 - the return of God's glory

The return of God's glory to the Temple in Jerusalem will only occur during His glorious reign during the Millennial Kingdom (see 43:2, 4).

Now, during the Global Kingdom, the Lord says "Heaven is my throne, and the earth is my footstool" and asks "what is the house that you would build for me, and what is the place of my rest?" (Isaiah 66:1 - ESV). But referring to the Millennial Kingdom, God tells Ezekiel the new Temple "is the place of My throne and the place of the soles of My feet, where I will dwell in the midst of the children of Israel forever" (Ezekiel 43:7a - NKJV; "forever" also applies this statement to the Eternal Kingdom).

A king's throne is located at his headquarters. So there is a shift of God's headquarters from heaven to earth, beginning to a degree during the Millennial, transitional Kingdom, then fully at the inception of the Eternal Kingdom. More specifically, Jesus' throne will be established over the earth during the Millennial Kingdom (Matthew 25:31), and God the Father's during the Eternal Kingdom (Revelation 21:3).

## [MK] Ezekiel 47 - the river of life

Ezekiel 47:1-12 describes a river which flows from under the Temple, traveling all the way down to the Dead Sea, where it brings life in the form of many fruit-bearing trees on either bank (the leaves of which never wither), turns the salt water into fresh water, and makes the Sea team with a variety of fish and living creatures. The fruit from the trees will serve as food and the leaves for healing.

This description is paralleled in Revelation 22:1-3 and the same river is referenced in Zechariah 14:8, a passage which refers to the time when "the Lord shall be King over all the earth" (Zechariah 14:9 - NKJV). No wonder the psalmist rejoiced, saying "there is a river whose streams make glad the city of God, the holy habitation of the Most High. God is in the midst of her" (Psalm 46:4-5a - ESV)!

# The Kingdom in Daniel

Daniel is a Kingdom book. The main theme throughout its pages is that the kingdoms of the earth are under God's control and one day God is going to set up His very own Kingdom which, unlike the earthly ones, will last forever! But until then, the kingdoms of the world are on a collision course with God's Kingdom.

There is no book in the Old Testament which has a larger percentage of its content dedicated to the Kingdom of God. In the chapter on the book of Daniel, the authors of "A Survey of the Old Testament" list "the Kingdom of God" as one of the two major themes of this prophetic-apocalyptic book.[7]

Jesus warned His followers about "the abomination that causes desolation, spoken of by the prophet Daniel" (Matthew 24:15 - HCSB; see Daniel 9:27; 11:31; 12:11). This indicates that Jesus accepted Daniel as the author of the book. The prophecies of Daniel run parallel to and are expanded by other prophecies, especially those in the book of Revelation.

## [GK] [MK]-[EK] Daniel 2 - God knows the future

Daniel provides the content and interpretation of Nebuchadnezzar's troubling dream. The dream provides a long-range, prophetic revelation about future events involving the successive rise and fall of kingdoms (usually interpreted to mean the Babylonian, Medo-Persian, Greek and Roman empires), and the coming of God's Kingdom which will be like a large stone. The stone crushes the others kingdoms, represented by a great metallic-coded statue, and grows—like a big mountain—to engulf the whole earth (see 2:44-45). Unlike the other human kingdoms, God's will never ever end.

Throughout the whole process of interpretation, Daniel consistently gave God the credit and glory and assumed a humble stance. The king was so grateful for the interpretation he told Daniel, "Surely your God is the God of gods and the Lord of kings and a revealer of mysteries, for you were able to reveal this mystery" (2:47; see 2:27-28).

## [GK] Daniel 3 - God alone is to be worshiped

Here we find the well-known story of the fiery furnace. Nebuchadnezzar ordered a 90 feet high image of gold and summoned all his provincial officials to participate in the dedication. They all were to bow down and worship the image. Daniel's three countrymen refused and were thrown in the furnace. A fourth person appeared, and the king was beside himself. (Daniel may have been permitted to stay at the palace to take care of the kingdom in the king's absence). Although the Aramaic is ambiguous, the King James version translates this portion as it appears in the original: "the fourth is like the Son of God" (Daniel 3:25 - KJV). This could mean "a son of the gods," or a celestial being (sometimes referred to as "sons of God" in Scripture) or, somehow, to *the* Son of God Himself. Nebuchadnezzar later refers to their God, Who "sent His Angel and delivered His servants" (Daniel 3:25 - NKJV). Was this the Son of God, the Angel of the Lord, or an ordinary angel? Whoever this was, it was clear God had extraordinarily intervened!

What followed was, in effect, a powerful "evangelistic service" which reached all the empire's heads of state and their administrators—"satraps, prefects, governors, advisers, treasurers, judges, magistrates and all the other provincial officials" (Daniel 3:3 - NIV)—who were present for the dedication. They had seen God in action and undoubtedly would take what they witnessed back to their provinces. This was God's way of taking advantage of an extraordinarily strategic event to further the cause of His Kingdom, with the participation of His faithful servants.

This was Nebuchadnezzar's reaction to this never-before-seen delivery from his fiery furnace: To praise their God publicly and acknowledge their unswerving faith and loyalty to Him. In his own words, "they trusted in him and defied the king's command and were willing to give up their lives rather than serve or worship any god except their own God. Therefore I decree that the people of any nation or language who say anything against the God of Shadrach, Meshach and Abednego be cut into pieces and their houses be turned into piles of rubble, for no other god can save in this way" (Daniel 3:28-29 - NIV).

To the skeptics who believe this story is simply a myth meant to encourage those who are undergoing persecution for their faith, comes the shocking story of a man who was torched three times but didn't burn. Not hundreds or thousands of years ago, but in 2019. "The Yazidi man says he was burned alive three times by ISIS after they found out he was a follower of Christ. He said his body 'didn't burn' a single time when he was imprisoned and tortured by the radical Islamic terrorists for two months."[8] One of those times "he was stoned and ISIS members drenched him in 20 gallons of gasoline. But even though he was burned alive, he said he inexplicably survived unharmed. He credited Jesus for surviving. 'And they burned me, but I didn't burn,' he said."[9]

## [UK] [GK] [EK] Daniel 4 - God controls those who are in control

Once again, we find Nebuchadnezzar eloquently singing God's praises in an open letter to "the peoples, nations and men of every language." After a brief salutation he declares:

> It gives me great pleasure to tell about the signs and wonders that the Most High God has done for me. How great are his signs! How powerful are his wonders! His kingdom is an eternal kingdom, and his dominion lasts from generation to generation. (Daniel 4:2-3 - ISV)

Nebuchadnezzar had just had another dream only Daniel could interpret. And the interpretation spelled out that the king would lose his mind for a certain period, "so that the living may know that the Most High is sovereign over human kingdoms and grants them to whomever he desires" (Daniel 4:17b - ISV). This is a reoccurring theme in Daniel and a key *Kingdom Principle*: *God is in control of all politicians, presidents, prime ministers, kings and even dictators. Nothing escapes His watchful eyes. No one can act outside of His preset boundaries. All will be held accountable.*

When Nebuchadnezzar got his wits back, his proclamation revealed he understood that God is eternal, His kingdom is everlasting, He detains absolute control over His domain, and everything He does is just and true:

> Then I praised the Most High, and I honored and glorified Him who lives forever: "For His dominion is an everlasting dominion, and His kingdom endures from generation to generation. All the peoples of the earth are counted as nothing, and He does as He pleases with the army of heaven and the peoples of the earth. There is no one who can restrain His hand or say to Him, 'What have You done?'"
>
> Now I, Nebuchadnezzar, praise and exalt and glorify the King of heaven, for all His works are true, and all His ways are just. And He is able to humble those who walk in pride (Daniel 4:34b-35, 37 - BSB)

## [GK] Daniel 5 - God is outraged at blasphemy

King Belshazzar, Nebuchadnezzar's grandson, offered "a great feast where the wine flowed freely" while using "the gold and silver cups taken long before from Solomon's Temple in Jerusalem." The king, "his princes, wives, and concubines drank toasts from them to their idols made of gold and silver, brass and iron, wood and stone" (Daniel 5:1-4 - TLB).

God had decided to crash their party, and a hand appeared before the king and his guests and, well, "the handwriting was on the wall." And Belshazzar wanted to know what it meant. Daniel is called in to the king's presence and gave it to him straight, letting him know how foolish it was to mess with the one true God, Who holds our lives and ways in His hands (Daniel 5:22-23). This led right in to the interpretation of the message on the wall. These were the words that had appeared and what they stood for:

*Mene*: "Mene means 'numbered'—God has numbered the days of your reign and has brought it to an end."

*Tekel*: "Tekel means 'weighed'—you have been weighed on the balances and have not measured up."

*Peres*: "Parsin means 'divided'—your kingdom has been divided and given to the Medes and Persians" (Daniel 5:25-28 - NTL).

The fulfillment of God's word came true immediately. That night Belshazzar was killed and Darius the Mede (possibly a title for Cyrus) annexed the Babylonian kingdom. God determines who will be in power and for how long. God does not take blaspheme lightly, and it was time for a change.

## [GK] [EK] Daniel 6 - God is able to deliver His own

Seen here is Kingdom living at its most important level: the personal one. Daniel, who now was probably in his eighties, was still a man of integrity and was loyal to his earthly king. Here is a *Kingdom Principle*: *when we love God and are loyal to Him above all, our ability to love and be loyal to others will actually be greater than if we had placed them first in our lives.*

Even his enemies "could find no corruption in him, because he was trustworthy and neither corrupt nor negligent" (Daniel 6:4b - NIV). So they convinced King Darius to outlaw praying to anyone—except to himself—for a month. Daniel simply could not comply.

Daniel was brought before the king by his envious colleagues. The king had him thrown to the lions. Darius was distressed and could not sleep that night. He rose early to find out if there was any hope of survival. He came to the den of lions and cried out: "O Daniel, servant of the living God, has your God, whom you serve continually, been able to deliver you from the lions?" (Daniel 6:20 - ESV). Daniel's faithfulness to God was greatly rewarded: his life had been spared, he was restored to his position of authority and his enemies were eliminated!

"Then King Darius wrote to all the peoples, nations, and languages that dwell in all the earth," proclaiming:

> Peace be multiplied to you. I make a decree, that in all my royal dominion people are to tremble and fear before the God of Daniel, for he is the living God, enduring forever; his kingdom shall never be destroyed, and his dominion shall be to the end. He delivers and rescues; he works signs and wonders in heaven and on earth, he who has saved Daniel from the power of the lions. (Daniel 6:25-27 - ESV)

## [GK] [MK] [EK] Daniel 7a - God delegates Kingdom authority

This chapter takes us back to the first year of Belshazzar's reign over the Babylonian empire. Daniel is having prophetic dreams and visions of his own, which present the basic framework for the transition from the last chapter of human history as we know it to the first chapter of God's Millennial Kingdom.

Daniel's vision includes four different beasts coming up out of the sea. The interpretation he is given is that they represent four earthly kingdoms. He is informed that "the saints of the Most High will receive the kingdom and possess it forever—yes, forever and ever" (Daniel 7:18 - BSB). That's great news but Daniel was still very troubled about the fourth beast, the 10 horns, and especially the little horn which "was waging war against God's holy people and was defeating them" (Daniel 7:21 - NLT). This took place only "until the Ancient of Days came and pronounced judgment in favor of the holy people of the Most High, and the time came when they possessed the kingdom" (Daniel 7:22 - NIV).

Daniel was told that the fourth beast is a fourth kingdom which will be different because its global, oppressive, and destructive power. The 10 horns are 10 kings belonging to this fourth kingdom, after which a different king will arise, will blaspheme God, oppress His people and try to change the set times and the laws. God will allow this to happen for three and a half years (Daniel 7:24-25). But God, the Ancient of Days, will exert His control by simply pronouncing judgment in favor of the saints (Daniel 7:22). The Heavenly Court will convene and, just like that, the fourth beast's power will be stripped away and he will be completely destroyed (Daniel 7:26).

When compared with Revelation, it becomes clear that Daniel was being told about the Tribulation period, when the Antichrist would be allowed to oppress God's people. But even that will be within God's control, so that when the time comes, God will place His people in authority: They will possess the Kingdom and reign with Christ in the Millennial Kingdom over the whole Earth.

### [UK]-[EK] Daniel 7b - God rules through His Heavenly Court

This is what Daniel saw in his awesome vision of the Heavenly Court:

> As I kept watching, thrones were set in place, and the Ancient of Days took his seat. His clothing was white like snow, and the hair of his head like whitest wool. His throne was flaming fire; its wheels were blazing fire. A river of fire was flowing, coming out from his presence. Thousands upon thousands served him; ten thousand times ten thousand stood before him. The court was convened, and the books were opened. (Daniel 7:9-10 - CSB)

You can't help but see the parallels between this passage and that of Revelation 4. But there is one Element which was still missing:

> I kept looking in the night visions, and behold, with the clouds of heaven One like a Son of Man was coming, and He came up to the Ancient of Days and was presented before Him. And to Him was given dominion, glory and a kingdom, that all the peoples, nations and men of every language might serve Him. His dominion is an everlasting dominion which will not pass away; and His kingdom is one which will not be destroyed. (Daniel 7:13-14 - NASB)

What a glorious sight this must have been! What a profound revelation! How could anybody miss the fact that this vision refers to Jesus, the Messianic King? It is from this passage that Jesus takes His preferred title of Son of Man during His earthly ministry, thereby helping us to make the connection.

> The kingdom, dominion, and greatness of the kingdoms under all of heaven will be given to the people, the holy ones of the Most High. His kingdom will be an everlasting kingdom, and all rulers will serve and obey him. (Daniel 7:27 - CSB)

The Son of Man will reign with His people over all the kingdoms of the world, first in His Millennial Kingdom, then in His Eternal Kingdom (Psalm 2:8-12; Revelation 2:26-27; 11:15; 21:1-3). Reigning with Jesus means worshiping God and serving Him and others, under His authority (Exodus 19:6; Revelation 1:5-6).

## [GK] Daniel 8 - God overseas the affairs of nations

Daniel receives a new vision about a ram with two long horns, one of them longer than the other at first, and a goat with one horn right between its eyes. They fight, the goat prevails, but loses his horn and four other horns sprout up in its place. From one of those a small horn grows and threatens Israel and places itself against God. Gabriel explains that the two horns on the ram represent the kings of Media and Persia, while the horn on the goat represents the king of Greece and the other four horns which take its place stand for the four kingdoms which spring from the first, but with diminished power.

Horns, in the Bible, signify power and, in this case, military superiority. After Alexander's untimely death at the age of 33, his vast empire was divided among four of his generals. One took over Macedon-Greece, another Thrace-Asia Minor, another Syria-Persia and yet another Egypt-Palestine, which included Israel.[10] But who was this terrible person in authority represented by the little horn which grew out of one of the four horns? A strong case can be made for interpreting this horn as Antiochus IV Epiphanes, the Seleucid general (under the Egypt-Palestine portion of Alexander's divided kingdom) who oppressed the Jews and suppressed the true worship of God, setting up a statue of Zeus in the Temple and sacrificing a swine on its altar. Many agree that Antiochus is a type who prefigures the coming Antichrist—the beast of Revelation and Paul's "man of lawlessness" (2 Thessalonians 2:3-4)—who will act in a similar fashion towards Israel in the end times.

God knows future historical events and what is going to happen in the end times. He gave His servant Daniel, in an act of mercy, a glimpse of this for our benefit.

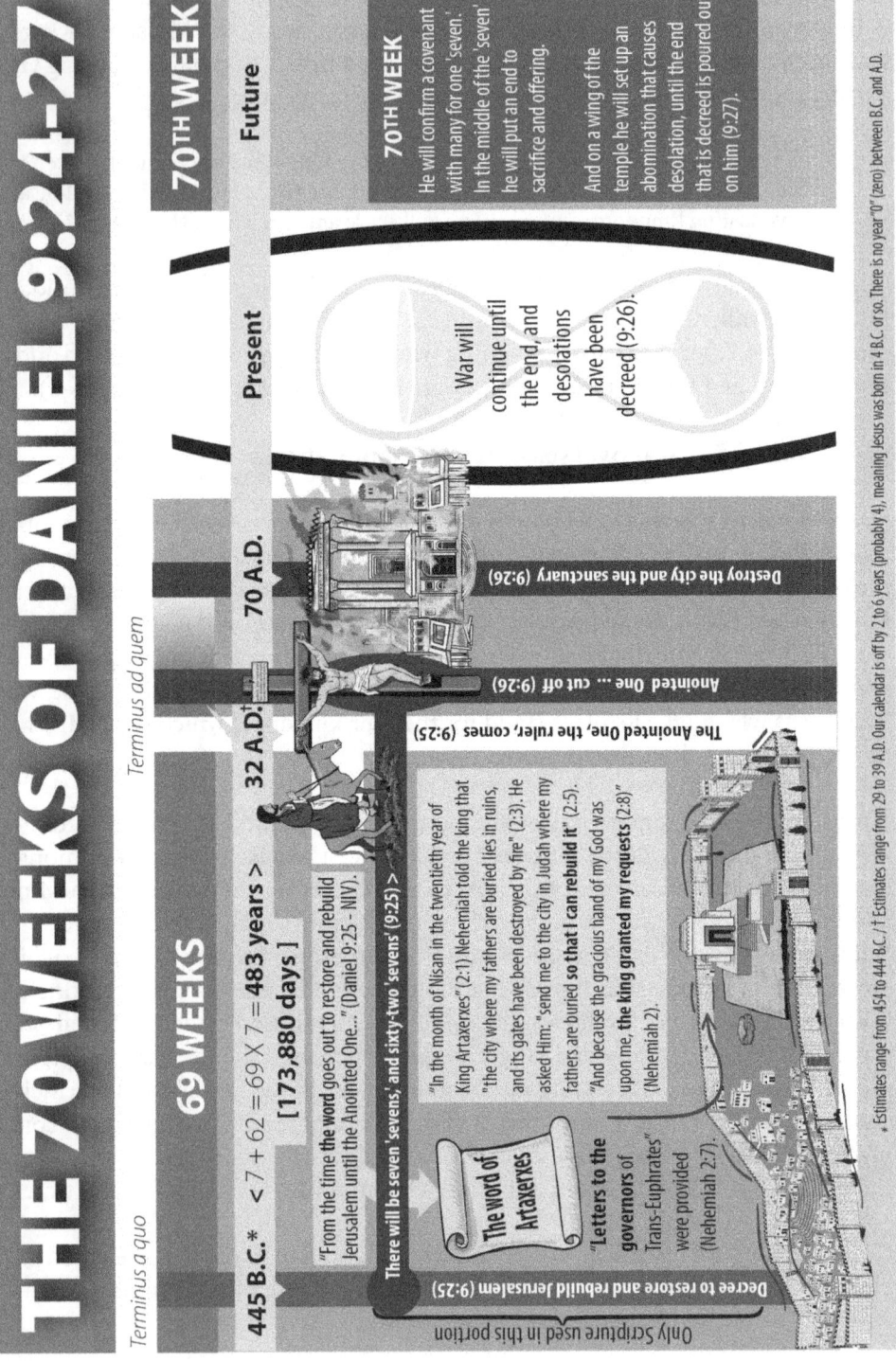

## [GK] Daniel 9 - God reveals when His Anointed would be coming and what will happen in the end

The authorship, date, and interpretation of the many visions in the Book of Daniel have generated a fair amount of controversy. That said, we must remember Jesus endorsed Daniel as a prophet and even made reference to Daniel 9:27, when He said, "So when you see the abomination of desolation, spoken of by the prophet Daniel, standing in the holy place" (let the reader understand)" (Matthew 24:15 - CSB), and went on to give instructions accordingly. This gives the followers of Jesus the authority to believe that Daniel was a real person and a genuine prophet who received a message having to do with the Messiah and the end-times.

While the prophecy of the 70 Weeks is one of the most specific in terms of the chronology of the coming of the promised Messiah, it presents some of the most difficult challenges to those who would like clarity concerning its dating system and symbolism. Much of what is said in the four crucial verses of Daniel 9:24-27 is enigmatic and ambiguous. Yet, the information received from Gabriel about the 70 Weeks is crucial not only because it refers to the timing of the coming Messiah but because the 70th Week serves as the framework for the Rapture, the Tribulation, the Great Tribulation, and the Day of the Lord in the Book of Revelation.

Daniel had been praying and inquiring about the future of Jerusalem (Daniel 9:20), when God's messenger Gabriel flew swiftly to his encounter. Gabriel told Daniel that a certain time limit had been "decreed" for God's purposes for "your people" and "your city." That God is in control means not only that He **knows** what is going to happen in the future, but that critical aspects of the future are **determined** ("decreed") by God, a prerogative He has as King. Six vital Kingdom objectives were to take place within the prophecy's time frame (Daniel 9:24):

**1. To finish (or restrain) transgression;** and **2. To put an end to sin.** These would require the inauguration of the Millennial Kingdom; **3. To atone for wickedness.** This speaks of Christ's atoning sacrifice on the cross. **4. To bring in everlasting righteousness.** Only "The Righteous One"—the Messiah—can achieve this goal. Again, a reference to the Millennial Kingdom. **5. To seal up vision and [the] prophecy.** The inference would be that vision and prophecy are needed no longer, because they had all been fulfilled. **6. To anoint the most holy.** The original language could indicate anointing the Holy of Holies, in which case it could refer to the Millennial Kingdom temple (see Ezekiel 40-44); or a most holy Person, in which case this would be Jesus the Messiah (the "Anointed One").

Gabriel tells Daniel that "seventy 'sevens' are decreed for your people" (Daniel 9:24). The Hebrew word *sabuim*, translated as "sevens" or "weeks" literally mean "units of seven" and, in this case, refers to years. Multiply 70 X 7 years and you

will get 490 years. The first 69 weeks (seven are mentioned, then another 62), or 483 years (490 minus one unit of 7), lead up to the first coming of Messiah.
**How much do we count?** In order to calculate the dates spoken of in prophecy, it is necessary to determine the duration of the "prophetic year." This has been done, among other ways, by comparing Daniel 7:25 and 9:27 and Revelation 12:6 and 14. The Revelation passages mention 1,260 days and a time, times, and half a time (three and a half years), simultaneously. If we divide 1260 (days) by 3.5 (years) we get 360 days.

*When do we start counting?* "The issuing of the decree to restore and rebuild Jerusalem" (Daniel 9:25 - HCSB) does not refer to rebuilding the Temple. "The edict in question was the decree issued by Artaxerxes Longitmanus in the twentieth year of his reign, authorizing Nehemiah to rebuild the fortifications of Jerusalem." And "the date of Artaxerxes's reign can be definitely ascertained... by the united voice of secular historians and chronologers."[11] Taking historical data into account, "the seventy weeks are therefore to be computed from the 1st of Nisan B.C. 445."[12]

*When do we stop counting?* Dr. Alva McClain argues that, taking into consideration the number of "weeks" mentioned in the passage and the prophetic year of 360 days, the equation would be 69 X 7 X 360 or 173,880 days, bringing us to April 6, 32 A.D.[13] It so happens that "April 6, 32 A.D., was the tenth of Nisan, that momentous day"[14] in which Israel's King would present Himself, righteous and victorious, riding into Jerusalem on a donkey (Zechariah 9:9). Reacting to His Triumphal Entry and the fulfillment of this prophecy, "the whole crowd of the disciples began to praise God joyfully with a loud voice for all the miracles they had seen: '**Blessed is the King who comes in the name of the Lord**. Peace in heaven and glory in the highest heaven!'" (Luke 19:37-38 - CSB).

However, "as Jesus approached Jerusalem and saw the city, He wept over it and said: 'If only you had known on this day what would bring you peace! But now it is hidden from your eyes.'" He then foretells Jerusalem's destruction, "because you did not recognize the time of your visitation from God" (Luke 19:41-44 - BSB). His own people had not recognized the official introduction to their true King and Messiah.

## Rejection foretold. Living in the gap.
Even this rejection was prophesied. "After this period of sixty-two sets of seven, the Anointed One will be killed, appearing to have accomplished nothing, and a ruler will arise whose armies will destroy the city and the Temple" (Daniel 9:26a - NLT; see also Isaiah 53:3). Here is a very clear declaration that after the Messiah is killed the city and Temple would be destroyed. It is an uncontested historical fact

that the Temple and the city of Jerusalem were destroyed in 70 A.D. (there's that number again). Therefore, the promised Messiah had to have come before that date. There are no other candidates who come even close to fulfilling this prophecy, other than Jesus of Nazareth.

We are now living in a gap and do not know when the 70th week will begin—the last seven-year period of human history as we know it. But when it does, a type of "the coming prince" who destroyed Jerusalem and the Temple in 70 A.D. (Daniel 9:26) "will make a firm covenant" with Israel, only to break it "in the middle of the week." And, as Antiochus IV Epiphanes, he will set up an abomination of desolation in the Temple, referred to by Jesus (Daniel 9:27; Matthew 24:15; see also Daniel 11:31 and 12:11).

The Good News is that this unsustainable situation will only last "until the decreed destruction is poured out on the desolator," who is Revelations' beast (Daniel 9:27 - HCSB; Revelation 19:20). Daniel's vision has to do with the focal points of the Global Kingdom: the coming of "the Messiah" Who would "be cut off" (Daniel 9:26), the dramatic last days of history, and the final defeat and destruction of the Antichrist.

### [GK] Daniel 10, 11 - God uses special messengers to warn of future events

The kingdom of darkness is a reality which will find its culmination in the end-times. Both this rebellious kingdom and end-time events will impact the Kingdom of God greatly, and for this reason are mentioned here. Chapters 11 and 12 are a continuation of chapter 10 and provide a detailed account of future events—mainly wars—which would and will greatly impact Jerusalem and the Jewish people. The future of Israel was, after all, what Daniel had so intensely been praying about. He wanted assurances that this chosen nation would survive and thrive under God's guiding hand, as a key element of God's Kingdom.

The prophecies contained in chapter 11, verses 2 through 35 have already been fulfilled with astonishing accuracy, being essentially a history lesson in advance concerning the period between 310 to 64 B.C. The messenger foretells the demise of the Persian empire, as its last sovereign ruler decides to "stir up everyone against the kingdom of Greece" (11:2). "The Persian king who invaded Greece was, of course, Xerxes, who reigned 485-464 B.C."[15]

### Tribulation and the Antichrist

Verse 35 ends by mentioning "the time of the end" which "will still come at the appointed time." These are eschatological terms and point to the end-times when the Antichrist will enter the picture. He is referred to as "the willful king" (Daniel

11:36-45), the "little horn" (Daniel 7:7, 8, 20, 24-26), and "the persecutor" (Daniel 9:27). "This section is the far fulfillment of God's prophetic plan. It summarizes details of Daniel's 70th week which are found nowhere else in Scripture. Antiochus Epiphanes, a type of Antichrist, is the perfect transition point to the actual Antichrist."[16]

As fearsome as this king is, "he will come to his end, and no one will help him" (Daniel 11:45 - NIV; see Revelation 19 and Zechariah 14:1-9).

## [GK] Daniel 12 - More trouble at the end times

The messenger informs Daniel there will be more trouble for his people "at that time"—again signaling the end times—"a time of distress such as has not happened from the beginning of nations until then." These words were echoed almost verbatim by our Lord, only adding: "and never to be equaled again" (Matthew 24:21 - NIV). Jesus then told His disciples about the sequence of events before His return and reminded them about "the abomination that causes desolation, spoken of through the prophet Daniel" (Matthew 24:15 - NIV; Daniel 9:27; 11:31; 12:11).

Daniel, whose great concern was the preservation and spiritual wellbeing of his people, is told that "at that time your people—everyone whose name is found written in the book—will be delivered" (Daniel 12:1).

Daniel is told about the resurrection and given a description of the glorified appearance of "those who have insight" and "who lead the many to righteousness:" They will "shine brightly like the brightness of the expanse of heaven" and be "like the stars forever and ever" (Daniel 12:3 - NASB). These are rewards worth living and waiting for! They motivate us to serve and bear much fruit. Leading "many to righteousness" is our Kingdom mission. And the best way to do so is to introduce others to "the Righteous One" Himself (Acts 22:14).

There is so much to learn from Daniel's life as a Kingdom model. His knowledge of God's sovereignty and limitless Kingdom power on the one hand and Daniel's character and wisdom on the other, has set a high standard for all citizens of the Kingdom. He was always willing, able and prepared to serve. He was truthful, gifted, disciplined and loyal to his earthly superiors. And, still, he never lost his passion for Israel's place in history and in God's plan, or his zeal when interceding for his people and homeland.

# Chapter 5

# Minor Prophets

## The Kingdom in Hosea

### [MK] [GK] Hosea 2, 3, 6 - God's Spirit poured out

God promises to make a covenant with the wild animals and other creatures (see Isaiah 11:6-7), and to "shatter bow, sword, and weapons of war in the land," and take His people as His wife forever, "in righteousness, justice, love, and compassion," and "in faithfulness" (Hosea 2:18-20 - HCSB; see Isaiah 2:4; 54:5; Micah 4:). These events reference a period in the future ("on that day," v. 18), when things will be very different. A time when wild animals will be tame, there will be no war, and God will "marry" His people. As these promises are compared to other similar statements, it becomes clear they refer to the Messianic Age.

In the shortest chapter of Hosea—chapter 3—it is foretold that Israel will be without a king for quite some time. It will be a period in which they will neither have the good and godly aspects of true worship (sacrifices and the ephod), *nor* the evil aspects of false religion (sacred stones and idols). Remember that after the Babylonian captivity, Israel never again had a problem with idolatry. But neither did they have a king. And, after the destruction of Jerusalem in 70 A.D.—and to this present day—they have not been able to hold sacrifices.

After this period, "the people of Israel will return and seek the LORD their God and David their king. They will come in awe to the LORD and to his goodness in the last days" (Hosea 3:5 - ISV). David is a reference to Messiah the King, as King David had died over 200 years prior to this prophecy. Besides, this will take place in the last days. This turning back to the Lord will happen just before or during the onset of the Millennial Kingdom (see "Zechariah 12—Jewish conversion," below).

In Hosea, chapter six, there is a reference to God's relationship with Adam as being a covenant. God says: "But like Adam, you broke my covenant and betrayed my trust." (Hosea 6:7 - NLT). The way the Kingdom works is by the King entering into a contract with His subjects. This applies not only to the known, formal covenants listed in the Bible, but to critical events and relationships as with Adam and Eve.[1]

# The Kingdom in Joel

### [GK] Joel 2 - God's Spirit poured out; the Day of the Lord

In Joel chapter two, God says that "in those days" He is going to pour out His Spirit on all people, sons and daughters will prophesy, old people have dreams, and youth see visions (Joel 2:28-29). When the Holy Spirit was poured out during the Day of Pentecost, Peter referred his audience (many of whom believed them to be drunk), to this passage in Joel. He also references the next few verses in Joel, which speak of the Day of the Lord (see Acts 2:14-21).

Specifically, Joel speaks of "the great and dreadful day of the Lord," before which there will be "wonders in the heavens and on the earth, blood and fire and billows of smoke," and says "the sun will be turned to darkness and the moon to blood" (Joel 2:30-31 - NIV). This expression is always associated with the outpouring of God's wrath in the final days. The difference in this passage is we are informed that "everyone who calls on the name of the Lord will be saved" as "there will be deliverance ... among the survivors whom the Lord calls" (Joel 2:32 - NIV). If you ever wondered if people will be saved during the Day of the Lord (which comes on the heels of the Great Tribulation), here is your answer.

### [GK] [MK] [EK] Joel 3 - "Bring down your warriors, O LORD!"

In Joel chapter three we are given a sequence of events having to do with the "in those days" era when the Lord will restore the fortunes of Judah. But before that happens, He will gather the nations and judge them because of the way they treated "My people, My inheritance Israel" and "divided up My land" (Joel 3:2 - HCSB). The chapter goes on to mention a time of war when plowshares will be beaten into swords (instead of the other way around, as in the Millennium. See Micah 4:3).

In the midst of the battle which occurs either right before or during the Day of the Lord, the cry goes out to "bring down your warriors, O LORD!" (Joel 3:11b - NIV). Compare this to Revelation 19, when the Lord comes back with "the armies who were in heaven" which also occurs in the context of "the press of the wine of the fury of the wrath of God the Almighty" (Revelation 19:14-15 - BLB). Jesus returns to finish the last war, Armageddon, which will still be in full swing at the end of the Day of the Lord.

Then the Lord says: "I will sit to judge all the surrounding nations" in the Valley of Jehoshaphat (Joel 3:12 - ESV; Jehoshaphat means "the LORD judges"). Compare this to what Jesus said about His return. He informed His disciples: "But when the Son of Man comes in his glory, and all the angels with him, then he will sit upon his glorious throne" and that "all the nations will be gathered in his presence" (Matthew 25:31-32a - NLT).

Multitudes will be drawn to the Valley of Jehoshaphat which will be "the valley of decision" (Joel 3:14 - NIV), perhaps because this will be the very last opportunity for repenting and placing one's faith and allegiance in the Lord. Remember, we have just seen that in this context, "everyone who calls on the name of the Lord will be saved." And if they do not, there will be no more time to do so because Messiah will be coming in His glory to judge. But before He does, "the sun and moon will grow dark, and the stars will cease their shining," and "heaven and earth will shake" but "the Lord will be a refuge for His people" (Joel 3:15-16 - HCSB).

As the book of Joel ends, the focus shifts to the Millennial and Eternal aspects of the Kingdom. Joel 3:17 tells of a future, holy and secure Jerusalem where God Himself has set up residence. Verse 18 speaks of a time of abundance and refreshment, when "a fountain will spring from the Temple of the LORD, to water the Valley of the Acacias" (Joel 3:18 - ISV), a theme recounted by other prophets and referred to by a psalmist.

On the flip side, Egypt and Edom (possibly modern-day Palestinians), will become "desolate" and "a desert wasteland" respectively. This will take place "because of the violence done to the people of Judah, in whose land they shed innocent blood" (Joel 3:19 - BSB; compare to current events). Yet "Judah will be inhabited forever" (Joel 3:20 - HCSB), a likely reference to the Eternal Kingdom.

# The Kingdom in Amos

**[GK] [MK] Amos 3, 5, 8, 9 - Righteousness to flow like a stream; the Day of the Lord; Restoration by Davidic King**

The people living in the days of Amos the prophet did "not know how to do what is right" (Amos 3:10). Their disdain for **Kingdom Values—God's** values—led the rich among them to "crush the poor under foot," "make them pay taxes with their grain," and "make trouble for those who are right and good," while receiving bribes "in secret for wrong-doing" (Amos 5:1-12 - NLV). Righteousness, the standard by which God measures everything in His Kingdom, was being thrown to the ground, the fruit of righteousness was being turned into wormwood, and the righteous were being oppressed (Amos 5:7,12; 6:12).

God told them He knew about the wrong they were doing and their many sins, and told them what He wanted them to do instead. "Look for good and not sin... hate sin, and love good," and "let what is fair be done" (Amos 5:14-15 - NLV). Or, as a central verse of this book has it, "let justice surge like waters, and righteousness like an unfailing stream" (Amos 5:24 - NABRE). Otherwise, God would not accept their worship rituals (Amos 5:21-23).

The Day of the Lord is also mentioned in Amos. Ironically, the people were longing for this day. They did not realize it would bring "darkness instead of light, very dark with nothing bright in it" (Amos 5:20 - NLV), that is, a day of judgment and wrath. They were educated on the subject and told it was "bad for you who want the day of the Lord to come" (Amos 5:18 - NLV). God promises that "in that day ... I will make the sun go down at noon and make the earth dark in broad daylight" (Amos 8:9 - NASB). God would bring mourning as a result of the injustice committed against the poor in the land (Amos 8:1-8), just as prophesied in the fifth chapter of Amos.

In chapter 9, verses 11 through 15 speak of a restoration which will be brought about by a Davidic King. By doing so, the book of Amos closes on a positive note, foretelling a time when the nation's fortunes will be restored, old cities rebuilt, vineyards and gardens again will be fruitful and plentiful, with the promise that "they will never again be uprooted from the land I have given them" (Amos 9:15 - NLT). This description is consistent with others which describe the Messianic Age or Millennial Kingdom.

# The Kingdom in Obadiah

[GK] [MK] **Obadiah 1 - Edom; God's Kingdom; Shalom; Hamas.**

Obadiah is a message to the nations about Edom and the last days. According to Dr. Brian Stephens, the main idea is a transition to the Kingdom. In his studies he has concluded that *Edom* (the descendants of Esau) refers to the modern day Palestinians. In July 2005, Stephens lectured on this small book. This whole section on Obadiah comes from the highlights of his talk and is used with his permission.

Obadiah is a great prophecy, and it ends with the best news. Look at the last phrase. It tells us the Good News, that the Kingdom is going to be established. It says that "the Kingdom will be the Lord's." Jews pray, "blessed are You, oh Lord our God, King of the universe." That means He is King over all things. He has no limitations. He has perfect resources. And what is His nature? He is a loving God. He likes to give. He is a generous God. The problem is that all too often you and I do not put ourselves in a position where God will bless us. The prophet is talking about this in this book: the position that specifically the world has to be in if God is going to open up the heavens and pour out blessings. The question is, are we willing to follow His conditions?

The main theme of this book is that God is going to establish His Kingdom. What is the main point of the book of Revelation? It is all about bringing God's throne from heaven to earth. It tells about the event that is going to bring that about. So does the book of Obadiah. It tell us that the last days are going to be about a war between the sons of Esau and the sons of Jacob. And that's what we are getting prepared for prophetically. Other [portions of] Scripture tell us that all the nations of the world are going to unite against Israel. And that is why God says He is speaking about Edom (Obadiah 1:1).

Let's talk about peace for a moment. I asked a group I was leading to define peace. "Peace is the absence of violence." It is not! Then they said: "peace is a feeling or an emotion." It is not! When God speaks about peace, He speaks not about the absence of something; He's talking about the fulfillment of His will. "Shalom" is a term of encouragement; it literally means an encouragement to fulfill God's will; to complete the purpose and plans of God. We see there is nothing Biblical about trying to bring about peace by telling Jewish people to get off their land.

Obadiah verse 10. God is angry with Esau, God is angry with his violence. That word in Hebrew is *hamas*. What does *hamas* mean? It is a specific type of violence. *Hamas* means violence for the sake of violence. Violence for the sake of seeing someone suffering in pain and hurt. That is the same type of spirit that Satan has.

He loves to devour, he loves to cause hardship and pain, he loves to make people suffer. That is his nature. And God says that is the spirit of Esau. That word *hamas* is a Semitic word. This terrorist organization that took on this name enjoys seeing Jewish people in pain. They don't want any peace agreement because they want to see Israel no more. They want to see every Israeli driven in the sea and they want to see, as they have said, the Mediterranean turned to blood, Jewish blood. Jeremiah mentions that in the last days Jacob will go through hardships (Jeremiah 30:7). But you see that the problems are going to bring Israel victory; they are a transition. Now, Messiah spoke about Jacob's trials (Matthew chapter 24, Mark chapter 13), and He tells us that these tribulations are likened to a woman in labor. From this time of trouble and darkness there will come the establishment of the Kingdom of God. And God warns the nations, "don't join with Esau." Why? He says, "I'm against Esau; I'm going to destroy Esau, and there's not going to be any remnant left of Esau as a nation."

Does that mean God hates the Palestinians? No. God loves all people the same. He loves the Arabs as much as the Jews. He rejoices the same way when an Arab or a Jew accepts Messiah. God is not a respecter of persons. God does not have a favorite pedigree or favorite ethnicity. He loves all people the same. And His Kingdom is going to be a Kingdom of nations. In fact, Israel is spoken of as a congregation of nations. What we see in the book of Revelations is the Kingdom of God is made up of people from every nation, tribe and language. That's the Kingdom of God!

# The Kingdom in Micah

### [GK] Micah 2, 3 - Stop cheating others and be fair

Justice is the social arm of righteousness. It includes treating others fairly. But in the time of Micah, there were those who were busy scheming how best to cheat other out of their fields, houses and even inheritance (Micah 2:1-2). The leaders in Israel, more than anyone, should have known and embraced a lifestyle of righteousness and justice. Isn't that what we expect from our leaders in Christian circles today?

I once received an e-mail from Moody Publishers about a survey they undertook that formed the basis for their book **Rising Above a Toxic Workplace**. What caught my eye was something I have suspected for years. "We discovered along the way," their message states, "that the worst stories came from churches and ministries, not businesses. We weren't looking for, or expecting, this result."[2]

Micah lashes out against the leaders of his nation. "Aren't you supposed to know what is just?," he asks. And yet, "you hate good and love evil," he scolds them (Micah 3:1-2 - HCSB). He describes their aggressive treatment of their followers in graphic terms, like shredding them to pieces and cooking them for lunch. He says their actions are "crimes" (Micah 3:4). Serious stuff. Do Christian leaders realize how seriously God takes their treatment of their staff, members and followers?

## [MK] Micah 4 - The Messianic Age

The Millennial Kingdom is described in Micah 4:1-8, and speaks of the personal presence of the Lord in Jerusalem as ruler over the nations (compare to Isaiah 2:1-4). Here are the main characteristics listed in the passage:

The description pertains to "the last days" when "the Lord's house" will be located on a mountain top which will be elevated above the others. Nations will stream to this place—Jerusalem—so the Lord "may teach us about His ways and that we may walk in His paths," because "from Zion will go forth the law, even the word of the Lord from Jerusalem." The Lord will settle disputes and "render decisions for mighty, distant nations." Nations will "hammer their swords into plowshares and their spears into pruning hooks" and "never again will they train for war" nor attack each other. Instead, there will be peace, security and prosperity, as people take it easy under their fig trees. People will "walk in the name of the Lord our God forever and ever" and "the Lord will reign over them in Mount Zion from now on and forever." To Zion will come "the former dominion" and the kingdom to Jerusalem (Micah 4:1-8 - NASB; contrast Micah 4:3 with Joel 3:10).

## [GK] Micah 6 - *Kingdom Values* and *Principles*

"He has told you, O man, what is good; and what does the Lord require of you but to do justice, to love kindness, and to walk humbly with your God?" (Micah 6:8 - NASB). This well-known verse from Micah lays out some **Kingdom Values** the Lord expects from His people.[3] Unfortunately, the following verses contrast God's ideals with the people's practices, and it doesn't look good. Their wealth was "ill-gotten," their scales were always tipped in their own favor with fraudulent weights. The rich were violent and had lying lips.

The **Kingdom Principle** applied to such sins, where there is the intent to take advantage of others, is that these people will come to ruin; they may eat, but they will never be satisfied; they "will store up but save nothing;" and they will "plant but not harvest" (Micah 6:9-15 - NIV).

# The Kingdom in Nahum

[GK] **Nahum 1, 2, 3 - God is against bloodshed and cruelty**

Nahum is an oracle against Nineveh and God's indignation with the bloodshed and "endless cruelty" Nineveh typified (Nahum 3:1, 19 - NIV). "I am against you" God tells Nineveh and threatens severe punishment (Nahum 2:13; 3:5 - NIV). In the midst of this rebuke, however, there are refreshing reminders that God is slow to anger, that "the LORD is good, a stronghold in the day of distress; He cares for those who trust in Him" (Nahum 1:3, 7 - BSB).

A contribution from Nahum to our focus on the Kingdom is the invitation to "behold, on the mountains the feet of him who brings good news, who announces peace!" (Nahum 1:15a - NASB). This verse echoes Isaiah 52:7, which adds "and brings good news of happiness, who announces salvation, and says to Zion, 'Your God reigns!'" These verses were fulfilled in Christ, Whose message was centered on the Good News of the Kingdom of God.

# The Kingdom in Habakkuk

[GK] **Habakkuk 1, 2 - Why does God tolerate evil and injustice?**

The book begins with the prophet logging a complaint with the Lord. He protests that God seems to not be listening to his plea. Why, he asks, does he have to put up with injustice, and why does God tolerate evil and violence? Plus, the wicked distort righteousness so that justice is perverted, the law stymied.

The Lord answers Habakkuk informing him He will be using the Babylonians to bring the judgment due his countrymen. Although we do not always know what God is up to, we can know that, as King, He will make sure justice prevails in the end. "Be sure of this: the wicked will not go unpunished, but the descendants of the righteous will go free" (Proverbs 11:21 - ISV).

Chapter 2 covers cases of injustice in relationships, especially due to greed, with warnings concerning the punishment which comes back to those who so treat others. There is also the warning against idol worship. The chapter ends with this reminder: "The Lord is in his holy temple; let all the earth be silent before him" (Habakkuk 2:20 - NIV). God is sovereign, is in control, and is worthy of respect.

# The Kingdom in Zephaniah

## [GK] [MK] Zephaniah 1, 3 - The Day of the Lord: total destruction

This is a book about the Day of the Lord and the Messianic Age. The prophet wastes no time in delivering the most dramatic statement about the destruction God will inflict on the world during "The Great Day of the Lord."

> I will completely sweep away everything from the face of the earth— this is the Lord's declaration. I will sweep away man and animal; I will sweep away the birds of the sky and the fish of the sea, and the ruins along with the wicked. I will cut off mankind from the face of the earth. This is the Lord's declaration. (Zephaniah 1:2-3 - HCSB)

There were (and are) those who think "the LORD will do nothing, either good or bad" (Zephaniah 1:12 - NIV), but that's a big mistake. Because the great Day of the Lord is surely coming. The sirens have been sounding by the prophets, who have consistently warned us through their writings. Zephaniah's message is consistent with the other prophets in his description of the Day of the Lord. He calls it "a day of wrath, a day of trouble and distress, a day of destruction and desolation, a day of darkness and gloom, a day of clouds and blackness" (Zephaniah 1:15 - HCSB). The Lord's day of wrath will bring such suffering on humanity "because they have sinned against the Lord" (Zephaniah 1:17 - HCSB). The problem was continual, rebellious, scandalous and—most importantly—unrepentant sin.

What humanity has done to the Lord's domain is unconscionable. Earthly rulers and common folk alike treat the planet as though it were their own. They speak of "Gaia," nature and evolution—anything to avoid any reference to its rightful Owner. They live lives which ignore the sovereign King and His ultimate authority over every living creature on earth. They play games, pretending God doesn't exist, and live as though they were not going to be called into account. Those who are more "mystical" believe in some form of energy or force. If they do believe in a "god" it would be the kind who never judges or condemns because He is all love and no blame. Still others use "God" and religion as an excuse to harm, a means to gain power, to abuse authority, to accumulate wealth while oppressing and enslaving others. The Day of the Lord is the day the Lord says "enough!"

No power, authority or resources will avail those caught in the way of God's holy wrath. Zephaniah's vision of total destruction is so complete it must be seen as "prophetic hyperbole" when he claims God "will make a complete, yes, a horrifying end of all the inhabitants of the earth" (Zephaniah 1:18b - HCSB; contrast with Zephaniah 2:9). Another example: After announcing "the whole world will be consumed by the fire of my jealous anger" (Zephaniah 3:8 - NIV), God declares He will then "purify the lips of the peoples" so they will begin to call upon Him (Zephaniah 3:9 - NIV).

Contrasting with the beginning of the terrible Day of the Lord is its culmination in the Messianic Era, when Jerusalem will be restored and protected by the Lord Himself. Not only is the Lord present in the capital city of the Kingdom, "He applies His justice morning by morning" (Zephaniah 3:5 - HCSB). The Day of the Lord's wrath is over. "The Lord has removed your punishment" and "the King of Israel, Yahweh, is among you" so there is no one and nothing to fear (Zephaniah 3:15 - HCSB). So close and loving is the Lord, that "Yahweh your God is among you" and "will rejoice over you with gladness. He will bring ... His love. He will delight in you with shouts of joy" (Zephaniah 3:17 - HCSB). As severe as the Lord's punishment will be, He is not turning His back on humanity, but weeding out the evil, saving the humble and repentant, and starting all over with them. It will be a time of restoration and delightful fellowship with His people.

# The Kingdom in Haggai

### [GK] [MK] Haggai 1, 2 - Temple to be built; The shaking of the heavens

Haggai's message has to do with the construction of the post-exilic Temple. The Lord promised Solomon the Temple was to be the place of the Lord's earthly throne (or the footstool of His throne). It was to be the King's headquarters on Earth, the center of His theocratic government. God's Presence and glory filled the Temple then, but because of Judah's rebellion, was lost and never regained (see 1 Kings 8:10-11 and Ezekiel 43:4-7).

In chapter one God tells the people to stop putting the construction off. In the second chapter God speaks to Haggai in a way that indicates the construction had begun and perhaps had been concluded. It was the best they could do with what they had, coming back from the Babylonian captivity. Yet there was no comparison with the former Temple build by Solomon.

Of course the contents are always more important than the packaging, and the Lord tells the prophet Haggai to cheer up because "in just a little while I will begin to shake the heavens and earth—and the oceans, too, and the dry land" (Haggai 2:6 - TLB), an apparent reference to the Day of the Lord. That may not sound so encouraging, but what follows does! God continues: "'I will shake all nations, and the Desire of All Nations shall come to this Temple, and I will fill this place with my glory,' says the Lord Almighty" (Haggai 2:7 - TLB).

As with the accounts of other Old Testament prophets, catastrophe comes before bliss, wrath before the awesome presence and majesty of the King living among His people. As for that future Temple (the "packaging"), Haggai was informed that "the future glory of this Temple will be greater than its past glory;" and God gave His word that "in this place I will bring peace" (Haggai 2:8-9 - NLT).

The catastrophe—the shaking of heavens and earth God will bring about—has as its purpose "to overthrow thrones" and to "destroy the strength of the kingdoms of the nations" (Haggai 2:22 - TLB). Whether there was a more immediate and symbolic application to this prophecy is not clear. But the language here takes us to the end of time, when there will be a literal shake up of earthly powers before the King arrives and sets up His own rule over all, which is consistent with Daniel 2:44-45.

# The Kingdom in Zechariah

Zechariah is an amazing collection of very vivid and specific prophecies. We will look at some of those pertaining to the first coming and glorious return of Messiah Jesus.

### [GK] Zechariah 3 - High Priest's sins taken away

Chapter three tells the story of a High Priest's sanctification from a privileged, heavenly standpoint. Joshua, the High Priest, is standing before the Angel of the Lord and Satan is there to accuse him. The way "the Angel of the Lord" (3:1) is interchanged with "the Lord" (3:2) and declares "see, I have taken away your sin" (3:4-5), indicates this is the pre-incarnate Christ. The Angel of the Lord then charges the High Priest to walk in God's ways and keep His requirements (3:7).

### [GK] Zechariah 8 - Basic *Kingdom Values*

Skipping over to chapter eight, there is the promise God makes to once again bless Israel. And He tells them what He expects from them. The things they are to do could be defined as **Kingdom Values**: Speak the truth and judge fairly with justice. They are to avoid thinking evil against those close to them, and should not enjoy swearing falsely (8:16-17). These last things the Lord despises.

## [MK] Zechariah 8 - Pilgrimage to Jerusalem

One day in the future the situation of Jerusalem will be so favorably reversed that "there will yet come peoples and inhabitants of many cities ... and say, 'come! let us go to implore the favor of the Lord and to seek the Lord of hosts. I too am going.'" The pilgrimage to Jerusalem will include "many peoples and strong nations" who "will come to seek the Lord of hosts in Jerusalem and to implore the favor of the Lord" (Zechariah 8:20-22 - NABRE). The reference is to the Messianic Age, when the Lord will reign and legislate from the throne of David, in Jerusalem.

## [GK] Zechariah 9a - The triumphal entry foretold

This highly detailed prophecy foretells the arrival of Messiah, or "The Coming of Zion's King," as the New International Version has it.

> Rejoice greatly, Daughter Zion! Shout, Daughter Jerusalem!
> See, your king comes to you, righteous and victorious,
> lowly and riding on a donkey, on a colt, the foal of a donkey.
> (Zechariah 9:9 - NIV)

Where the NIV translates the Hebrew *yasha* from this verse as "victorious," the New American Standard Bible has "endowed with salvation." The King comes to Jerusalem the first time on a donkey, humbly demonstrating He was coming in peace. Matthew described Jesus' perfect fulfillment of this prophecy. He wrote that "Jesus sent two disciples, saying to them, 'Go into the village opposite you, and immediately you will find a donkey tied, and a colt with her. Loose them and bring them to Me'" (Matthew 21:1, 2 - NKJV). The disciples go, bring Him the donkey and the colt and He rode into Jerusalem as the onlookers shouted "Hosanna to the Son of David!" and "Blessed is He who comes in the name of the Lord!" (Matthew 21:9 - NKJV). These are Messianic greetings from Psalm 118:26.

## [MK] Zechariah 9b - What happens when Messiah comes back

The very next verse describes what will happen after Messiah's second coming. The Lord will take weapons of war away from Israel and "He will proclaim peace to the nations. His rule will extend from sea to sea and from the River to the ends of the earth" (Zechariah 9:10 - NIV).

There is the promise of deliverance and protection when "the Lord will appear over them; his arrow will flash like lightning. The Sovereign Lord will sound the trumpet" (Zechariah 9:14 - NIV). "The Lord their God will save his people on that day;" they will be beautiful and "will sparkle in his land like jewels in a crown" (Zechariah 9:16-17 - NIV).

After condemning idols and diviners that do a disservice to people and leave them wandering, confused and oppressed, we are told the Lord Himself will tend to His flock and that from the tribe of Judah will come the Cornerstone, a Messianic title (Zechariah 10:1-4).

## [GK] Zechariah 12 - Jewish conversion

The question arises: will the Jewish nation ever come to acknowledge Jesus as Messiah? If so, when and how? The following prophecy addresses this issue, 500 years before Messiah was even born. God told Zechariah: "I will pour out on the house of David and on the inhabitants of Jerusalem, the Spirit of grace and of supplication, so that they will look on Me whom they have pierced; and they will mourn for Him, as one mourns for an only son, and they will weep bitterly over Him like the bitter weeping over a firstborn" (Zechariah 12:10 - NASB). God will convict the Jewish nation which will repent when they look on the Lord ("Me") whom "they have pierced" (crucified), and mourn deeply and genuinely, as when one mourns for an only or firstborn child.

This is not anti-Semitism or an indictment on the Jewish nation. Quite the contrary. It is a message of hope, in that God's chosen people will finally recognize God's chosen Messiah, Son and King. And "on that day" when they come to this realization, mourn and repent, "there shall be a fountain opened for the house of David and the inhabitants of Jerusalem to cleanse them from sin and uncleanness" (Zechariah 13:1 - RSV). (For more on Israel's turning to Messiah, see Romans 11:25-29).

## [GK] Zechariah 13 - The Shepherd is struck, the sheep scattered

Another prophecy dealing with Messiah's first coming is so important that Jesus quotes it to His closest disciples. Here is the prophecy: "'Awake, O sword, against My Shepherd, against the Man who is My Companion,' says the Lord of hosts. 'Strike the Shepherd, and the sheep will be scattered ...'" (Zechariah 13:7 - NKJV).

Here is what Jesus told His disciples it meant, during the Last Supper: "then Jesus said to them, 'All of you will be made to stumble because of Me this night, for it is written 'I will strike the Shepherd, and the sheep of the flock will be scattered'" (Matthew 26:31 - NKJV). Jesus knew His disciples would flee once He was struck and warned them ahead of time.

## [MK] Zechariah 14 - Messiah returns to reign

Zechariah Chapter 14 contains one of the clearest, most detailed accounts of the Lord's return. The NIV adds the title "The LORD Comes and Reigns" above this passage, for good reason. Although many prophetic passages skip around, introduce other subjects in the text, and may not be presented in chronological order, this passage is an exception to that rule.

Zechariah begins this final section by declaring that "the day of the LORD is coming" and that the Lord "will gather all the nations to fight against Jerusalem," with dire consequences for the city and its population (Zechariah 14:1-2 - NLT). He informs us that "the Lord my God will come, and all his holy ones with him," that "the Lord will go out to fight against those nations," and that "on that day his feet will stand on the Mount of Olives" (Zechariah 14:3-4, 6 - NLT).
What Zechariah describes, we learn in the Lord's revelation to the Apostle John, is the battle of Armageddon, referred to by name in Revelation 16:16. That the Lord fights against the nations at that time is perfectly paralleled in Revelation 19:11-16, which tells of Jesus' return with His saints to conquer the Earth and set up His Millennial Kingdom. And, "his feet" touching down on the Mount of Olives is also foretold by the two angels who appeared to the Apostles and told them: "This same Jesus, who has been taken from you into heaven, will come back in the same way you have seen Him go into heaven." They were on the Mount of Olives when Jesus' ascension took place (Acts 1:9-12 - BSB).

In summary, after the Great Tribulation comes the Day of the Lord, which culminates with the battle of Armageddon and the Lord's return with His saints to stop the aggression of the nations which had come together to attack Jerusalem and to set up His Millennial Kingdom headquarters there.

### The events "on that day"
The prophets warned about the darkness that would occur as a result of the Lord's wrath. Zechariah confirms that "on that day there shall be no light, cold, or frost" (Zechariah 14:6 - ESV; see Matthew 24:29). But when Jesus comes back, He brings the light with Him, because, He claimed, "I am the light of the world. Whoever follows me will never walk in darkness, but will have the light of life" (John 8:12b - NIV). Imagine the lights going out on the whole planet for the duration of the Day of the Lord, then a light appearing in the sky, brighter than the sun (as in Acts 26:13). That will catch the world's attention! The Prophet Isaiah confirms this phenomenon. He said: "The moon will grow dark, and the sun will no longer shine, for the LORD Almighty will be king. He will rule in Jerusalem on Mount Zion, and the leaders of the people will see his glory" (Isaiah 24:23 - GNT; see also Isaiah 60:19).

Light enables vision and signifies knowledge. All truth will emanate from the Millennial Kingdom's throne in Jerusalem. Isaiah speaks of the mountain of the Lord's temple in the last days, and people streaming to it so He can teach them

His ways. He said the law and the word of the Lord will go forth from Jerusalem at that time (Isaiah 2:1-4). Because Jesus is the light of the world, when He arrives in Jerusalem, "it will be a day known only to Yahweh, without day or night, but there will be light at evening" (Zechariah 14:7 - HCSB). Light will emanate from Jerusalem and illuminate the whole world at the same time. Does this mean people around the world will be in the same time zone?

There will be another phenomenon designed to manifest Jesus the King's Presence and blessings. "On that day living water will flow out from Jerusalem, half of it toward the eastern sea [the Dead Sea] and the other half toward the western sea [the Mediterranean Sea], in summer and winter alike" (Zechariah 14:8 - HCSB). There are more details about this river in Ezekiel 47:1-12, which explains that the water comes from the Temple, near the throne, and everywhere it flows, it brings life (see also Psalm 46:4 and Joel 3:17-18). Revelation 22:1 speaks of this river in the context of the Eternal Kingdom which is no surprise, since that Millennial Kingdom is meant to be a transition and therefore will already display many of the traits found permanently in the eternal state.

The river of life brings rich meaning to Jesus' invitation and claim, when "on the last day, the climax of the festival, Jesus stood and shouted to the crowds, 'Anyone who is thirsty may come to me!'" Jesus announced that "anyone who believes in me may come and drink! For the Scriptures declare, 'Rivers of living water will flow from his heart'" (John 7:37-38 - NLT). Here is the piece to the puzzle that makes Jesus' words even more significant: the Feast of the Lord mentioned in the Gospel of John, as well as the context of the glorious return of the Lord in Zechariah, are both the Feast of Tabernacles. Jesus is not only the light of the world, He is the living water (see John 4:10, 14).

## The Lord will be King over all the Earth

The long awaited return has finally happened and everything is in place. Now comes the announcement that will change everything. "On that day Yahweh will become King over all the earth—Yahweh alone, and His name alone" (Zechariah 14:9 - HCSB). This is what every friend of God and follower of Jesus desires with his or her whole heart. This is what we have been praying for over the years: "Our Father in heaven, Hallowed be Your name. Your kingdom come. Your will be done on earth as it is in heaven" (Matthew 6:9-10 - NKJV). Beginning "on that day" it will! There will no longer be false religions, faithless philosophies, idols or gods to be pursued. "On that day there will be one Lord, and his name the only name" (Zechariah 14:9b - NIV).

Seismic activity generated when the Lord touches down on the Mount of Olives will cause it to "split apart, making a wide valley" (Zechariah 14:4). Meaning

"Jerusalem will be raised up in its original place" because the mount on which it is built will be taller than the surrounding others (Zechariah 14:10 - NLT; see Psalm 2:6; 15:1; 68:16; 99:9; Isaiah 66:20). Again, Isaiah's prophecies corroborate and elucidate those of Zechariah: "In the last days, the mountain of the LORD's house will be the highest of all— the most important place on earth. It will be raised above the other hills, and people from all over the world will stream there to worship" (Isaiah 2:2 - NLT). From then on, "Jerusalem will be filled, safe at last, never again to be cursed and destroyed" (Zechariah 14:11 - NLT).

Recapping, the Lord comes back with His saints, ends the Armageddon assault on Jerusalem, brings light to Earth again, opens a fountain of living water from His throne in Jerusalem, which is now on what is the tallest mountain in the area— which would have to be Mount Zion or Mount Moriah—or both.

But what about all the nations that came against Jerusalem in the Battle of Armageddon? "The Lord will send a plague on all the nations that fought against Jerusalem," the description of which sounds like nuclear fallout. Those affected will be "like walking corpses, their flesh rotting away. Their eyes will rot in their sockets, and their tongues will rot in their mouths." Their animals will suffer the same effects and fate. At that point, "the wealth of all the neighboring nations will be captured—great quantities of gold and silver and fine clothing" (Zechariah 14:12-15 - NLT).

**First deliberations**
What will be some first deliberations from Messiah's throne? It is revealed that "the survivors from all the nations that have attacked Jerusalem will go up year after year to worship the King, the Lord Almighty, and to celebrate the Festival of Tabernacles" (Zechariah 14:16 - NIV).

The King will begin to reign by demanding acts of restitution. The world always ganged up on Israel and looked the other way when its enemies attacked. At the end of history as we know it things will get much worse, with Antichrist and the world turning on Israel like never before. During the Day of the Lord and the battle of Armageddon Jerusalem's "possessions will be plundered" and "the city will be captured, the houses ransacked, and the women raped. Half of the city will go into exile" (Zechariah 14:1-2 - NIV). A righteous reign demands there be proportional restitution.

The King will also demand that the surviving population of the nations that attacked Jerusalem make a yearly pilgrimage there to worship the King, during the Feast of Tabernacles. This will be a sign of loyalty to the King and a reminder of the injustice done to Israel in years past. All families of the earth will be expected to appear before the Lord each year to worship the King. If they do not, rain will be withheld from their nation (Zechariah 14:16-19).

It used to be that everything came stamped with "Made in USA." Nowadays just about everything in the western hemisphere says "Made in China." But when the Lord begins to reign, every object in the Temple area and in Jerusalem will have "HOLY TO THE LORD" inscribed on it (see Exodus 28:35-36). Everything will be completely dedicated to the Lord and separated from regular use and set apart for Kingdom purposes, and nobody who is unclean or defiled will be allowed in the Temple area (Zechariah 14:20-21).

# The Kingdom in Malachi

### [GK] Malachi 1, 2, 3, 4 - The Great King; the marriage covenant; the Day of the Lord

God identified Himself as a Father and Master, yet was not receiving the honor and respect He deserved from the people of the kingdom of Israel (Malachi 1:6). The Lord also identified Himself as a Great King and made it clear He was not pleased with those who promised to give Him their best (an acceptable animal for sacrifice), only to renege when the time came to make the sacrifice (they would give a blemished animal instead) (Malachi 1:14).

God shares with Malachi a very profound and strategic piece of information. He is so serious about marriage because it is a covenant through which God is "seeking godly offspring" (Malachi 2:14-15). This has implications for the family because couples that are united in love, respect and godliness create the kind of environment where children can take on this same character and these same traits. The reason God, the King, values the godly family so much is that He is "seeking godly offspring" for Himself.

The purpose of marriage is to illustrate—tangibly—the intimate relationship God desires to have with us. The purpose is also to generate godly children who can become **God's** children. Which is why the first mission God gave the first couple was to "be fruitful, multiply, and fill the earth" (Genesis 1:28), and the first institution he provided as the ideal place for this to happen was marriage (Genesis 2:24). But a fallen race like ours must be redeemed, repossessed and repurposed. And that could only happen through the sacrificial death of Jesus. Once regenerated, we do indeed become God's children (see 1 John 3:1).

This being His ultimate purpose for marriage and the family answers many of our deepest questions about the purpose of life on Earth, like why we are here and what God wants from us. It also helps us to understand why the family is under such fierce attack by the enemy.[4]

The announcement of the Lord's coming is made in Malachi chapter three. There appear to be elements of the first and second coming there. The Lord comes to refine, judge and receive offerings made in righteousness. He will testify against those who practice what could be said to be the opposite of **Kingdom Values**, such as sorcery, adultery, perjury, dishonest wages, the oppression of widows and the fatherless, and the withholding of justice from foreigners. That is, the exploitation of the weak (Malachi 3:1-15).

One of God's attributes is that He remains constant. "I the LORD do not change," He tells His prophet (Malachi 3:6 - NIV). This is great news for His faithful followers and brings enormous security. But for those who prefer to change with the times, this can be a problem. Because, if God doesn't change, neither do His will and values.

Malachi also speaks of the Day of the Lord. It is a future reality ("surely the day is coming") that will burn the arrogant and evildoers as if in a furnace, leaving no trace of their roots behind. "But for you who fear My name, the sun of righteousness will rise with healing in its wings" (Malachi 4:1-2 - HCSB). The Day of the Lord begins with His retribution, the pouring out of His wrath on those who have refused to repent and believe. The second phase brings relief, healing and celebration. Because, as we understand from other passages, that will be the time of the Lord's coming in glory to set up His Millennial Kingdom, a time eagerly anticipated and which will be earnestly celebrated by His own.

# The Old Testament comes to a close

Although King Cyrus of Persia had allowed the people of Judah to go back to their homeland and rebuild the Temple, they remained unfaithful and plagued with great guilt. They had forsaken the commands of the Lord and were still under the dominion of Persia and slaves in their own land (Ezra 1; 9:4, 9, 10). Nehemiah also laments this fact, claiming the returned exiles had not abandoned their evil ways and that the Persian empire continued to rule over their crops, bodies and cattle. This resulted in great distress (Nehemiah 9:36-37).

All the glorious prophecies of a golden age, with a new Davidic king, and a people with transformed hearts and spirits (Ezekiel 11:19; 36:26), had not been realized. They had their new Temple, but the glory of the God of Israel was not there. They had their land, but were not free to enjoy it as they wished. The Old Testament, therefore, ends in disappointment. Worse: A tumultuous 400 years lay ahead of them, when the voice of prophets would not be heard, and the nation would be forced to wait for their long-anticipated Messiah while enduring the oppression inflicted by foreign powers.

The Persian domination lasted from 536 to 333 BC. The Greeks—via the Alexandrian Empire, then the Ptolemaic Dynasty of Egypt, and finally through the Seleucids of Syria—governed the Jewish people from 333 to 166 BC. The Maccabean or Hasmonean Revolt brought independence and freedom to Judea from 166 to 63 BC. But this was short-lived, as the Roman empire occupied and dominated Judea from 63 BC to 313 AD.

The Jewish people were tired of being oppressed and eagerly anticipated the Messianic Age. Yet, once the Messiah came, many would not acknowledge Him as Israel's King, since He did not come as a political conqueror, but as a humble Servant—even though this had been foretold (Isaiah 42:1; Zechariah 9:9). The historical fact remains: The last Jewish leader to receive the title of king was Mattaniah, whose name Nebuchadnezzar changed to Zedekiah (2 Kings 24:16-17). The next One to receive the title of King of the Jews would be Jesus the Christ.

# *SECOND DIVISION*

# New Testament Kingdom Highlights

# The Genealogy of Jesus

A record of the genealogy of Jesus Christ the son of David, the son of Abraham
Matthew 1:1

## Before Abraham
(mentioned only in Luke 3)

*Not mentioned in Matthew Account*

- God
- Adam
- Seth
- Enosh
- Kenan
- Mahalalel
- Jared
- Enoch
- Methuselah
- Lamech
- **Noah**
- Shem
- Arphaxad
- Cainan
- Shelah
- Eber
- Peleg
- Reu
- Serug
- Nahor
- Terah

## Abraham to David

*Same in Matthew and Luke*

| In Matthew 1: | In Luke 3: |
|---|---|
| **Abraham** | Abraham |
| Isaac | Isaac |
| Jacob | Jacob |
| **Judah** | Judah |
| Perez | Perez |
| Hezron | Hezron |
| Ram | Ram |
| Amminadab | Amminadab |
| Nahshon | Nahshon |
| Salmon | Salmon |
| Boaz | Boaz |
| Obed | Obed |
| Jesse | Jesse |
| **David** | David |

## After King David

*Very Different Lineages*

| Lineage through **Joseph** — In Matthew 1: | Lineage through **Mary** — In Luke 3: |
|---|---|
| Solomon | Nathan |
| Rehoboam | Mattatha |
| Abijah | Menna |
| Asa | Melea |
| Jehoshaphat | Eliakim |
| Jehoram | Jonam |
| **(x)Uzziah (Azariah)** | Joseph |
| Jotham | Judah |
| Ahaz | Simeon |
| Hezekiah | Levi |
| Manasseh, | Matthat |
| Amon, | Jorim |
| Josiah, | Eliezer |
| Jeconiah* | Joshua |
| *Shealtiel,* | Er |
| Zerubbabel, | Elmadam |
| Abiud, | Cosam |
| Eliakim, | Addi |
| Azor, | Melki |
| Zadok, | Neri |
| Akim, | *Shealtiel* |
| Eliud, | *Zerubbabel* |
| Eleazar, | Rhesa |
| Matthan, | Joanan |
| Jacob, | Joda |
| Joseph [the husband of Mary] | Josech |
|  | Semein |
|  | Mattathias |
|  | Maath |
|  | Naggai |
|  | Esli |
|  | Nahum |
|  | Amos |
|  | Mattathias |
|  | Joseph |
|  | Jannai |
|  | Melki |
|  | Levi |
|  | Matthat |
|  | Heli |
|  | *Joseph* |

(x) Three Kings' names ommitted by Matthew: Ahaziah, Joash, Amaziah (1 Chronicles 3:11-12)

*or, Jehoiachin

---

"Now Jesus himself was about thirty years old when he began his ministry. He was the son, so it was thought, of Joseph..." (Luke 3:23)

**Genesis 3:15:** The Messiah would be reckoned after the "seed of the **woman**" – not the father.

**Isaiah 7:14** foretold that the Messiah would be **born of a virgin** – therefore, without a human father.

**Galatians 4:4** – GNT: *But when the right time finally came, God sent his own Son. **He came as the son of a human mother** and lived under the Jewish Law.*

Jesus' humanity came solely through His mother. Therefore, Joseph's genealogy, while important, was not decisive.

---

"Thus there were fourteen generations in all from Abraham to David, fourteen from David to the exile to Babylon, and fourteen from the exile to the Christ" (Matthew 1:17).

© John Hatton 2019

# Chapter 6

# Matthew: The Gospel of the Kingdom

*But when the right time finally came, God sent his own Son.*
*He came as the son of a human mother*
*and lived under the Jewish Law.*
*Galatians 4:4 – GNT*

**The Kingdom in the Gospel of Matthew**
The New Testament, or "New Covenant," records the fulfillment of the Old Testament prophecies of a Messiah who would be both King and Suffering Servant, as described by Isaiah. Although a king—or better, *the* King—Jesus was on a mission that was initially not understood even by His closest disciples and family. Hoping against hope, Israel wanted a conquering king who would free them from Roman domination. They were not expecting a humble carpenter from Nazareth or prepared for a servant preacher from Galilee, whose mission included dying on a cross—although both had been foretold (Isaiah 9:1-2; 42:1-4; 53:3-11; Matthew 2:23; Mark 1:9).

But what is a king without subjects? A father without children? Before He could reign over people, Jesus had to save them by justifying and making them righteous. And, so "shall the righteous one, my servant, make many to be accounted righteous, and he shall bear their iniquities" (Isaiah 53:11b - ESV). The Gospels bear witness as to how Jesus accomplished this, and the rest of the New Testament details how this righteousness was lived out by His followers.

## Matthew, the Gospel of the Kingdom

Matthew is widely recognized as the Gospel of the Kingdom because of its emphasis on what was the central theme of Christ's message. For this reason there will be more to cover here than from other Gospels and books in the New Testament, where only Kingdom highlights will be pointed out, with brief comments where appropriate.

Because the entire Gospel of Matthew is Kingdom-centered, it would make sense to begin with an overall view of this book, by glancing at an outline of its content:

> **1. The King's birth - 1:1–4:11:** Genealogy; birth announcement; Jesus is born; the Magi visit; to Egypt, then Nazareth; John the Baptist; Jesus' baptism and temptation.
>
> **2. The King's principles (Galilean ministry) - 4:12–7:29:** Beginning of Jesus' ministry; first disciples called; sick healed; Sermon on the Mount.
>
> **3. The King in action - 8:1–11:1:** Preaching, healing, teaching, and casting out demons; commissioning the Twelve.
>
> **4. Mounting opposition to the King - 11:2–13:53:** Jesus and John the Baptist; withdrawal; Jesus versus Beelzebub; Kingdom parables.
>
> **5. The King's reaction to opposition - 13:54–19:2:** Jesus: A Prophet without honor; John the Baptist beheaded; Jesus feeds five thousand; Jesus feeds four thousand; Transfiguration; greatest in the Kingdom; parables.
>
> **6. Formal presentation and rejection of the King (Jerusalem and Judean Ministry) - 19:3–25:46:** About divorce; little children and the rich; instructions to disciples, formal presentation of the King in the Triumphal Entry; the nation's rejection of the King; the King's rejection of the nation; the Olivet Discourse.
>
> **7. Crucifixion and resurrection - 26:1–28:20:** Plot to kill Jesus; the Lord's Supper; Peter's denial; trial; crucifixion; resurrection; Great Commission.

## [GK] Matthew 1 - The King's genealogy

Jacob was on his deathbed when he called his sons and prophesied about their future. When he got to Judah, he said "the scepter will not depart from Judah, nor the ruler's staff from his descendants, until the coming of the one to whom it belongs, the one whom all nations will honor" (Genesis 49:10 - NLT). From then on it became clear that the promised Messiah would come from the line of Judah.

So when Matthew provides Jesus' genealogy, it is no wonder he quickly moves from Jesus back to David, then further back to Abraham, and then forward to Isaac, Jacob and Judah. The connection between Jesus and King David was of fundamental importance because it was common knowledge the Messiah would be "the son of David" (Matthew 15:2; 21:9; 22:42; Mark 10:47). The Lord had promised David a special Descendant Who would be on his throne forever (Psalm 89:3-4, 27-29), an impossible accomplishment for a mere mortal.

After going through 42 generations in the Lord's genealogy (three sets of 14), Matthew turns to the story of the birth of Jesus. The story is also told in Luke 1:26-2:20 where different details are provided, details that are of fundamental importance when discussing the Kingdom. We will be going back and forth between the two accounts, stressing those statements that speak to the kingship of Jesus.

Joseph, a descendant of King David, was engaged to Mary, also a descendant of David, by all indications. Luke 3:23-38 almost certainly contains Mary's genealogy (see chart above). Mary was visited by the angel Gabriel and told she would give birth to a son Who would be called Jesus, "the Son of the Most High, and the Lord God will give Him the throne of His father David. He will reign over the house of Jacob forever, and His kingdom will have no end." When Mary asked how that could be possible, since she was a virgin, Gabriel told her this would be the work of God and, "therefore, the holy One to be born will be called the Son of God" (Luke 1:31-335 - HCSB). Mary accepted all she was told by faith and made herself available for God's purposes.

When Mary had conceived by the Holy Spirit, Joseph was warned by an angel in a dream not to leave her, as he had secretly planned to do. He was told to name the son Jesus, as He would save His people from their sins. This would fulfill Isaiah's prophecy (Matthew 1:18-25; Isaiah 7:14). Joseph obeyed the vision he received and took Mary as his wife.

## [GK] Matthew 2 - The King is born!

Joseph and Mary leave Nazareth and go to Bethlehem, the city of David, to register, since Joseph was David's descendant. While there, Jesus is born, as foretold hundreds of years before (Micah 5: 2). Angels appear to shepherds in the field and tell them that "today a Savior, who is Messiah the Lord, was born for you in the city of David" (Luke 2:11 - HCSB). After Jesus was born in Bethlehem, probably close to two years later, wise men came to Jerusalem and asked "where is He who has been born King of the Jews? For we saw His star in the east and have come to worship Him" (Matthew 2:2 - HCSB).

These "wise men" (we are not told how many they were), are called *magos* or *magus* (plural *magi*) in the original Greek text, a word "now regarded by many as of Babylonian origin" which is "the name given by the Babylonians (Chaldaeans),

Medes, Persians, and others, to the wise men, teachers, priests, physicians, astrologers, seers, interpreters of dreams, augurs, soothsayers, sorcerers etc."[1]

Dr. Brian Stephens believes it is possible these *magos* could be understood to be "specialists of the Talmud," who were knowledgeable of Daniel's prophecies about the coming Messiah. They would be descendants of Jews who decided not to return to Jerusalem after the 70 years of captivity, but to stay on in Babylon or Persia.

Be that as it may, they went to Jerusalem with the right idea. They knew about the birth of the King of the Jews, they traveled from far away to see Him, and "falling to their knees, they worshiped Him" when they found Him. "Then they opened their treasures and presented Him with gifts: gold, frankincense, and myrrh" (Matthew 2:11 - HCSB). Jesus is worthy to be sought, worshiped, and to receive our very best.

## [GK] Matthew 3 - The King's forerunner and anointing the King

### A call to repentance and faith; a call to the Kingdom

God's solution for humanity's sin problem is based on true repentance and faith.[2] And that was the emphasis of John the Baptist's message, as he preached "repent, for the kingdom of heaven is near" (Matthew 3: 1-2). As he did so, he was fulfilling the prophecy of Isaiah 40:3, which spoke of a voice calling in the desert and preparing the way for the Lord. "Then, after John had been thrown into prison, Jesus came into Galilee proclaiming God's Good News." In what was His first sermon on record, Jesus proclaimed: "'the time has fully come,' He said, 'and the Kingdom of God is close at hand: repent, and believe this Good News'" (Mark 1:14, 15 - WNT).

But before Jesus' ministry began, He had to go through two defining moments: His baptism and His temptation in the wilderness.

### The King's Anointing

Jesus' baptism (Matthew 3:13-17) was vital for His earthly ministry and position as Messiah because it was there He was anointed with the Holy Spirit. While prophets, kings and priests in the Old Testament were anointed with olive oil as a symbol of the Holy Spirit, Jesus received a special anointing by the Spirit Himself, Who came down in the visual aspect of a dove. Jesus, fully God and fully human, received the fullness of the Spirit and *all* the gifts of the Spirit needed for His ministry. John would later testify that "God gives the Spirit without limit" to Him (John 3:34 - NIV).

Also of pivotal importance was the Father's endorsement of His Son's identity and ministry as the prophesied Suffering Servant and Ruling King, two paradoxical characteristics of the Messiah. The Father said: "This is My beloved Son. I take delight in Him!" (Matthew 3:17 - HCSB).

The first declaration reverts us to the second Psalm which speaks of the Lord's "anointed one," of Whom the Lord says, "You are my son; today I have begotten you." The One Who the Lord will install as His king on Mount Zion and to Whom He will give the nations as an inheritance, over which He will rule with an iron scepter, a code-image associated with the Messianic Age or Millennial Kingdom (Psalm 2:2, 6-9 - NABRE; see Revelation 12:5, 19:15). When the voice from above said Jesus was His Son, He was also saying He was the Anointed King Who will one day rule over the whole earth (John 3:35).

The second declaration, "I take delight in Him!," takes us back to the Servant of the Lord, spoken of by Isaiah. Through the prophet the Lord exclaimed, "behold! My Servant whom I uphold, My Elect One in whom My soul delights! I have put My Spirit upon Him; He will bring forth justice to the Gentiles" (Isaiah 42:1 - NKJV). The prophecy speaks to the exact moment of Messiah's baptism and anointing, as this was when the Father placed His Spirit upon Him. And the Father's delight relates to the Son's obedience and loyalty to the Father's will and plan.

John the Baptist was hesitant to baptize Jesus at first, not realizing all that was involved in this important event. John's baptism was for repentance and Jesus didn't need repenting. But Jesus insisted that "it is fitting for us to fulfill all righteousness" (Matthew 3:15 - NKJV), and John complied. Jesus' goal was to fulfill all righteousness—whether as a loving Son, a righteous King, or a humble and obedient Servant of the Lord.

## [GK] Matthew 4 - The King's testing

### The test

Jesus had just been anointed by the Holy Spirit. Now the Spirit led Him out into the desert to be tested. Jesus had just been declared to be God the Father's Son. Satan would try to exploit that position. "If You are the Son of God, tell these stones to become bread," he proposed (Matthew 4:3 -HCSB).

"The form of the 'if' clause in Greek ... does not so much challenge his sonship as assume it to build a doubtful imperative. Satan was not inviting Jesus to doubt his sonship but to reflect on its meaning; ... it was a temptation to use his sonship in a way inconsistent with his God-ordained mission."[3] "Satan's aim was to entice Jesus to use powers rightly his but which he had voluntarily abandoned to carry out the Father's mission. Reclaiming them for himself would deny the self-abasement implicit in his mission and in the Father's will."[4] (See Paul's discussion on how Christ voluntarily humbled Himself and how God highly exalted Him, in Philippians 2:1-11).

## Ready for ministry

Baptized in water, anointed by the Spirit, affirmed by the Father, and tested by the devil. Jesus was now ready to begin His ministry. Besides, He was, by all indications, 30 years old, the age rabbis could begin teaching. The Mishnah stated one was fit "at thirty for authority," meaning they were "able to teach others."[5]

Jesus was being prepared all His life for His ministry. Moses was prepared for 40 years in Egypt and another 40 in the desert. Only then did he minister for 40 years, leading the people of Israel through the desert, to the Promised Land. Jesus, on the other hand, was prepared for 30 years and then exercised His public ministry for only 10% of that time, teaching, preaching and healing for three years. Though little is stated about his childhood, we know Jesus matured and grew intellectually, physically, spiritually and socially (Luke 2:52). He participated in Passover, in Jerusalem, at age twelve (Luke 2:41). He learned a trade, becoming a carpenter (Mark 6:3). And He began his ministry when He was about thirty years old (Luke 3:23).

After being tempted by the devil and coming away victoriously, Jesus returned to Galilee—to Nazareth and then Capernaum—which would be His headquarters for a time, fulfilling Isaiah 9:1-2. "From that time on Jesus began to preach, 'Repent, for the kingdom of heaven has come near'" (Matthew 4:17 - NIV). It is of utmost importance that Jesus' first sermon was about the Kingdom. Mark reports John had been preaching "repentance for the forgiveness of sins" and baptizing. John had since been thrown in prison and Jesus was proclaiming "'the time promised by God has come at last!' he announced. 'The Kingdom of God is near! Repent of your sins and believe the Good News!'" (Mark 1:15 - NLT). That is the King's message in a nutshell. If you strip everything away to the most basic essence of the Good News, it is that one must repent and believe.

But that wasn't just Jesus' *first* message, it was His *only* message, at least in the beginning, as "Jesus traveled throughout the region of Galilee, teaching in the synagogues and announcing the Good News about the Kingdom. And he healed every kind of disease and illness" (Matthew 4:23 - NLT).

## [GK] Matthew 5 - Life in the Kingdom: The sermon on the mount

## The King begins to teach

I was there with my father, brother, and a group of Christians from Arkansas. Our "tour guide" was Mike Huckabee. It was 1994, and as we looked down on the Sea of Galilee, someone in the group suggested I go down the hill a ways and say something in a low voice. I did, and they heard me perfectly. Jesus used the water in the background and the slope to carry His voice, as a natural megaphone, as He preached the greatest sermon in the world. When a rabbi was about to speak, he would sit down to make it official. That's what Jesus did before His proclamation of what God expects from those who enter the Kingdom.

The Sermon on the Mount begins with the Beatitudes, which are **Kingdom Values.**[6] The King blesses those who are poor in spirit (humble), who mourn (are repentant), are meek (gentle), those who have a strong desire for righteousness, who are merciful (forgiving), pure in heart (people of integrity), peacemakers (reconcilers) and who are persecuted because of righteousness. Part of their blessing comes from living according to the King's rules for life. And part comes from the rewards they will receive, namely possessing the Kingdom, being comforted, inheriting the Earth, being filled or fulfilled, receiving mercy, seeing God and being called sons of God.

The Lord sets some limitations, it seems, on His followers and the church when it comes to politics, when He states "you are the salt of the earth" and "you are the light of the world" (Matthew 5:13-14). Salt is a preservative and seasoning but not the main course. The saints will dominate the scene only during the Millennial Kingdom and beyond, not during the Global Kingdom. Now Christians are salt. Proportionately a minority, many times unseen by society, but who make a vital difference, just as salt does in food. How insipid and rotten everything would be without the influence of God's people! Even notorious atheists have recently recognized this. "Dawkins has now come out and repudiated his previous belief that Christianity should be banished from society even more firmly. In fact, he told *The Times*, ending religion—once his fervent goal—would be a terrible idea, because it would 'give people a license to do really bad things.'"[7] Other atheists, the article notes, have seen the frightening descent of society as they witness the diminishing influence of Christianity, and are alarmed.

God's people are also to be light. In a pitch dark room, even a little candle can make a world of difference. Without that light people would stumble in the dark and lose their way. We can be influencers. We should be contagious. We are called to make a difference and make a contribution to humanity.

Through the ages, when the church tried to assert its political power and force its will on society, it usually abused its authority, with disastrous results. But the church, as the light of the world, should allow itself to be seen, so that people "may see your good works and glorify your Father in heaven" (Matthew 5:16 - NKJV).

## The enduring value of God's law

God doesn't change; neither do His laws. They are constant. And anyone who breaks them and encourages others to do the same, will be considered "least in the kingdom of heaven" (Matthew 5:19a - NKJV). Man's opinions and values may "evolve," but not the Lord's. When people question and discredit God's values and teach others to do the same, soon the whole nation is thinking the same way. The same *wrong* way. "Everybody can't be wrong," and "everybody does it" are used to evaluate the value. But nothing justifies breaking God's law.

The reverse principle pertaining to God's commandments is, "but whoever does and teaches them," and that person will "be called great in the kingdom of heaven" (Matthew 5:19b - NKJV). Part of being salt and light is modeling and teaching obedience to God's Law.

## Kingdom hierarchy

Being "called great" in the Kingdom begs the question: will there be hierarchies or levels of greatness in the eternal state? Jesus seems to indicate that there will. Jesus speaks here of being called great in the Kingdom and being called least in the Kingdom. The use of "kingdom" here probably refers to the Eternal Kingdom where rewards will be awarded according to faithfulness and fruitfulness.

Jesus told the parable of the talents where He revealed that the Master will say, "you were faithful over a few things; I will put you in charge of many things" (Matthew 25:23 - HCSB). In the parable of the minas, the Master says "because you have been faithful in a very small matter, have authority over 10 towns" (Luke 19:17 - HCSB). To another He gives authority over 5 towns. It is faithfulness that determines the rewards to be received as well as the level of greatness one will have in the Eternal Kingdom.

One last consideration would be to look at Jesus' earthly ministry and extrapolate to His heavenly ministry. While Jesus loved all equally, out of the crowd of followers He appointed 72 worker-evangelists (Luke 10:1), and chose 12 disciple-apostles (Mark 4:10). From "the Twelve," who accompanied Him during His three-year earthly ministry, three were especially close: Peter, James, and John (Mark 5:37; Matthew 17:1). Out of the three, Peter and John were closest. Between the two, John was the very closest (John 20:2).

## Righteousness needed to enter the Kingdom

Jesus must have shocked His audience when He declared that one must be more righteous than the Pharisees in order to enter the Kingdom (Matthew 5:20). Although the Pharisees were considered very devout, they were mostly "holier-than-thou." The bottom line about this issue, however, is that only with Jesus' credited righteousness can one ever hope to enter His Kingdom.

## Jesus condemns verbal abuse

Murder is punishable in the Law, but Jesus said that getting angry with your brother and name calling are also punishable before God, and that before one can adequately relate to the Lord (bring their gift to the altar), they must make things right with their brother. Jesus encouraged settling out of court with your adversary whenever possible, before things get ugly. Jesus was making it clear that human affairs are intimately connected to our relationship with the Father, and verbally and emotionally abusing others is a serious offense before the Lord. Such a person will be held accountable, being "in danger of the judgment," "in danger of the council," or "in danger of hell fire" (Matthew 5:22 - NKJV).

## Jesus condemns virtual adultery

The Law spoke against physical adultery (Exodus 20:14), but Jesus was also interested in the motivation of the heart. "You have heard that it was said to those of old, 'You shall not commit adultery.' But I say to you that whoever looks at a woman to lust for her has already committed adultery with her in his heart" (Matthew 5:27-28 - NKJV).

Chastity is a lost value, while lust is Hollywood's bread and butter. But for the serious follower of Jesus, refraining from and conquering lust is a Kingdom rule to live by. The oldest book of the Bible already contained this principle. Job "was a man of perfect integrity, who feared God and turned away from evil" (Job 1:1 - HCSB). He showed this in practical ways, such as when he declared "I made a covenant with my eyes not to look with lust at a young woman" (Job 31:1 - NLT).

Ignoring this warning can lead to serious consequences. When Jesus said that "if your right eye causes you to sin, pluck it out and cast it from you," He was obviously speaking figuratively, because one would still have their left eye to see with. He meant, I believe, that even if great sacrifice is needed, it would certainly be "more profitable for you that one of your members perish, than for your whole body to be cast into hell" (Matthew 5:29 - NKJV).

## Marriage, oaths, going the second mile, loving your enemies, and giving to the needy

Jesus goes on to clarify an issue concerning divorce. Divorce is not intended to be the final solution for a difficult marriage. The only justification for divorce that our Lord provided here, was "sexual immorality" (Matthew 5:32; from *porneia*, meaning "illicit sexual intercourse in general;").[8] This is a difficult and controversial subject and there are other Scripture verses to be taken into consideration, but this is not the intent of this study.

Jesus prohibits the use of oaths, especially because there are things that are out of our control. Our present day movies are replete with interesting examples of the protagonist promising victims they will always be there to protect them and invariably failing because things simply got out of their control. Citing three essential Kingdom areas, Jesus said not to swear "by heaven, for it is God's throne; nor by the earth, for it is His footstool; nor by Jerusalem, for it is the city of the great King" (Matthew 5:34 - NKJV). Yet He commanded us not to swear by our own head, because we cannot even control the color of our hair. We are to say simply "yes" or "no," as anything in addition to these proceeds from the evil one (Matthew 5:34-37).

The *go the second mile and love your enemies Kingdom Principle*: Going the second mile and loving your enemy principles are some of the most radical and hard to follow in Jesus' message. These **Kingdom Values** go against our grain, our sense of justice and fairness, and our desire for revenge. But Jesus taught His followers not to resist evil people but to turn the other cheek. Kingdom citizens are to love, bless, do good, and pray for their enemies! That is the way to be sons of their Father in heaven—reflecting His actions and imitating Him—because that is what He does.

The *be complete and mature like God Kingdom Principle*: "Therefore you shall be perfect, just as your Father in heaven is perfect" (Matthew 5:48). This verse has been misquoted and misunderstood, according to Dr. Bill Goff. He teaches in his conferences that the word translated as "perfect" (Greek *teleios*), means "complete" and, when applied to the Christian life, "mature." It does not mean having no flaws. We are to be imitators of God. One version says: "Watch what God does, and then you do it, like children who learn proper behavior from their parents" (Ephesians 5:1 - MSG).

## [GK] Matthew 6 - The power of Kingdom prayer

Jesus endorses giving to the needy, yet not as the hypocrites who do so only to show off. They wanted to be seen and so they were. That, and only that, was their reward. But when done in secret, God sees and rewards.

### The Lord's Prayer

Paul Smailis woke up at three o'clock in the morning with a very clear impression: he was to contact 31 men from our church and have them pray and fast for Bill Billingsley, our pastor, on a specific day of the month for the next six months.

A week later our pastor was diagnosed with cancer and given two months to live.

The next year would see a massive amount of prayer in our church. The Lord extended Pastor Billingsley's life, and he lived for a little over a year after the first diagnosis. During that time our pastor grew even closer to the Lord and taught us many things about faith and prayer. One of his sermons was about praying for God's Kingdom to come. He asked us: "Is it not God's will that His Kingdom come? Is it not in His plans and is He not surely going to bring it about, anyway? Why then would He have us pray that His Kingdom come?"

Before giving us the answer he asked us to open our Bible to Daniel 9:2. There Daniel was reminded through his reading of Jeremiah, that "the desolation of Jerusalem would last seventy years." Daniel's reactions was not to fold his arms in complacency and wait to see God act. Instead he took an active role and, in his own words, "I turned to the Lord God and pleaded with him in prayer and petition, in fasting, and in sackcloth and ashes" (Daniel 9:3 - NIV).

Daniel went on to confess not only his people's sins, but his own. He pleaded with the Lord to have mercy on Jerusalem—which was desolate—and His people, who remained in captivity. He ended by calling on the Lord to perform His mighty work. "O Lord, listen!," he cried. "O Lord, forgive! O Lord, hear and act! For your sake, O my God, do not delay, because your city and your people bear your Name" (Daniel 9:16-19 - NIV).

So why pray for something that is God's will? Why ask for something He has promised and is planning to do, anyway? Because, Pastor Billingsley explained, God *wants* us to pray and He waits on our prayers to act. There is a special authority He has given us which we exercise when we pray. So we should not be reluctant to pray for something as sure as Christ's return. Because He told us to.

When we pray, we are participating in the advancement of the Kingdom. Prayer is the main way we exercise the Kingdom authority God has entrusted us, here and now. In a sense, when we pray we are doing in the present, in a limited way, what we will do fully when we reign with Christ forever.

Just a few months after preaching this message, Pastor Billingsley slipped into God's glorious Eternal Kingdom. At his memorial service, his wife Betty Jean looked me straight in the eye and said: "We are still praying that His Kingdom come." She knew I was still reflecting on that sermon.

## Praying that God's Kingdom come
The Lord's model prayer, which He taught His disciples, contains one of the most

often quoted passages on the Kingdom of God: "Our Father which art in heaven, Hallowed be thy name. Thy kingdom come. Thy will be done in earth, as it is in heaven" (Matthew 6:9b, 10 - KJB).

Jesus always had a special way of saying a lot in just a few words. Each one of His words was packed with rich and profound meaning. His model prayer was no exception. His prayer puts our lives in perspective, because it shows we can approach God as "our Father," that His throne is "in heaven," that we are to maintain the utmost respect and honor towards His name, and should pray often that His Kingdom come or be established on Earth, so that His will may be done as completely and perfectly here as it is there.

There are two natural divisions in the Lord's prayer: the first part is made up of petitions that relate to God—His glory, kingdom, and will. The second has to do with our physical, relational and spiritual needs. This is consistent with our Lord's teaching at the end of this same chapter where He tells us to "seek first his kingdom and his righteousness, and all these things will be given to you as well" (Matthew 6:33 - NIV).

After Jesus begins His prayer by referring to God as "our Father," He says "Your name be honored as holy" (Matthew 6:9b - HCSB). God's name should be set apart from the ordinary and treated as special. Jesus loved His Father dearly and wanted people to speak highly of Him. Yet today there are so many who take the Lord's name in vain, use His name with curse words, and blaspheme His holy name.

As a missionary to Brazil for 40 years, one of the main ministries my father had was that of camp administrator. He bought the land, built the camp site and began the "Royal Ambassador" organization in there, which would fill the camp grounds with Christian boys between the ages of 9 and 16. Sometimes there were five camps in a roll, with close to 350 campers in each. Most of the time these campers would speak highly of "Pastor Alvin Hatton." But sometimes they would criticize the camp food, or make fun of my father during the camp "skits." That didn't sit well with my father. Yet I think it actually saddened and irritated me even more.

It is reasonable to assume Jesus was saddened to see people of His day mocking, criticizing and speaking irreverently of His Father. So He prayed, "hallowed be your name."

Next, Jesus asks that "Your kingdom come. Your will be done on earth as it is in heaven" (Matthew 6:10 - HCSB). These two requests are synonymous: God's will being done perfectly on earth is the same as God's Kingdom coming in full strength to Earth. This special "coming" or establishing of the Kingdom on Earth could only be referring to the Millennial Kingdom, since His Global Kingdom is a present reality. Jesus is not teaching us to pray for the **introduction** of God's Kingdom but for its fullness. This is looking forward to the day when "the kingdom of the world has become the kingdom of our Lord and of his Christ, and he will reign for ever and ever" (Revelation 11:15).

Jesus didn't want us to lose sight of the final outcome of History. He acknowledged that our present state is not ideal, and that God is not content to leave the earth under the authority of the "prince of this world"—the evil one. What Jesus started when He came the first time He will finish when He comes the second time! After all, "the Son of God came to destroy the works of the devil" (1 John 3:8 - NLT; see also John 12:31).

Satan would like for us to think praying for this matter is an exercise in futility. But if it were, why would Jesus ask us to do so?

Jesus switches to our personal needs when He teaches us to ask the Father to "give us today our daily bread" (Matthew 6:11 - HCSB). A benevolent king provides for his subjects and a caring father provides for his children. Children usually do not concern themselves with where their next meal will come from. They just know their father will take care of that.

Once our physical or "survival" needs are taken care of, Jesus teaches us to concentrate on our spiritual ("forgive us our debts") and relational needs ("as we also have forgiven our debtors") (Matthew 6:12 - HCSB). The need to forgive is so important that it is the only part of the model prayer which receives special attention. Jesus warns that "if you don't forgive people, your Father will not forgive your wrongdoing" (Matthew 6:15 - HCSB).

To understand just how serious Jesus is about this, He told the parable of an unmerciful servant in Matthew 18:23-35. Appropriately, the story is of a king who calls his servants in to settle their accounts with him. One of the servants is forgiven a debt that would have been impossible to pay, only to demand payment from a colleague who owed him a sum that was minimal in comparison. Since he could not pay, the servant had him thrown in prison until he could. The king finds out and cancels the servant's pardon, having him handed over to torturers until his debt is paid in full.

Another spiritual need is our call to live the overcoming life, characterized by obedience and faithfulness in the face of trials and temptations. Although Jesus warned that "temptations are inevitable" (Matthew 18:7 - NLT), He shows us it's okay to ask the Father to deliver us from these each day. He prayed, "do not bring us into temptation, but deliver us from the evil one" (Matthew 6:13 - HCSB; see 1 Corinthians 10:13).

Our Lord's model prayer ends with the triumphant declaration that "for Yours is the kingdom and the power and the glory forever. Amen" (Matthew 6:13 - HCSB). God gives us the Kingdom, but never relinquishes the ultimate authority over it. It will always be "the Kingdom *of God*." Only He enjoys omnipotent power, and glory is due to Him alone. He declared: "I will not give my glory to another" (Isaiah 42:8).

This is cause for relief and celebration. We can rest assured, knowing our loving and righteous God will always be in control. He will never retire, abdicate or delegate His ultimate authority as King of kings. He will never be overthrown. And He will never change. This dispels any fear of Him someday tiring of us or changing His disposition towards us. This is indeed "eternal security" for us.

### Fasting, treasures, worrying, seeking the Kingdom
Jesus did not say *if* but *when* you fast (Matthew 6:16) The emphasis here is to avoid being a show-off; to fast with the right motivation. When done discretely, "your Father, who sees everything, will reward you" (Matthew 6:18 - NLT). The **Kingdom Principle** in this and other similar passages is: ***don't be religious to impress others but to serve God with a sincere heart.***

### The *you can't serve two masters* Kingdom Principle
Jesus warns His listeners not to store up treasures here on earth, but to store them in heaven, where they will be safe and last forever. "You cannot serve both God and money" because "no one can serve two masters," He told them (Matthew 6:24 - NLT). Doing so would mean being pulled in two opposite directions.

### The *stop worrying and start trusting* Kingdom Principle
If God, then, is our Master, we don't have to worry about the provisions of life, such as food and clothing. All our worrying, Jesus insists, will do us no good and get us nowhere. God takes care of His creation and will certainly take care of us. So, Jesus asks His disciples, "Why do you have so little faith?" (Matthew 6:30 - NLT; see verses 25-29).

Since God is aware of our needs, we must stop worrying and start to "seek the Kingdom of God above all else, and live righteously, and he will give you everything you need" (Matthew 6:33 - NLT). Here is the **Kingdom Principle** we see here: ***If we prioritize our needs over God's interests, both we and the Kingdom*** *suffer. But if we seek God's interests first, He will take care of ours as well.* We concentrate on serving Him and He concentrates on our wellbeing.⁹

When we worry, it is usually about the future, about "tomorrow." But Jesus tells us to live one day at a time. That's hard enough as it is.

## [GK] Matthew 7 - Kingdom "dos and don'ts"

### Judging, casting pearls, seeking, and the golden rule
The sermon is not over yet. Jesus speaks about judging others. How He understands human nature! Of course He does! "All things were created by him, and apart from him not one thing was created that has been created" (John 1:3 - NET Bible). He begins with a stern warning, which we will see below as a **Kingdom Principle**.

### The *don't judge or you'll be judged* Kingdom Principle
Don't judge, but know that if you do, you too will be judged. ***You will be judged using the standards you used to judge others*** (Matthew 7:1-2). That's a **Kingdom Principle**. That is how things work in God's domain.

Here's where human nature comes in. Jesus said to stop looking at the speck in someone else's eye while totally ignoring the plank in our own. That sounds absurd until we realize that is what most people do. It is a common problem that destroys friendships and marriages. We can readily see all the shortcomings of those closest to us, while we remain oblivious to our own.

Think about it: if you can see their character flaws so clearly, don't you think they can see yours as well? Usually, what we see in others are our own shortcomings projected on them. The worse the problem of the beholder, the less he will see his own faults and the more he will magnify the faults of others. Jesus said that behaving like this makes us hypocrites. He tells us to first get rid of the plank in our own eye so we can see how to deal with the speck in our brother's eye.

### The *don't give pearls to pigs* Kingdom Principle
Avoid offering what is sacred to dogs and throwing your pearls to pigs. It is important to know when to witness and share **Kingdom Values** with others, and when hearts are so rebellious and closed, they will only take your words and distort them to ridicule your faith.

### The *seeking, knocking, and asking* Kingdom Principle
The **Kingdom Principle** of earnestly seeking God, knocking at His door, and ask-

ing Him for something you need, says that He will answer you and give you good things, as your good Father in heaven.

### The *do unto others* Kingdom Principle
The so called "golden rule" is a **Kingdom Principle** which contains the essence of everything found in the Old Testament ("the Law and the Prophets"). This principle teaches that we should treat others as we would *like* to be treated (Matthew 7:12), not as we *are* treated. For this, we must be proactive, not reactive.

### The *enter through the narrow gate* Kingdom Principle
Here is a sobering **Kingdom Principle**: "The gateway to life is very narrow and the road is difficult, and only a few ever find it," while "the highway to hell is broad" and its gates are wide open, and many choose it (Matthew 7:13-14 - NLT). The road to the Kingdom is like a narrow, uphill, rocky pathway; the road to destruction is more like an interstate highway which is downhill all the way.[10]

### The *fruit inspection* Kingdom Principle
While Jesus said we are not to judge others, He does allow us to reach a logical conclusion about someone or their ministry based on the results they are producing. In fact, Jesus warns us to "beware of false prophets who come disguised as harmless sheep but are really vicious wolves." How can we know who and how they really are? "You can identify them by their fruit, that is, by the way they act," Jesus explained (Matthew 7:15, 16 - NLT). Jesus said good trees produce good fruit, bad trees bad fruit, and never the other way around. The same goes for people.

### The *just calling Him "Lord" is not enough* Kingdom Principle
Alert! Just because someone calls Jesus "Lord" doesn't mean they are getting in "the Kingdom of Heaven." This principle is similar to the one seen in Jesus' story of Lazarus and the rich man (Luke 16:19-31). Just because the rich man called Abraham "father" doesn't mean he was released from his place of torment, even though Abraham, ironically, responded by calling him "son." The people in Jesus' example claimed to have done many wonderful things in His name. The problem was not that they had fallen from grace, but that: a) They did not care about keeping God's Law; and b) Jesus had never known them in the first place. Such people are contrasted with those who are wise (similar to what is done in Proverbs).

### The *build on the rock* Kingdom Principle
Jesus declared that "anyone who listens to my teaching and follows it is wise," and is comparable to "a person who builds a house on solid rock." On the other hand "anyone who hears my teaching and doesn't obey it is foolish, like a person who builds a house on sand" (Matthew 7:24, 26 - NLT). Listening is not enough. It is

essential to practice the **Kingdom Principles** Jesus taught. Building on His Person and teaching is the solid rock which prepares us for the storms in life. Building on the sand means collapsing and being washed away when the storms hit home.

And with that application and illustration, Jesus ended His famous sermon. After hearing His message, "the crowds were amazed at his teaching, for he taught with real authority" unlike the religious teachers of the day (Matthew 7:28-29 - NLT).

## [GK] Matthew 8 - Faith and authority in the Kingdom

**The *it's better to be an outsider with faith than a faithless insider* Kingdom Principle:**
When a Roman commander demonstrated great faith in the Lord, amazed, Jesus declared He had not seen such faith in Israel. Which prompted Him to speak of the day many other "outsiders" or non-Jews "will come from the east and the west. They will take their places at the feast in the kingdom of heaven. They will sit with Abraham, Isaac and Jacob" (Matthew 8:11 - NIRV). As for some "insiders," who are "subjects of the kingdom" because they are descendants of Abraham, "those who think they belong to the kingdom will be thrown outside, into the darkness. There they will sob and grind their teeth" (Matthew 8:12 - NIRV).

"The feast in the kingdom of heaven" is probably the same as mentioned in Isaiah 25 (see comment above, under "Isaiah 25—A banquet prepared"). Those who do not believe in a literal Millennial Kingdom on Earth must answer why Jesus would reference cardinal coordinates ("from the east and the west") when speaking of this Kingdom of Heaven banquet. Abraham, his son, and his grandson will all be there, so this will be either in the Millennial or Eternal Kingdom. Isaiah 25:6 speaks about destroying the shroud that enfolds all peoples, referring to nations. This would be more in line with the Messianic Age than the eternal state.

At the end of this story the Lord tells the centurion his request will be granted, and in so doing states another **Kingdom Principle**: *"Go! Let it be done just as you believed it would"* (Matthew 8:13 - NIV). Faith is a **Kingdom Value**. The principle is that God answers our prayers according to our faith (see Matthew 9:22, 29; 13:58). The context is faith that is exercised according to God's will.

## Jesus calms storm, casts out demons, restores demon-possessed man
In an amazing string of events, Jesus heals many, states "the Son of Man has no place to lay his head," and calms a storm over the lake by commanding the wind and waves to die down. This leads His disciples in the boat to exclaim "what kind of man is this? Even the winds and the waves obey him!" (Matthew 8:20, 27 - NIV).

On the other side of the lake Jesus expels demons from an outcast. The demons, obviously horrified, challenge Jesus: "'what do you want with us, Son of God?' they shouted. 'Have you come here to torture us before the appointed time?'" (Matthew 8:28, 29 - NIV). Jesus casts the demons into a large herd of pigs numbering about 2,000, which rush into the lake and drown. Jesus restores the demon-possessed man and gives him the mission of going to his family and telling them what had just happened (Mark 5:1-20). Missionaries tell this Bible story to demonstrate that Jesus has authority over the spirit world and the power to restore lives broken by Satan.

## [GK] Matthew 9 - A King Who heals

When Jesus went back to Capernaum, His home base, a paralytic was brought to Him. He told him his sins were forgiven. Some religious leaders present felt Jesus was blaspheming. "Knowing their thoughts" Jesus said "I want you to know that the Son of Man has authority on earth to forgive sins." He then demonstrated His power to heal by telling the paralytic to pick up his mat and go home, which he did (Matthew 9:4, 6 - NIV). Jesus called Himself the Son of Man and declared His divine nature, as all were in agreement that only God can forgive sins.

In another sequence of miraculous events, Jesus heals a woman who touches His cloak as He presses through a crowd. He tells her "'take heart, daughter,' he said, 'your faith has healed you.' And the woman was healed at that moment" (Matthew 9:22 - NIV). Jesus was on His way to bring the synagogue leader's daughter back to life, which He did to the astonishment of all (Matthew 18-26). "As Jesus went on from there, two blind men followed him, calling out, 'Have mercy on us, Son of David!'" (Matthew 9:27 - NIV). After healing both of them, He cast out a demon from a mute man, who was then able to speak (Matthew 9:32, 33).

These were all signs of the Kingdom and a clear indication the King was in their midst: Jesus demonstrated power over nature, evil spirits, illness and authority to forgive sins. He showed compassion, knew what people were thinking in secret, raised the dead, and carried the titles of "Son of Man" and "Son of David."

Jesus was on a mission which had Him going "through all the towns and villages, teaching in their synagogues, proclaiming the good news of the kingdom and healing every disease and sickness" because "he had compassion on them" (Matthew 9:35-36 - NIV). The King's three-year mission was to proclaim the Kingdom and to heal the sick and oppressed.

## [GK] Matthew 10 - Kingdom authority delegated

## The Twelve receive authority

Jesus called the Twelve together and delegated Kingdom authority to them. "He gave them authority over unclean spirits, to drive them out and to heal every disease and sickness" (Matthew 10:1 - HCSB). He instructed them how to proceed when they went out and told them "as you go, announce this: 'The kingdom of heaven has come near'" (Matthew 10:7 - HCSB). The Kingdom was near because the King was in their midst and because Kingdom power was invading the darkness, reclaiming what rightfully belongs to the King. The power the disciples now possessed and the signs they performed were proof of this new reality.

## The *Kingdom Principle* of discipleship

"When Christ calls a man, he bids him come and die." So said theologian Dietrich Bonhoeffer, a modern day martyr, who was hanged in a German prison, under Hitler's rule.[11] Christ's disciple must die to self and to the world.

This *Kingdom Principle* requires one to love God more than parents and children, otherwise being unworthy of the Lord. It demands taking up the cross and following Jesus, otherwise being unworthy of Him. Here it is, stated as a rule or principle: *"the one who finds his life will lose it, and the one who loses his life because of me will find it"* (Matthew 10:37-39 - ISV).

## More *Kingdom Principles*

Jesus sets forth a list of *Kingdom Principles* concerning rewards for serving those who represent the Lord:
1) If you welcome Jesus, you welcome God the Father;
2) If you welcome a prophet you receive a prophet's reward;
3) If you welcome a righteous person you receive a righteous person's reward;
4) Even if you just give one of Jesus' disciples a cup of water you will never lose your reward (Matthew 10:40-42).

## [GK] Matthew 11 - The Kingdom suffers violence

## The greatness of John the Baptist

When John the Baptist was in prison, he sent his disciples to ask Jesus if He was indeed the One they were expecting. Jesus points John's disciples to a list of signs of the Kingdom He had been performing and said those who are not scandalized by Him are indeed blessed (Matthew 11:1-6). Jesus told His listeners that John marked the end of an era of prophets (11:13), that John was a prophet and even more than a prophet: He was the herald sent to prepare the way of Messiah (11:9-10). Jesus declared that no one greater than John had ever been born, "yet even the least person in the Kingdom of Heaven is greater than he is!" (Matthew 11:11 - NLT).

This and the next verse are of difficult interpretation. To which aspect of the Kingdom of Heaven is Jesus referring? Is He referring to the Global Kingdom or to the Eternal Kingdom? I believe the Lord is saying that there is none greater than John in the Global Kingdom (the present age), but even the least in eternity, in the Eternal Kingdom, will be purer and more righteous than John could ever have been as a human living on planet earth. Even the least in heaven will be closer to God and live in a continual state of victory and bliss unknown to the best of saints on earth.

John the Baptist was a transitional figure, and ever since he came on the scene to prepare the way for King Messiah, God's Kingdom had come under attack. John had been arrested, Jesus was about to face fierce opposition and rejection, and His disciples would be persecuted. Jesus said that "from the days of John the Baptist until now, the kingdom of heaven has been suffering violence, and the violent have been seizing it by force" (Matthew 11:12 - HCSB). Is this the best way to understand this difficult passage? Why does this passage present problems of interpretation?

> The difficulties arise because *biazomai* and *biastēs* ("forcefully advancing" and "forceful men") can be taken as either positive or negative terms. ... *Biazomai* is most commonly negative and passive, meaning to suffer violence. The *de* (but) that introduces v. 12 suggests a contrast with v. 11, also making v. 12a more likely negative. *Biastai* in conjunction with *harpazousin* ("lay hold of," but more commonly *attack*) seems likely to be negative too: violent people attack the kingdom. This combination of translations would then lead the verse to be rendered something like "from the days of John the Baptist until now, the kingdom of heaven suffers violence, and violent people attack it."[12]

The older versions of the NIV have "the kingdom of heaven has been forcefully advancing" but the newer version has "from the days of John the Baptist until now, the kingdom of heaven has been subjected to violence, and violent people have been raiding it." The versions which understand the beginning of this verse to mean "forcefully advancing" may or may not be a correct interpretation of the original meaning, but the fact remains that, led by Jesus, the Kingdom was indeed advancing against enemy strongholds and territory.

### The King's authority
Jesus denounced those who rejected John and Himself, as well as the unrepentant population of the towns where He performed many miracles. He praised the Father "because You have hidden these things from the wise and learned and revealed them to infants" (Matthew 11:25 - HCSB). It is a **Kingdom Principle** that **God has chosen to humble the haughty and reveal His Kingdom Secret to the**

***humble, poor, and "insignificant" to society.*** "For what this world considers to be wisdom is nonsense in God's sight. As the scripture says, 'God traps the wise in their cleverness'" (1 Corinthians 3:18 - GNT).

Jesus describes His relationship with the Father, says He reveals the Father to whoever He desires, and declares that "all things have been entrusted to Me by My Father" (Matthew 11:27 - HCSB; see 28:18 and John 13:3). Authority is not autonomous power. It is intimately connected with the source. Jesus had total authority because He received it from the Father. Jesus' disciples had authority because it was delegated to them by Jesus. *You only have authority if you are under authority* (see Matthew 8:9).

Jesus describes Himself, stating: "I am gentle and humble in heart" (Matthew 11:29 - HCSB). This was evident through His whole life and ministry. That the King, to Whom the Father had entrusted all things, could be this meek and humble is surprising and lies in contrast with power-hungry leaders across the ages.

## [GK] Matthew 12 - The King is rejected by the establishment

While in a place of retreat, Jesus' tender loving care is again displayed by healing the sick who were brought to Him (Matthew 12:15-21). This fulfilled the Messianic prophecy found in Isaiah 42:1-4.

### The King is slandered and rejected

After seeing Jesus heal a demon-possessed man who was blind and mute, the onlookers wondered, "Could this be the Son of David?" (Matthew 12:23 - NIV). This Messianic title speaks of the promised descendant who would reign forever on David's throne. The Pharisees stepped in and reached an unprecedented low point by willfully blaspheming against Jesus and the Holy Spirit. They accused Him of driving out demons by the power of the chief of demons instead of recognizing Jesus had just fulfilled Isaiah's Messianic prophecy, which states: "God ... is coming to save you. And when he comes, he will open the eyes of the blind and unstop the ears of the deaf. The lame man will leap up like a deer, and those who could not speak will shout and sing!" (Isaiah 35:4b-6a - TLB).

But the Pharisees resisted the truth and blasphemed the Lord—and that was a game changer.

Jesus claimed He was driving out demons by another Power. He said "but if I am expelling devils by the Spirit of God, then the kingdom of God has swept over you unawares!" (Matthew 12:28 - Phillips New Testament). The Pharisees could not deny the fact of the healing, so they denied the source of the power. By doing so, they demonstrated they were closed to God, insensitive to His Spirit, and against His Son, in an absolute and final manner.

Jesus proceeded to give them a stern warning, letting them know "men may be forgiven for every sin and blasphemy, but blasphemy against the Spirit cannot be forgiven. A man may say a word against the Son of Man and be forgiven, but whoever speaks against the Holy Spirit cannot be forgiven either in this world or in the world to come!" (Matthew 12:31-32 - Phillips New Testament).

From this point forward Jesus began to teach through parables so that only the "initiated" could understand His teachings, and as a form of judgment on the "outsiders."

## [GK] Matthew 13 - The Kingdom chapter and Kingdom parables

If Matthew is the Gospel of the Kingdom, Matthew 13 is the chapter of the Kingdom, containing seven parables and a series of explanations about the Kingdom. After the first parable is told, Jesus' disciples are obviously confused and not acquainted with that style of teaching. They ask Him why He was speaking in parables. Jesus told them, "You are permitted to understand the secrets of the Kingdom of Heaven, but others are not'" (Matthew 13:11 - NLT; see Isaiah 6:9-10). The name of this series and the title of the first volume are taken from this passage as it appears in the Gospel of Mark: "The secret of the kingdom of God has been given to you" (Mark 4:11a - NIV).

The first parable—of the different kinds of soil or hearers—is found in Matthew 13:1-23. According to Jesus' interpretation of His parable, we understand the Global Kingdom is made up of four different kinds of people, categorized according to their response to the Good News of the Kingdom.

The first are those who reject the message outright. The second kind accept the message on impulse. But when they see the commitment that is required, they back out. The third kind get entangled with daily chores, concentrate on getting rich, or pursue other distractions. They do not "seek first the Kingdom." The fourth kind are those who accept the message, commit to the Kingdom, and go about bearing much fruit, which glorifies the Father (John 15:8).

A clarification is in order. Since the Global Kingdom is God's reign on earth, and everything and everybody on earth belong to the Lord, the Global Kingdom is not synonymous with salvation. Everyone who has ever lived—or now lives—on Earth is part of the Global Kingdom. Yet, the vast majority of Earth's population was not—and is not—saved because they have not "entered" or "inherited" the Kingdom, even thought they are still under God's rule and domain.

The other parables in this chapter compare the Kingdom of God with: A plantation field of wheat and weeds or tares (Matthew 13:24-30; 36-43); A mustard seed (Matthew 13:31-32); Yeast (Matthew 13:33); Finding a hidden treasure and a priceless pearl (Matthew 13:44-46); A net full of good and worthless fish (Matthew 13:47-50); and A storehouse of new and old (Matthew 13:51-52). For a brief comment on each of these, please see chapter 2 of *The Secret of the Kingdom of God*, the first volume of this series, under the section "What can the Kingdom be compared to?" (Pages 38-41).

## [GK] Matthew 14 - The King's power over the physical world

### The King's forerunner, is executed

John the Baptist, the Herald of the King, is beheaded (Matthew 14:1-12). The attack on the Kingdom took an ugly turn with the execution of one of its key mortal members. But God plays by different rules and what seems to be a setback by human standards becomes a story of inspiration for countless followers of Jesus Christ through the ages.

### Jesus feeds 5,000, walks on water

Jesus demonstrates His compassion and Kingdom power over matter by feeding a crowd of 5,000 men, plus women and children (Matthew 14:13-21). Jesus, the Bread of Life, provided abundantly for the needs of those who went out to hear Him. The miracle was also designed to teach the disciples to trust Him as their sufficient provider. There were 12 baskets left over. Could it be that the Lord gave one to each of the Twelve to make an unmistakable and tangible point?

Jesus sends His disciples on ahead of Him to the other side of the lake. Their boat is making little headway, given the strong winds (Matthew 14:22-33). Jesus walks on water to meet up with them. Jesus is full of surprises! But this was so out of the ordinary the disciples were terrified and thought they were seeing a ghost. Jesus calms their fears and Peter tries to walk over to Him. When he started sinking Jesus takes him by the hand and asks him why he doubted. As soon as they got in the boat, the wind died down and the disciples worshiped Him and confessed: "truly you are the Son Of God" (v. 33). Once more Jesus demonstrated He is Lord over the elements of nature. That would make sense, "for everything was created by Him, in heaven and on earth, the visible and the invisible, whether thrones or dominions or rulers or authorities– all things have been created through Him and for Him" (Colossians 1:16 - HCSB).

## [GK] Matthew 15 - Three *Kingdom Principles*

### The *not planted by the Father Kingdom Principle*

Jesus told His disciples that *"every plant that my heavenly Father has not planted will be pulled up by the roots"* (Matthew 15:13). They were concerned because the Pharisees had taken offense to something Jesus had said, and they let Jesus know. Although the Pharisees were well known, well established, and well thought of in the Jewish society, they did not have God's approval and were doomed to see their cause ultimately fail and their organization vanish with the passing of time.

This calls for serious refection and begs the question: "am I doing what God has called me to do? Is it His will for me or my own idea of serving Him?" Because ministries that were not planted by the Father will be pulled up by the roots.

### The *blind leading the blind Kingdom Principle*
*"If one blind person leads another blind person, both will fall into a ditch"* (Matthew 15:14 - ISV). This principle literally speaks of leadership. When leaders are in spiritual darkness and propose to lead others who too are in darkness, the result is disastrous for those who lead and those who follow. The principle applies to leadership in general. The Pharisees looked right at the evidence and still did not would allow it to convinced them. Is it any different today?

### The *it's what comes from the heart that matters Kingdom Principle*
*"But what comes out of the mouth proceeds from the heart, and this defiles a person"* (Matthew 15:18 - ESV). The Kingdom is not made up of a bunch of legalistic rules for the sake of rules. The King is interested in the heart. Ceremony and rituals may have their place, but what determines a person's character emanates from the heart, the center of his or her being (see verses 19 and 20).

## [GK] Matthew 16 - Keys to the Kingdom and more principles

### The Church and the keys to the Kingdom
Peter confesses Jesus as Messiah, the Son of God (Matthew 16:16). Jesus blesses Peter and states this was revealed to him by the Father. Jesus declares: "On this rock I will build My church, and the forces of Hades will not overpower it" (Matthew 16:18 - HCSB). The Church, despite its imperfections, will continue to be victorious to the end against the kingdom of darkness. Jesus calls it "My church" and promises *He* will build it on "this" rock (either Peter's confession that Jesus is Messiah and Son of the living God, or on Peter as representative of the apostles, who were tasked with carrying on Jesus' mission in the world, or both; see Acts 2:42; Ephesians 2:20; and Revelation 21:14).

As we will see below, the Church would become the Kingdom's agency in the Global Kingdom. As such, it is vital to recognize that, as the Kingdom itself, the Church belongs to Jesus. Although an obvious statement, it's a good reminder since many pastors and leaders treat their local congregations or associations as though they were their own.

Jesus tells Peter "I will give you the keys of the kingdom of heaven" (Matthew 16:19 - NIV). More than authority, the keys represent access. How can a person enter the Kingdom? Why does Jesus refer to keys in the plural? These and other related issues are considered in *The Secret of the Kingdom of God*, chapter 3, "Kingdom Access: How Do I Get in?," under "Kingdom access granted: what gets you in" (page 48). In summary, Jesus is the Door to the Kingdom, and the keys that open the Door are repenting and believing.

### The *we can be used by God or be used by the devil* Kingdom Principle
Jesus commended Peter for identifying Him as Messiah. He told His closest disciples He would soon be facing suffering and death but would come back to life three days later. "Peter took Him aside and began to rebuke Him" (Matthew 16:22 - HCSB), saying this must not be allowed to happen. However, Jesus was quick to put Peter in his place and identify the source of such an idea. Jesus "turned and told Peter, 'Get behind Me, Satan! You are an offense to Me because you're not thinking about God's concerns, but man's'" (Matthew 16:23 - HCSB).

Even those closest to the Lord must always be on their guard, because even during a season when they are being blessed and inspired by God, they can turn almost as quickly and be used, in a moment of weakness, by the enemy. The irony in the contrast is almost too much to take in. Peter had just been blessed by Jesus for saying something the Father had revealed to him. Now Jesus is rebuking him for saying something that was inspired by the devil! Yet there is a Peter in all of us.

### The *deny self, carry cross and follow* Kingdom Principle
In response to Peter's attempt to "protect" Him from suffering and death, Jesus says those who wish to be His disciples must deny themselves, carry their cross (a symbol of death), and follow Him (Matthew 16:24). Stated as a principle, Jesus said: **"Whoever wants to save his life will lose it, but whoever loses his life for my sake will find it"** (Matthew 16:25 - ISV).

### The *getting paid back upon the second coming* Kingdom Principle
Even though Peter had just confessed Him as Messiah, Jesus again uses His eschatological title to speak of His glorious return. He tells His disciples that "the Son of Man is going to come with his angels in his Father's glory, and then **he will repay everyone according to what he has done**" (Matthew 16:27 - ISV). It will be pay back time. That will be good news for His faithful followers, and terrible news for His enemies. The glorified Jesus repeated His promise, saying, "look! I am coming quickly, and **My reward is with Me to repay each person according to what he**

*has done*" (Revelation 22:12 - HCSB). Although the first reference seems to be to the Second Coming and the second verse to the Rapture, either way, this **Kingdom Principle** is both a promise and a threat. It all depends on what each person has done and whose side they are on.

## [GK] [MK] Matthew 17 - A preview of the coming Kingdom
### The transfiguration

Jesus warned that "whoever is ashamed of Me and of My words in this adulterous and sinful generation, the Son of Man will also be ashamed of him when He comes in the glory of His Father with the holy angels" (Mark 8:38 - HCSB). It's the *if you're ashamed of Me now, I will be ashamed of you then Kingdom Principle*.

Then Jesus promises that some there would not die before "they see the Son of Man coming in His kingdom" (Matthew 16:28 - HCSB), with Mark stating that they would "see the kingdom of God come in power" (Mark 9:1 - HCSB). The idea of bringing His Kingdom with Him would seem to refer to the time when Jesus returns to set up the Millennial Kingdom. But in a more immediate sense, we can infer Jesus used the verb "come" as synonymous with "manifest." When He told people to "repent, because the kingdom of heaven has come near!" (Matthew 4:17 - HCSB), He was declaring that the Kingdom was being manifest by His presence. When He promised the Kingdom would come in power before some of those present died, He meant the King would very soon manifest Himself in His glory to a limited audience. These would see Him in a sort of preview, a rehearsal of the coming and setting up of His Kingdom. For this reason, everything that happens and is said during the time of our Lord's transfiguration is potentially prophetic of the end times.

Six days after this prediction, Jesus took His inner circle—Peter, James, and John—with Him to a mountain top where "He was transformed in front of them, and His face shone like the sun. Even His clothes became as white as the light" (Matthew 17:2 - HCSB). Just as soon as He was transfigured, Moses and Elijah also appeared and began talking with Him. These two Old Testament heroes are closely tied to end-time events. Elijah was expected to come before the Messiah appeared (Mark 9:11; Mark 8:27; John 1:25) and was equated to John the Baptist in the case of Jesus' first coming (Luke 1:17; Matthew 17:12). And the two witnesses of Revelation 11:3 are described as having some of the main characteristics of Elijah and Moses (Revelation 11:6).

Jesus, the King, was appearing in His glorified state before His closest disciples, when Peter said, "Lord, it's good for us to be here! If You want, I will make three tabernacles here: one for You, one for Moses, and one for Elijah" (Matthew 17:4

- HCSB). It is true that Peter "said this because he didn't really know what else to say, for they were all terrified (Mark 9:6 - NLT). And it seems clear he spoke out of turn (the Father's command to "listen to Him!," as seen below, was almost certainly aimed at him). But what many preachers and commentators fail to see is that what Peter said was not the product of random rambling but stemmed from prophecy and Jewish tradition. He spoke of building three tabernacles because, Messianic Jews explain, "The Feast of Tabernacles speaks of the day when the Messiah Himself will tabernacle among men, wipe away every tear, and bring in the utopian age or 'golden age' of which men have dreamed since time immemorial."[13]

Zechariah 14 is a description of the installation of the Messianic Kingdom and mentions that the survivors (of the Tribulation and the Day of the Lord) will be expected to participate in a yearly pilgrimage to Jerusalem "to worship the King, the Lord of hosts, and to keep the Feast of Tabernacles or Booths" (Zechariah 14:16 - AMP).

Surely Peter had this connection to the Feast of Tabernacles and the ushering in of the Messianic Age in mind but was cut off by the appearing of a bright cloud and the Father's voice, reaffirming what He had said at His Son's baptism (Matthew 3:17): "This is My beloved Son. I take delight in Him," with the added order to "listen to Him!" (Matthew 17:5 - HCSB). The "beloved Son" refers to Jesus' calling as King (Psalm 2), while "I take delight in Him" speaks of His role as Suffering Servant (Isaiah 42:1). God was again indicating Jesus was both.

As with Daniel, when he was visited by celestial beings, the disciples were terrified with the experience. Jesus told them not to be afraid and, while walking back down the mountain, instructed them to keep this to themselves, "until the Son of Man is raised from the dead" (Matthew 17:9 - HCSB). By referring to Himself as the Son of Man, Jesus could have been reminding them of Daniel's Kingdom vision in Daniel 7:13 and 14.

## Tax-free children

Peter was asked if Jesus paid the Temple tax. Peter said He did. Jesus asked Peter what he thought: "from whom do the kings of the earth collect duty and taxes—from their own children or from others?" (Matthew 17:25 - NIV). Peter replied that they collect from others. Jesus went on to explain that indeed the children are exempt, but since they did not want to offend the authorities, they would pay taxes anyway. Two lessons seems clear: a) If there are certain privileges enjoyed by the children of earthly kings, how much more for the sons and daughters of the King of kings; and b) While the royal children have not yet come into the glorified Kingdom, they must submit to earthly authorities.

## [GK] Matthew 18 - The greatest in the Kingdom; conflict resolution in the church; the *Kingdom Values* of prayer and forgiveness

Jesus had declared John the Baptist to be the greatest among humans, but that even the least in the Kingdom of heaven is greater than he (see above, under "Matthew chapter 11 - The Kingdom suffers violence"). A logical follow-up question would be "who then is the greatest in *the Kingdom of heaven*?" That is what the disciples now want to know. Jesus' answer is as simple as it is surprising: "whoever humbles himself like this child—this one is the greatest in the kingdom of heaven."[14]

Jesus said that if a person doesn't become like a child, he or she will not enter the Kingdom in the first place. Ever. Not only is it important to be *like* children, but children themselves have a special place in God's heart. How can we know this? Jesus said that "whoever welcomes one child like this in My name welcomes Me" (Matthew 18:5 - HCSB).

Jesus instructs the Church on how to handle brothers who fall into sin (Matthew 18:15-17). Following His guidelines will help the Church community avoid pitfalls and all sorts of relationship problems which tend to never go away when there is ambiguity and issues are not faced head-on.

### The *connected on earth, connected in heaven Kingdom Principle*
Still speaking in the context of the Church, Jesus promises that "whatever you bind on earth is already bound in heaven, and whatever you loose on earth is already loosed in heaven" (Matthew 18:18 - HCSB). By this Jesus was delegating authority to the Church; but it seems clear the Church must be in tune with heaven.

To reinforce and clarify the authority He was giving, Jesus continued by saying that "when two of you get together on anything at all on earth and make a prayer of it, my Father in heaven goes into action. And when two or three of you are together because of me, you can be sure that I'll be there" (Matthew 18:19-20 - MSG). The connection principle happens through prayer. Prayer is a **Kingdom Value**.[15]

Jesus tells the story of the unmerciful servant to illustrate how the Kingdom operates (Matthew 18:23-35). He begins by explaining that "the kingdom of Heaven is like a king who decided to settle his accounts with his servants" (Matthew 18:23). The moral of the story is that we have been forgiven, so we must forgive. If we refuse to forgive others, God will refuse to forgive us as well. Forgiveness is a **Kingdom Value**.[16]

**[GK] Matthew 19 - Divorce, renouncing marriage, welcoming little children, riches, entering the Kingdom, and the earth's renewal**

## The matters of divorce and choosing not to get married

After refuting the idea of simply dismissing one's wife, Jesus declares for a second time that "whoever divorces his wife, except for sexual immorality, and marries another, commits adultery" (Matthew 19:7-9 - NKJV). Jesus' disciples comment that in that case it would be better not to marry. Jesus said marriage wasn't for everyone. There are those who remain celibate because they were born or became eunuchs, and there were "those who choose to live like eunuchs for the sake of the kingdom of heaven" (Matthew 19:12 - NIV). Those who feel they are perfectly able to remain single as a way of better serving the King and His Kingdom should do so, according to this word from the Lord.

Jesus had already taught about the importance of being like little children and welcoming them in His name. Yet when little children were brought to be blessed by Him, His disciples shooed them away. **Jesus told them to let the children come to Him because "the kingdom of heaven belongs to people like them"** (Matthew 19:14 - NIRV). The **Kingdom Principle** here is that we should evangelize and disciple children because the Kingdom is to be filled with them and those like them. I am privileged to be serving with a ministry called *The Mailbox Club*, which reaches over 3 million children a year, in over 80 countries, with "Explorers Club" Bible lessons. Children are so much more open to the Gospel than adults! Most Christians who are now adults made a decision to follow Christ before or during their mid teens.

## Entering the Kingdom

The rich young leader serves as an example of how "it will be hard for a rich person to enter the kingdom of heaven!" (Matthew 19:23 - HCSB; see v.v. 16-30). There are many nuances in the story of this encounter. In the Gospel of Mark, we see that this rich leader "knelt down before Him, and asked Him, 'Good Teacher, what must I do to inherit eternal life?'" (Mark 10:17 - HCSB).

Jesus asks him why he is calling Him "good" and says only God is good (Psalm 14:2-3; 143:2). What response would Jesus be trying to evoke with this statement? I believe Jesus knew that seeing Him as a "teacher" just wasn't enough. The response I believe Jesus was looking for would have been something like this: "Yes, Lord, only God is good. And that is why You are good, because you are the Son of God."

The question was about inheriting eternal life, which Jesus equated with entering the Kingdom. Jesus tells him that to "enter into life," he has to "keep the commandments" (Matthew 19:17 - HCSB). "Which?," he asks. Jesus gives him a list that includes "do not bear false witness" (v. 18). Still, the young leader claimed to have kept all the commands Jesus cited. We all know that is highly unlikely and that he was probably, at that very moment, bearing false witness.

What if, instead of trying to justify himself, the young leader confessed: "I have been unable to keep all the commandments and need to repent and believe. I need a Savior. Please have mercy on me, a sinner"?

Instead, he challenges Jesus, as if to say, "is that all?" He asks what else there might be. "Then, looking at him, Jesus loved him and said to him, 'You lack one thing: Go, sell all you have and give to the poor, and you will have treasure in heaven. Then come, follow Me.' But he was stunned at this demand, and he went away grieving, because he had many possessions" (Mark 10:21, 22 - HCSB).

This is not, necessarily, a demand made on every rich person who wishes to enter the Kingdom. This was specific to this person and situation, though Jesus does require denying self and leaving behind whatever needs to be let go. And yes, at one point when He taught we should seek the Kingdom, He also told the crowd to sell their possessions and give to the poor because one's heart will be where one's treasure is (Luke 12:31-34). This, however, is not the focal point in Jesus' exchange with the wealthy youth.

Here is what is usually missed in this passage: Jesus loved this young man. He did not challenge his claim to have kept all the commands cited, but offered him the chance to show he meant business. Jesus made him an offer He did not make very often to individuals during His earthly ministry. He invited this youth to come and follow Him. This amounted to joining His company of disciples. What a priceless privilege! But, in order to do so, he would need to give away his wealth. Though not formerly wealthy, the Twelve had left all behind to follow Jesus, and having a wealthy young man flaunting his riches as they journeyed together would just not work.

What if this young, rich leader recognized the once-in-a-lifetime opportunity that was being afforded him, and demonstrated he valued Jesus more than his possessions? What if he had taken Jesus up on His offer and followed Him closely as one of His disciples? Then he would have been like the man in one of the Kingdom parables: "when he discovered a pearl of great value, he sold everything he owned and bought it!" (Matthew 13:46 - NLT).

Instead, "he went away grieving." He was pulled in Jesus' direction but decided the price of following Him was just too high. He had not understood that the price of not following Him is even higher. The thing about successful investors is they are usually shortsighted. More times than not they cannot see past their time on earth and fail to invest in what lasts forever (read Luke 12:13-21).

## The invitation to follow Jesus

As for personal invitations, Jesus personally and individually invited the Twelve to follow Him, become fishers of people, and proclaim the Kingdom (Matthew 4:18-22; 9:9; 10:2-7). Their response was to leave everything behind and to follow immediately.

The invitation to follow Jesus was also made to a few others, as seen in Luke 9:59-62 and partially in Matthew 8:19-22. One person Jesus invited wanted to delay his following until his father had died. But Jesus told him to "let the dead bury their own dead, but you go and spread the news of the kingdom of God." To another one who wanted to go back and say his goodbyes to his family, Jesus warned that "no one who puts his hand to the plow and looks back is fit for the kingdom of God" (Luke 9:60, 62 - HCSB).

If Jesus' response seems a little harsh or radical, remember that He was on a mission and time was running out. And then, consider that when the Son of God, the promised Messiah and King is standing in front of you and inviting you, there simply could be nothing more important to do with your life! Also, saying "wait" to any boss is like saying "no."

Then there was Jesus' generic "whoever" invitation in Luke 9:23; 14:27; as in Matthew 16:24. This was an open invitation to the public. Jesus did not offer just a handful of exclusive invitations. His invitation is open to all who will come. But he who follows must be willing to "put aside his own desires and conveniences and carry his cross with him every day and keep close to me!" (Luke 9:23 - TLB).

## The Son of Man sits on His throne of glory at the renewal of all things

Once the rich young leader was gone Jesus told His disciples just how hard it was for the rich to enter the Kingdom of Heaven or the Kingdom of God (used interchangeably here, so we know they mean the same thing). His disciples, influenced by their culture, were in shock. If the rich couldn't get in, who could? Jesus told them that indeed for human beings getting in to the Kingdom is impossible but that with God all things are possible. This is a clear indication that salvation is a God thing, not a performance or merit-based achievement. Which means Jesus knew the young rich leader could never have entered the Kingdom by keeping all the Law, since no one is capable of doing so.

With this, Peter reminds the Lord that they had left everything to follow Him and wanted to know what they were going to get out of it. Jesus' answer is what should have astonished them, because He revealed to them the role they would have in His Kingdom. When He, the Son of Man, is on His throne of glory, then the Twelve, who have faithfully followed the Lord, will also sit on thrones, governing over Israel (see also Luke 22:29-30). And everyone else "who sacrifices home, family, fields—whatever—because of me will get it all back a hundred times over, not to mention the considerable bonus of eternal life" (Matthew 19:29 - MSG).

### *Kingdom Secret: There will be a renewal of all things on earth*
When will the apostles reign with the Son of Man? At or during "the regeneration when the Son of Man will sit on His glorious throne" (Matthew 19:28 - NASB). The renewal or regeneration will occur at the beginning of the Millennial Kingdom. It is distinct from the creation of the New Heaven and the New Earth, which happen at the outset of the Eternal Kingdom.[17]

To better understand this future reality, we see there will be a certain parallel between the Christian experience and the Millennial and Eternal Kingdom. The Bible tells us that, "Therefore if anyone is in Christ, he is a new creation. The old has passed away. Behold, the new has come!" (2 Corinthians 5:17 - BSB). Are you saved and in Christ? When that happened did you get a new body? No, but you are a new creation with a new nature and a new destiny and are in the process of being sanctified. You are a different person but you are not "another" person (as being someone else). You are the same but changed, transformed and, yes, regenerated. Something similar will happen with planet Earth. During the Millennium, the Earth will be converted and sanctified. It will be regenerated and the curse will be lifted (Romans 8:18-25).

One day we will receive our glorified bodies, either after dying or being raptured. We will enter the eternal state and never sin or suffer again. That is similar to what will happen after the Millennial Kingdom and at the outset of the Eternal Kingdom. The Earth will *die* (be destroyed) and the universe along with it will "pass away" (2 Peter 3:10-13). There will be a New Earth, somehow tied to the old one but completely different, like receiving a glorified body of its own (Revelation 21:1-2, 5).

### A *Kingdom Principle: Some who are first will be last and vice versa*
Jesus told His disciples that "many who [now] are first will be last [then], and many who [now] are last will be first [then]" (Matthew 19:30 - AMP). There are many that are in high places in the world system who are mostly loyal to themselves, and others who are at the bottom of "the food chain" who are faithful to the Lord above all. In the Kingdom the latter will have prominence over the former. God will not take social status into account when He distributes His rewards.

Faithfulness and fruitfulness will be the key factors for receiving rewards.

## [GK] [MK] Matthew 20 - What the Kingdom is like; sitting at the King's side; and the compassionate King

### A *Kingdom Principle*: *God's grace places all saved on the same level*
In this parable a landowner goes out several times during the day to hire workers for his vineyard. He first goes out early in the morning, then at nine in the morning, about noon, at three in the afternoon, then finally at about five. Each time he offers one denarius for the day of work. Each worker is happy to accept his offer and goes to work for him.

When it came time to pay the workers, the 5 PM crew got paid one denarius, even though they started so late. So the ones who arrived earlier thought they would receive more. When they did not, they started griping, saying that the newcomers had worked much less, and yet "you made them equal to us" (v. 12). But the landowner told him he was not being unfair and was giving them the agreed amount. And asked, "don't I have the right to do what I want with my business? Are you jealous because I'm generous?" (v. 15). Jesus finished by again saying that "last will be first, and the first last" (v. 16) (Matthew 20:1-16 - HCSB).

There is a truth which is brilliantly illustrated here: God's grace and generosity place all of His people on the same level when it comes to His offer of salvation. Whether it comes and is accepted early or late in life, entering the Kingdom is offered on the same terms and is based on God's grace, not years of service (see Romans 9:15). While there are different levels of rewards, the gift of salvation by grace is the same for all who receive it.

### Sitting beside Jesus in His Kingdom requested
Jesus forewarns His disciples, in very direct terms, that He (the Son of Man) would soon be faced with betrayal, mockery, flogging and crucifixion, being raised to life again on the third day. The reaction of James, John and their mother? The request that the boys sit on either side of the King in His Kingdom (Mark 10:35)! Talk about bad timing. And being clueless. Jesus had to put it to them bluntly, though gently: "you have no idea what you are asking for." And asked them if they could drink the cup He was about to drink and, further demonstrating they had not understood the gravity of the moment, replied they could.

Jesus tells them they indeed would be drinking from His cup, but "to sit at My right and left is not Mine to give; instead, it belongs to those for whom it has been prepared by My Father" (Matthew 20:23 - HCSB). With this, Jesus confirms there is an established hierarchy in the Kingdom, with positions to be filled which already have someone's name on them.

The request was out of place and showed these disciples and their mother had no idea of the scope of Messiah's Kingdom. Neither had they grasped the Kingdom's way of doing things. Unlike human governments, where rulers are authoritarian and ruling means being served, in the Kingdom, having a position of leadership means serving those under your care. Jesus told them that "whoever wants to become great among you must be your servant" (Matthew 20:26 - HCSB). Jesus had modeled this to them for the last three years and reminded them that "the Son of Man did not come to be served, but to serve, and to give His life—a ransom for many" (Matthew 20:28 - HCSB).

This is an extraordinary statement when we go back and see where the title "Son of Man" comes from. The prophet Daniel had been given a vision where he saw "One like the Son of Man" Who "was given dominion and glory and a kingdom, that all peoples, nations, and languages should serve Him" (Daniel 7:1-14 - NKJV; see v.v. 9-14). Did you catch that? Serve **Him**. And yet Jesus is saying that He came to serve **us**. And we, as His followers and imitators, are to serve one another.[18]

When Jesus said He not only came to serve but "to give His life—a ransom for many," this is one of the rare times Jesus spoke of His death as being vicarious. The other would be during the Lord's Supper, when He said, "This is My blood of the covenant, which is poured out for many for the forgiveness of sins" (Matthew 26:28 - BSB).

## Compassionate Messiah: the blind see and follow
The healing of two blind men has implications for the Kingdom not only because of what was done but for what was said (Matthew 20:29-34). Jesus fulfilled the prophecy that foretold that "when he comes, he will open the eyes of the blind" (Isaiah 35:5a - NLT; see also Isaiah 29:18). As Jesus was leaving Jericho and heading towards Jerusalem, the two men cried out for mercy, calling Him "Lord" and "Son of David," a Messianic title. While everybody was telling them to be quiet, Jesus asked them what they wanted. They wanted to see. Though blind, spiritually they had the insight to recognize Jesus as Lord and the promised Messiah.

Jesus had compassion on them and touched their eyes. Their sight was immediately restored, and they followed Him. Though Jesus had shared His heart about the trials He would soon be facing, His own inner circle showed no sympathy. He could have felt sorry for Himself but instead felt compassion for others. Indeed "He was despised and rejected by mankind, a man of suffering, and familiar with pain" (Isaiah 53:3a - NIV).

## [GK] Matthew 21 - The King's triumphal entry

Matthew 21:1-11 records the triumphal entry of Jesus into Jerusalem, the special occasion Gabriel must have been alluding to (Daniel 9:25-26), and which was foretold with precision by Zechariah close to 500 years before (Zechariah 9:9). This was a sign, a cue for those aware of Old Testament prophecy, signaling the official appearing of the Messiah, the ruler. A ruler Who came gently and in peace, as demonstrated by riding in on a donkey, instead of a white horse which is what a war-time conquering king would have done. Appropriately, Jesus is hailed as "the Son of David," the Blessed One Who comes in the name of the Lord (Psalm 118:26).

Alva McClain reminds us that as He slowly made His trek to Jerusalem, probably a few months before His triumphal entry, "the Lord appointed 70 others, and He sent them ahead of Him in pairs to every town and place where He Himself was about to go" and preaching that "the kingdom of God has come near you" (Luke 10:1, 9 - HCSB). "The impact of the ministry of the Seventy, followed by that of our Lord personally, must have been tremendous and would account in part for the large crowds on the way when He entered Jerusalem."[19] This crowd was made up of people who had heard the Kingdom being proclaimed by the 70 disciples of Jesus, who had gone from town to town. These were not the same crowds that later would yell, "Crucify him!" (Matthew 27:23).

Luke adds that when the crowds cried out "God has given us a King!" and "long live the King!" there were Pharisees there who told Jesus to rebuke His followers for making statements like that. But Jesus told them that "if they keep quiet, the stones along the road will burst into cheers!" (Luke 19:38-40 - TLB). Jesus was not going to tell His followers to keep quiet about His identity any longer. It was His official entry into the city of the Great King, and this had to be shouted from the rooftops (see Matthew 5:35; Psalm 48:2).

Jesus went on into Jerusalem and while He cleansed the Temple area again, driving out the merchants and turning over their tables, healing the blind and the lame, some children there began to shout "Hosanna to the Son of David" (Matthew 21:15 - NIV). This caused the chief priests and teachers of the law to become angry and question Jesus. But Jesus quoted Psalm 8:2 to them, which speaks of children spontaneously praising the Lord. With this, He was accepting the Messianic title.

In what may be the only time Jesus used His power for destruction during His earthly ministry, Jesus placed a curse on a fruitless fig tree, which immediately withered. This prophetic act was meant as a warning to Israel, though performed in the presence of the disciples only. The warning was related to the nation not producing the "fruit" which their Messiah should have found when He came. This fruit would be that of repentance and belief in the Good News (Mark 1:15). See the parallel to Jesus' action in a parable He told about the order to cut down a fruitless fig tree, right after declaring: "I tell you, no! But unless you repent, you too will all perish" (Luke 13:5 and 6-9 - NIV).

As Jesus and His disciples arrived in Jerusalem and entered the temple courts, Jesus' authority was questioned. He told the leaders a parable concerning themselves and then told the chief priest that "the tax collectors and the prostitutes are entering the kingdom of God ahead of you" (Matthew 21:31 - NIV).

He told them another parable about the owner of a vineyard who prepared it and rented it out, then went on a journey. When it was harvest time, the owner sent servants to collect his portion of the fruit. But the tenants beat and killed them. Finally, he sent his own son, but they killed him as well. Jesus asked the religious leaders what they thought the owner should do next. They said "He will put those wretched men to a wretched death and lease his vineyard to other tenants who will give him the produce at the proper times" (Matthew 21:41 - NABRE). By their own words they pronounced a guilty sentence upon themselves.

Jesus followed up by quoting Psalm 118:22-23, a Messianic psalm that refers to the stone rejected by the builders which became the capstone. The builders being the Jews and Jesus being the capstone, the most important and determining stone in the whole structure.

Then, in line with the condemnation suggested by the religious leaders themselves, Jesus declared: "Therefore, I say to you, the kingdom of God will be taken away from you and given to a people that will produce its fruit" (Matthew 21:43 - NABRE). What a terrible indictment! Jesus was, of that moment, taking the Kingdom away from Israel as a nation. The Apostle Paul said "a partial hardening has come upon Israel, until the fullness of the Gentiles has come in" (Romans 11:25 - ESV). Therefore, although the Kingdom was not taken from Israel forever, Israel lost its position as the earthly representative of the Kingdom to "a people that will produce its fruit," as the Church has taken on that ministry, "until the fullness of the Gentiles has come in." We will see more about the Church Age below.

## [GK] Matthew 22 - What the Kingdom is like: a King's invitation; no marriage; the Messiah as son of David and Lord

### The Kingdom of Heaven is like a King
Continuing in a similar thread, Jesus addressed the religious leaders with another

parable. "The kingdom of heaven is like a king" who offered a wedding banquet for his son. Those invited ignored the invitation, went about their busy lives and mistreated and killed the King's servants who delivered the invites. The King was outraged and sent his army to destroy those people. He then invited others so the banquet would be filled with guests. Some entered without the proper wedding garb and were kicked out.

Commentators point out that the host provided the wedding clothing for those who needed it in those days. The idea is that those who should have been citizens of the Kingdom (the Jewish nation) rejected the King's Son. So, the Kingdom was offered to others (the gentiles). But there were certain conditions and, reading between the lines, we can understand that the proper wedding garments represent God's credited righteousness (Isaiah 61:10), without which no one can stand before God. A **Kingdom Principle** that relates to this parable is: "For many are called, but few are chosen" (Matthew 22:1-14 - NASB).

The Saducees, who didn't believe in a resurrection (or angels), questioned Jesus by presenting Him with a theoretical problem. "Jesus answered them, 'You are deceived, because you don't know the scriptures or the power of God. For in the resurrection they neither marry nor are given in marriage, but are like angels in heaven" (Matthew 22:29-30 - NET Bible; see Luke 20:35). "In the resurrection" refers to the Eternal Kingdom. Were it not for this statement by our Lord, we would not know there will be no marriage in the eternal state.

The Pharisees took their turn in trying to trap Jesus into committing a theological blunder, to no avail. When He got through with them, "no one was able to answer him a word, and from that day on no one dared to question him any longer" (Matthew 22:46 - NET Bible).

How did Jesus have them stumped? He took a question to *them*. He asked them whose son they thought the Messiah was. David's son, they replied. Jesus asked why would David, inspired by the Spirit, call Him "Lord"? And Jesus quoted Psalm 110:1 to them: "The Lord declared to my Lord, 'Sit at My right hand until I put Your enemies under Your feet.'" In a final blow, Jesus asks, "If David calls Him 'Lord,' how then can the Messiah be his Son?" (Matthew 22: 41-45 - HCSB).

## [GK] Matthew 23 - Jesus condemns false religious leaders, cries over Jerusalem, and says farewell

As Jesus is about to leave His earthly ministry behind, He declares His seven "woes" over the teachers of the law and Pharisees who are nothing but hypocrites and blind guides. He begins by accusing them of hindering people from entering the Kingdom. Jesus tells them, "Woe to you, scribes and Pharisees, you hypocrites! You shut the kingdom of heaven in men's faces. You yourselves do not enter, nor will you let in those who wish to enter" (Matthew 23:13 - BSB). These religious leaders were legalism personified, and Jesus condemns them most severely. He told them, "you take a small bug out of your cup but you swallow a camel!" The solution would be to "clean the inside of the cup and plate, then the outside will be clean also" (Matthew 23:24, 26 - NLV). Jesus states they will kill the prophets and teachers sent to them, and refers to them as, "You snakes, you children of serpents! How can you escape being condemned to hell?" (Matthew 23:33 - ISV).

Then Jesus cries out, "Jerusalem! Jerusalem! Murderer of prophets! Killer of the ones who brought you God's news! How often I've ached to embrace your children, the way a hen gathers her chicks under her wings, and you wouldn't let me. And now you're so desolate, nothing but a ghost town. What is there left to say? Only this: I'm out of here soon. The next time you see me you'll say, 'Oh, God has blessed him! He's come, bringing God's rule!'" (Matthew 23:37-39 - MSG).

## [GK] Matthew 24 - The end of the age: signs and what to expect

Jesus prophesied the destruction of the Temple. When pointing in its direction He told His disciples that "not one stone shall be left here upon another, that shall not be thrown down" (Matthew 24:2 - NKJV). When they reached the Mount of Olives, which has the most magnificent view of the Temple area, the disciples asked Him when this would happen and what would be the sign of His return and the end of the age.

Jesus began by telling them that first will come "the beginning of birth pains" characterized by false messiahs, wars, earthquakes and nations and kingdoms rising against each other (Matthew 24:1-8). Then His followers will be persecuted, put to death and hated by all the nations because of Jesus. Many will abandon the faith, hate and betray each other. False prophets will appear. Wickedness will increase and love will become cold. But those who remain faithful to the end will be saved. The Gospel of the Kingdom will be proclaimed the world over, followed by the end (Matthew 24:9-14).

Jesus describes the tribulation as a time of unparalleled distress; next comes the Day of the Lord, followed by the sign and coming of the Son of Man. Jesus says "they will see the Son of Man coming on the clouds of the sky with power and great glory" (Matthew 24:30b - NASB), at which time angels will gather the elect. Jesus warns His coming will be unexpected, and calls for preparation and faithfulness (Matthew 24:15-51).

# [GK] [MK] Matthew 25 - Parables about the Rapture, rewards, and the Millennial Kingdom

## The parable of the ten virgins

Jesus warns His disciples to be prepared and anticipate His return by telling the parable of the ten virgins (Matthew 25:1-13). He says the bridegroom took a long time to come for his bride and the bridesmaids fell asleep. This is another hint that Jesus' return would be a long time in coming (see Matthew 24:48). The main theme here, however, is the need to keep watch since the hour of the Groom's return is unknown. In the parable, although all fell asleep, half were prepared and had enough oil for their lamps and the other half did not, and was unable to enter the wedding banquet. Oil usually represents the Holy Spirit. Since half of this group was spiritually prepared, we understand they had heeded Messiah's call to repent and believe. The other half would represent the outwardly religious but inwardly empty.

## The parable about putting talents to good use

Next, Jesus tells the parable of the talents (Matthew 25:14-30). He says the Kingdom will be like a man going away on a journey and entrusting one of his servants with five talents, another with two and the third with one, according to their abilities. The parable demonstrates how Jesus' servants will be evaluated and rewarded for the way they invested that which was entrusted to them while living in the Global Kingdom. Here, too, the focus of the Lord's evaluation is based on faithfulness and fruitfulness. Here, too, Jesus hints first that He would be going away, then that He would delay in coming back. He says that "after a long time the lord of those servants came and settled accounts with them" (Matthew 25:19 - NKJV).

Those who are fruitful double the worth of their talents and are called "good" and "faithful," being handsomely rewarded by their Lord. The one who is not faithful (fruitful) proves not to be one of Jesus' disciples, is called wicked, and loses the little he had to begin with.

## The glorious coming of the Son of Man

Jesus revealed that "when the Son of Man comes in his glory, and all the angels with him, he will sit on his throne in heavenly glory." All nations will appear before Him and He will separate the sheep from the goats, the blessed and righteous from the cursed. "Then the King will say to those on his right, 'Come, you who are blessed by my Father; take you inheritance, the kingdom prepared for you since the creation of the world." The sheep are identified as "the righteous." The King is the "Lord" and "the Son of Man." The goats, the ones "on his left," will be "cursed" and thrown "into the eternal fire prepared for the devil and his angel," which is their "eternal punishment" (Matthew 25:31-46 - NIV).

### The meaning of these parables
Jesus alludes to the Rapture—and the need to be ready for it—in the parable of the ten virgins, as "the cry" warning of the arrival of the bridegroom "parallels the trumpet blasts of [Matthew] 24:31; 1 Cor 15:52; and 1 Thess 4:16 (which contains both trumpet and shout)."[20]

The parable of the talents speaks of the rewards to be given out after the Rapture takes place. The rewards are based on what the servants did while alive, but the settling of accounts takes place only after the Master returns.

And, finally, Jesus speaks of His return in glory, at which time He will judge and separate the "sheep" and the "goats." This takes place after the tribulation, at the end of the Day of the Lord, when Jesus comes back to earth (Revelation 19) to set up His Millennial Kingdom (Revelation 20). "This judgment takes place on earth immediately after the Battle of Armageddon" and "before the kingdom is established on earth, for the saved are told to 'inherit the kingdom' (Matt. 25:34)."[21] The sheep, humans who are still alive and are followers of Jesus, enter the Millennial Kingdom, while the goats do not, but are sent off to eternal punishment.

### [GK] Matthew 26 - Jesus and the New Covenant; the ordeal begins

### Jesus shares the Passover meal with His disciples
Jesus told His inner circle of disciples He desired to celebrate Passover with them before His suffering began. During the Lord's Supper Jesus explained that the bread represents His body, and the cup His "blood of the covenant, which is poured out for many for the forgiveness of sins" (Matthew 26:26-28 - NIV). Luke's Gospel says "this cup is the new covenant established by My blood; it is shed for you" (Luke 22:20 - HCSB). Jesus was inaugurating the promised new covenant (Jeremiah 31:31–34). Every Biblical covenant includes shedding of blood. Jesus pointed to the cup of wine which represented His own blood which He would soon shed for the sins of the world.

Jesus declared that the next time He would "drink of this fruit of the vine" would be "with you in my Father's kingdom" (Matthew 26:26-29 - NIV), and that "I will not eat it again until it is fulfilled in the kingdom of God" (Luke 22:16 - HCSB). Jesus is probably referring to "the feast in the kingdom of heaven" (Matthew 8:11; Isaiah 25:6-8), to take place in the Millennial Kingdom.

### Jesus prays in the Gethsemane
Jesus and the disciples left and went to the Garden of Gethsemane. Contrasting with the cup of the fruit of the vine yet intimately related to it, is the symbolic cup of suffering which represented the ordeal Jesus had predicted He would have to

endure. Jesus tells His disciples, "My soul is crushed with horror and sadness to the point of death," and He cries out to God, "My Father! If it is possible, let this cup be taken away from me. But I want your will, not mine" (Matthew 26:38-39 - TLB). Jesus asks the Father a second time to be spared the cup of suffering (Matthew 26:42) but understands He must submit to the Father's will and go through with the crucifixion, being faithful to the end (Matthew 26:42).

While in the garden, Judas arrives with the armed Temple guards, sent by the chief priests and elders. Jesus is arrested and taken to the Sanhedrin. There the high priest questions Jesus, charging Him under oath to declare if He is indeed the Christ and Son of God. Jesus answered affirmatively and told them that "in the future you will see the Son of Man sitting at the right hand of the Mighty One and coming on the clouds of heaven." The high priest tore his clothes and accused Jesus of blasphemy (Matthew 26:62-64 - NIV). This signified there was no doubt Jesus had declared Himself to be Messiah, the Son of God and the Son of Man.

Peter denies Jesus (Matthew 26:69-75), and Judas, having betrayed the Lord, hanged himself (Matthew 27:1-10).

## [GK] Matthew 27 - King of the Jews: tried, mocked, crucified

Jesus is taken before Pilate, who asks if He is the king of the Jews. Jesus answers "yes," but remains silent when accused by the chief priests and elders. Jesus publicly acknowledges being the King of the Jews, a title Pilate would order placed above His head on the cross (Matthew 27:37). Pilate also refers to Jesus as "Christ" (Matthew 27:17, 22). The soldiers mock Jesus, hailing Him as "King of the Jews," spit on Him, place a crown of thorns on Him and beat Him on the head. (Matthew 27:27-31).

Jesus is crucified. Above his head was a sign with the written charge against him: **"THIS IS JESUS, THE KING OF THE JEWS"** (Matthew 27:37 - NIV). Passers-by hurled insults at Him and the chief priests, teachers of the law and elders cried, "He's the king of Israel and He can't even save Himself" (Matthew 27:38-44). While on the cross Jesus quotes Psalm 22, a strong earthquake shakes the area, tombs break open, holy people are raised to life and appear in Jerusalem to several people (Matthew 27:45-56).

Joseph of Arimathea, who had become one of the disciples, asks Pilate for Jesus' body, takes it, wraps it in clean linen cloth and places it in a new tomb cut out of rock with a big stone in front of its entrance. The chief priests and Pharisees understand Jesus' claim that He would rise on the third day, so they ask Pilate to secure the tomb with a seal and have it guarded.

## [GK] Matthew 28 - Resurrection, Kingdom authority, and the great commission

On the first day of the week, an angel with the appearance of lightening comes, rolls back the stone at the entrance and sits on it. The guards are so terrified they play dead. The angel tells the women who had come on the scene that Jesus had risen, like He said He would. They are afraid yet full of joy when "suddenly Jesus met them. 'Greetings,' He said. They came to him, clasped his feet and worshiped him." He told them to not be afraid, but to go and tell His brothers to meet Him in Galilee (Matthew 28:1-10 - NIV).

### Messiah's absolute authority

The Eleven went to Galilee as instructed earlier by Jesus. When they saw Him, they worshiped Him. Jesus told them, "I have been given all authority in heaven and earth" (Matthew 28:18 - TLB). We have seen that Jesus claimed to have "authority on earth to forgive sins" (Matthew 9:4, 6 - NIV), and that He exerted His power and authority over: Evil spirits (by casting them out); nature (the wind and waves ceased); matter (bread and fish were multiplied); and the body (people were healed and raised from the dead).

Jesus had already declared that "all things have been entrusted to Me by My Father" (Matthew 11:27 - HCSB). Before washing His disciples' feet and telling Peter he would betray Him, Jesus knew "that the Father had given all things into His hands, and that He had come forth from God and was going back to God" (John 13:3 - NASB). So it is clear His authority over "all things" extends to everything **on Earth** and **in heaven**."

### Jesus commands followers to *go!*

Because Jesus has absolute authority, He tells His followers to "go and make disciples in all the nations" and "teach these new disciples to obey all the commands I have given you" (Matthew 28:19, 20 - TLB). Teaching them to **obey** adds practicality to this charge. This now is the business of the Kingdom of God on Earth and is happening through the Church. It is no coincidence that the focus of Jesus' time with His disciples, between His resurrection and ascension, was the Kingdom of God; and that the focus of the book of Acts is the inauguration and expansion of the Church.

Jesus promises to be with His disciples, and therefore His Church, "to the end of the age" (Matthew 28:20 - NIV). The One Who holds all authority and power in heaven and on Earth will always be with His people. Forever.

# Chapter 7

# The Gospels of Mark, Luke and John

## The Kingdom in the Gospel of Mark

### [GK] Mark 15 - Crucified for being "THE KING OF THE JEWS"

The passages in Mark having to do with the Kingdom are almost identical to those in Matthew, making it unnecessary to look at them again in this Gospel. Yet, there are some nuances in chapter 15 we should not overlook. The multiple references to the Kingdom in this chapter, where Jesus faces Pilate, cannot be a coincidence. It is God's authority meeting man's authority. God's Kingdom versus a man-made and a man-powered dominion. Ultimate power over limited and local strength. It is the character of Christ contrasted with the politics of people. And yet, the outcome is not at all what one would expect, because Jesus willfully lays His life down for a greater purpose: to save us and to please His Father (John 10:11, 17, 18; 15:13).

First, notice how Pilate begins by asking Jesus, "Are You the King of the Jews?" Jesus answers affirmatively ("You have said it") (Mark 15:2 - HCSB). Second, Pilate asks the crowd, "Do you want me to release the King of the Jews for you?" They shout back to release Barabbas instead. Pilate insists: "Then what do you want me to do with the One you call the King of the Jews?" To which the crowd responds with a call for His crucifixion (Mark 15:9-13 - HCSB).

Third, Jesus is handed over to the Roman soldiers. "They dressed Him in a purple robe, twisted together a crown of thorns, and put it on Him. And they began to salute Him, 'Hail, King of the Jews!' They kept hitting Him on the head with a reed and spitting on Him. Getting down on their knees, they paid Him homage (Mark 15:16-20 - HCSB). Although Pilate seemed to want to release Jesus, these soldiers were happy to begin His process of humiliation and suffering in earnest. The contrast between their arrogance, ignorance and violent nature and Jesus' meekness could not be greater. Standing before them was indeed the King of kings and Lord of lords and, having all power and authority in heaven and on earth, He chose not to respond in kind but to go through the ordeal for which He had come (John 12:27).

Fourth, it is communicated for all to see that Jesus is being crucified for being "THE KING OF THE JEWS." Passers-by insulted and mocked Him while the chief priests and scribes challenged Him. "Let the Messiah, the King of Israel, come down now from the cross, so that we may see and believe," they said (Mark 15:25-32 - HCSB).

But even in History's darkest hour, there were those who saw the light and kept on believing. The centurion who was standing guard saw how Jesus had died and exclaimed, "This man really was God's Son!" The women who had followed and served Jesus were eye-witnesses of these events. And, "Joseph of Arimathea, a prominent member of the Sanhedrin who was himself looking forward to the kingdom of God," mustered up the courage to ask Pilate for Jesus' body so he could give Him an honorable burial. Joseph was a Kingdom seeker. And though he probably did not understand what had just happened to His King, he was ready to serve Him in the best way he could (Mark 15:39-47 - HCSB).

Next, Mark tells of Jesus' resurrection and ascension, proving He was victorious during His earthly ministry, up to the very last moment. As the Suffering Servant (Isaiah 53), Jesus was a true overcomer. And as the royal King (Psalm 2), He was, is and ever will be triumphant!

# The Kingdom in the Gospel of Luke

Though similar to Matthew and Mark, Luke has a few unique accounts that directly involve the Kingdom. We will skip over the similar passages, meaning not all chapters in Luke will be considered below.

### [UK]-[GK] Luke 2 - Jesus, age 12, journeys to Jerusalem with parents

We have seen highlights from both Matthew's and Luke's account concerning

Jesus' birth. Luke adds that Jesus "grew up and became strong, filled with wisdom, and God's grace was on Him" and that He "was obedient" to His parents "and Jesus increased in wisdom and stature, and in favor with God and with people" (Luke 2:40, 51-52 - HCSB). That is to say that Jesus grew intellectually, physically, spiritually, and socially.

This was certainly a first for the Second Person of the Holy Trinity, Who is uncreated, without beginning and, like God the Father, had always been all-knowing and all-powerful. This passage demonstrates Jesus was also human, and as such He was growing, His knowledge was increasing, He was limited by His dependence on His parents and related to them in obedience. He also had to grow spiritually, increasing in favor with God. Understanding how Jesus' two natures—the divine and the human—could perfectly coexist is one of the most baffling and mysterious aspects of Christology.

Case in point, He journeyed to Jerusalem with His parents and kinfolks when He was 12, for the Feast of Passover. His folks went back home, thinking He was with them, only to discover He had stayed behind. He was at the Temple, listening to the teachers. Both His questions and His answers amazed everyone who heard Him. When His mother finally found Him, she told him how worried Joseph and she had been. He told her He needed to be in His *Father's* house.

## [GK] Luke 3 - John the Baptist on *Kingdom Values*

John the Baptist preached God's judgment on those who did not produce good fruit. The crowds asked him what they should do. John gave them ways to put **Kingdom Values** into practice: share your extra clothes and food with those in need; don't collect more than required (he told tax collectors); don't extort money and don't accuse falsely, he told his listeners (Luke 3:9-14).

## [GK] Luke 6 - Jesus questions crowd's loyalty

Jesus asked the crowd, "Why do you call Me 'Lord, Lord,' and don't do the things I say?" (Luke 6:46 - HCSB). He went right to the center of our double-minded, half-hearted tendency as human beings. You can almost hear Elijah in the background, crying out, "'How long are you going to waver between two opinions?' he asked the people. 'If the Lord is God, *follow* him!'" (1 Kings 18:21a - TLB). If Jesus is Lord and King, do what He says! If we do, we'll be digging deep and building on the rock. If not, we'll have no foundation and will not withstand the storms of life (Luke 6:47-49). Jesus would later say, "Blessed ... are those who hear the word of God and obey it" (Luke 11:28 - NIV).

## [GK] Luke 8 - Women support Jesus' ministry

The Gospel writer informs us that when Jesus went out into the villages "preaching and telling the good news of the kingdom of God," not only were the Twelve with Him, but "some women who had been healed of evil spirits and sicknesses: Mary, called Magdalene (seven demons had come out of her); Joanna the wife of Chuza, Herod's steward; Susanna; and many others who were supporting them from their possessions" (Luke 8:1-3 - HCSB). These women were instrumental in the spreading of the Good News of the Kingdom.

## [GK] Luke 9 - Twelve sent out to proclaim Kingdom, deliver, heal

Jesus called the Twelve, gave them power and authority over demons and diseases, provided specific instructions, and "sent them out to tell everyone about the Kingdom of God and to heal the sick" (Luke 9:2 - NLT). They did as Jesus told them and, when they came back, He took them on a retreat. But the crowds found out where they were. Jesus "welcomed them and taught them about the Kingdom of God, and he healed those who were sick" (Luke 9:6, 10-11 - HCSB). A connection between the Gospel of the Kingdom, healing and deliverance is established. The disciples are given authority to preach and power over demons and sickness. This has implications for Kingdom citizens today as well.

## [GK] Luke 10 - Seventy two sent out, return with good report

Next, Jesus commissions the seventy two, sends them out two by two, to the towns He would soon be visiting. He tells them to pray to the Lord of the harvest to send more workers to help and told them He was sending them out like lambs among wolves. They were supposed to "heal the sick, and tell them, 'The Kingdom of God is near you now' " (Luke 10:9 - NLT). Jesus pronounces judgment on the towns that rejected the Kingdom message. The seventy two return, rejoicing that even the demons submitted to them, in Jesus' name. Jesus said He saw Satan fall from heaven like lightening, and that they had authority over the enemy. They should, however, rejoice that their names are written in heaven. Jesus tells them, "My Father has entrusted everything to me" (Luke 10:22 - NLT).

## [UK] [GK] Luke 12 - Many *Kingdom Principles* revealed

This chapter presents many ***Kingdom Principles***, proclaimed by the King Himself. Of course, most of what Jesus said contained principles to live by. It would be difficult to extract every single one from everything He said, as registered in the Gospels. Below are a few examples which by no means are exhaustive.

– **The *nothing concealed* Kingdom Principle**
This principle reminds us of the omniscience of God. When it comes to human activity (and everything else), God sees all and knows all (Job 28:24; 34:21). If you do something good and keep it a secret (to avoid attracting attention to yourself and showing off) "your Father, who sees everything, will reward you" (Matthew 6:4, 18 - NLT). The opposite is also true: He sees and will punish all evil, even that which is done in private.

Here Jesus tells the people to beware of the Pharisees' hypocrisy, because "there is nothing covered up that will not be revealed, and hidden that will not be known." More specifically, "whatever you have said in the dark will be heard in the light, and what you have whispered in the inner rooms will be proclaimed upon the housetops" (Luke 12:1-3 - NASB; see also Luke 8:17).

– **The *fear God, not others* Kingdom Principle**
The chief priests and Pharisees were plotting together to take Jesus' life. No doubt they bullied others to submit to their misguided leadership and threatened to punish non-conformists with death. They had become stumbling blocks, trying their best to demoralize Jesus and keep others from following Him (see Luke 11:37-54).

Yet, Jesus would have nothing of it. He would not be intimidated and warned others not to be either. "I say to you, My friends, do not be afraid of those who kill the body and after that have no more that they can do. But I will warn you whom to fear: fear the One who, after He has killed, has authority to cast into hell; yes, I tell you, fear Him!" (Luke 12:4-5 - NASB). This was a principle that always guided our Lord's ministry, more so now than ever. The temptation to use His power and prove His enemies wrong, exposing them in the presence of the crowds, must have been enormous. But Jesus remembered that His enemies had it coming, and God would judge and condemn them soon enough.

This principle is also very appropriate for us today, as Christians are increasingly being persecuted, mocked and killed. We should not ultimately fear what men can do to us, since they can "only" go so far as killing us. On the other hand, God's ability to deal with us does not end with our death.

– **The *sparrow* Kingdom Principle**
Jesus had just spoken about how nothing is concealed before God. Now He applies the Father's omniscience to encourage His listeners. "Are not five sparrows sold for two cents?," He asks them. They were plentiful and cheap, meaning they were not very significant. "Yet not one of them is forgotten before God," Jesus

revealed. Not only does God keep up with the entire population of sparrows, but "indeed, the very hairs of your head are all numbered," Jesus told the crowd.

That is a very tangible way of expressing God's absolute knowledge and control. "The average person's head has up to 150,000 hair follicles (the entire adult body has 5 million). That number is constant over a lifetime" but "whether you lose the actual strands that come from those follicles can change."[1] That's a lot to keep up with. And if God can keep up with every strand of hair on everybody's head on planet earth (today that would stand at 7,752,656,660,000,000, if the average person has 100,000 strands), wouldn't you think He can keep up with each one of *us*?[2]

Jesus reassures His crowd, with a touch of humor no doubt: "Do not fear; you are more valuable than many sparrows" (Luke 12:6-7 - NASB).

## The *acknowledge Jesus and be acknowledged by Him Kingdom Principle*

While Muslims are permitted—even encouraged—to conceal or deny their faith under difficult circumstances, Christians are warned in Scripture to avoid denying their Lord.

Walid Shoebat, a former Muslim terrorist turned Christian, explains this little-known practice in his book, "God's War on Terror:"

> The two doctrines that encourage this insidious form of religiously sanctioned deception are called *Kitmand* and *Taquiyya*. The first is a command to deliberately conceal one's beliefs. It is a particular form of lying practiced primarily by Shi'ites and to a lesser degree by Sunnis.
> Shi'a Muslims are commanded to purposefully hide what they truly believe in order to mislead outsiders as to the true nature of their religion.
> Taqiyya is virtually the same. A Shi'ite Encyclopedia describes Taqiyya as "concealing or disguising one's beliefs, convictions, ideas, feelings, opinions, and/or strategies at a time of eminent danger, whether now or later in time, to save oneself from physical and/or mental injury." A one-word translation would be "Dissimulation."[3]

Jesus sternly warned His followers to confess and not to deny Him, spelling out the rewards and consequences of these actions. "And I say to you, everyone who confesses Me before men, the Son of Man will confess him also before the angels of God; but he who denies Me before men will be denied before the angels of God (Luke 12:8-9 - NASB). This, of course, would not be referring to a slip or a momentary weakness, as exemplified even in Peter's very serious denial of Christ, as he was later restored by our Lord (John 18:15-27; 21:15-19). It would concern those who more blatantly or permanently deny and reject the Lord.

Jesus had already declared that "whoever is ashamed of Me and My words, the Son of Man will be ashamed of him when He comes in His glory, and the glory of the Father and of the holy angels" (Luke 9:26 - NASB). Denying the Lord is to be avoided at all costs. Confessing Him before others, on the other hand, is a **Kingdom Value** relating to faithfulness, proclaiming the Kingdom, witnessing, integrity, courage, and others.[4]

## The *blasphemy against the Holy Spirit Kingdom Principle*
Jesus calls this the unpardonable sin. The religious leaders had seen Jesus fulfill prophecy before their very eyes. This could not be denied so, because of their calloused hearts, they denied the Source of Jesus' power (see Matthew chapter 12, above, under "The King is slandered and rejected").

Jesus explained that "everyone who speaks a word against the Son of Man, it will be forgiven him; but he who blasphemes against the Holy Spirit, it will not be forgiven him" (Luke 12:10 - NASB). To this statement, Matthew adds "either in this age or in the age to come" (Matthew 12:32).

For those who worry (as I did as a kid) about the possibility of having ever committed this sin, here is a very quick and easy test: If you are concerned about this, it means you have *not*. Because people who have blasphemed the Holy Spirit are no longer sensitized and convicted by Him. They have become utterly calloused and "immune" to God's presence, and God will have given up on them.

## The *life above possessions Kingdom Principle*
As the saying goes, "he who dies with the most toys is still dead." Wealth should be used as a means to supply one's own personal and family needs, to bless others (especially those in need), and to further the Kingdom, mostly through the local church. Making money an end in itself, to have it as a life goal, goes against **Kingdom Values**. Jesus proclaimed, "beware, and be on your guard against every form of greed; for not even when one has an abundance does his life consist of his possessions" (Luke 12:15 - NASB; see accompanying parable about the foolish rich man in Luke 12:16-21).

One of the big problems with society today is greed. Yet Jesus calls "the man who stores up treasure for himself, and is not rich toward God" a fool (Luke 12:20-21 - NASB). When you look at wealth from a Kingdom perspective, everything changes. You can't take earthly possessions with you, but you *can* take your spiritual inheritance. Those who invest in the Kingdom are "rich toward God" in this life and the next. Now, that is investing in the future and an investment that will last!

### The *do not worry about life* Kingdom Principle
We live in a world of constant change, and change is accelerating like never before. Change creates uncertainty, which leads to stress and worry. But Kingdom citizens have a constant in their life: "I the LORD do not change" (Malachi 3:6 - NIV). Now, the Kingdom is characterized by righteousness, and God says "my righteous ones will live by faith" (Hebrews 10:38 - NLT; also Habakkuk 2:4; Romans 1:17; and Galatians 3:11). Faith is what we need to face the storms of life (Luke 8:25).

This is not to say that we are to be devoid of emotion, never affected by difficult challenges, never concerned in the slightest. The psalmist felt painful distress and cried out to the Lord for help (Psalm 31:9; 43:5; 42:6, 11; Psalm 43:5). Jesus shared with His disciples He was feeling "overwhelmed with sorrow to the point of death" because of the ordeal that was lying just ahead (Matthew 26:38 - NIV). Jesus also told His disciples, "I have a baptism to be baptized with, and how great is my distress until it is accomplished!" (Luke 12:50 - ESV).

Yet, worry is different in that it implies doubt and lack of faith in God's provision and protection. "For this reason I say to you, do not worry about your life," He told His disciples. That included not worrying about what they would eat or wear. Jesus reminded them that their heavenly Father feeds the birds and clothes the grass and flowers, even though their life span is so short. How much more will He take care of people. Then Jesus goes right to the heart of the problem and exclaims: "you men of little faith!" Jesus said, "Your Father knows that you need these things" (Luke 12:22-30 - NASB). God keeps up with our needs. We don't have to fret and waste our energy on this. Instead, we should focus on the Kingdom and the King will focus on supplying our needs.

### The *seek the Kingdom first* Kingdom Principle
The principle goes like this: if we concentrate on God's Kingdom, He will concentrate on our needs. If, instead, we concentrate on our own needs and not on the Kingdom, God will concentrate on His Kingdom and not on our needs.

It's kind of like marriage: if the husband concentrates on the wife's needs and wife on her husband's, the relationship thrives and both get what they need. However, if either concentrates only on their own needs, neither will get what they need. Although this all may sound pragmatic and selfish (doing something to get something), the truth is that it is counter-intuitive to human nature and depends on a relationship where there is trust, love and altruism.

Here is how Jesus states the principle: "but seek His kingdom, and these things will be added to you" (Luke 12:31 - NASB). Not only will "these things" (food and clothing) be added to you, but the Kingdom itself will too! You are investing in God's Kingdom and guess what? God's giving it to you as a present. It's **His** Kingdom, but in a sense it's *your* Kingdom as well. That's why Jesus could tell His disciples, "do not be afraid, little flock, for your Father has chosen gladly to give you the kingdom" (Luke 12:32 - NASB).

If the Kingdom is our focus, we would naturally think: "Oh boy! I'm coming into an incredible inheritance. I'm going to be rich!" But the next thing Jesus says can be a stumbling block for some. He tells His followers: "Sell your possessions and give to charity" in order to have "an unfailing treasure in heaven, where no thief comes near nor moth destroys" (Luke 12:33 - NASB). This was seemingly meant primarily for those who would physically move about with Jesus and secondarily for the Primitive Church, the members of which routinely sold their possessions to help the poor among them, as seen in the book of Acts. The principle of storing up treasures in heaven instead of focusing on accumulating material goods here on Earth was meant for every Christ follower through the ages.

You've heard of vicious cycles. Well, here is a **Kingdom Principle** that is a blessed cycle: because you seek God's Kingdom first, you invest in your treasure in heaven; and because your treasure is in heaven, that is what you concentrate on. Because, "where your treasure is, there your heart will be also" (Luke 12:34 - NASB).

**The** *don't be caught off guard when Jesus comes back* **Kingdom Principle**

There's nothing quite like being caught off guard. It is a disconcerting feeling. It can be humiliating. You want to just kick yourself and say, "why didn't I prepare for this? Why wasn't I ready?" As we think of this principle, we must prepare for the inevitable: death and the return of Jesus. He promised repeatedly that He would return. Unfortunately, there is something in the fallen human nature that seeks to betray our best intentions. And there is the enemy who wars against our souls.

If life is a test, this is the final exam. Jesus made some comparisons to illustrate the importance of being ready for His return. He said it will be like men waiting for their boss to come back from a wedding and being able to open the door immediately him when he gets back. He added, "blessed are those slaves whom the master will find on the alert when he comes" (Luke 12:37a - NASB). Jesus said the boss will invite them to dine and will come over and wait on them. The other comparison was with a break in. If the head of the household knew when the thief was coming, he wouldn't have allowed him to get in. Jesus warned: "you too, be ready; for the Son of Man is coming at an hour that you do not expect" (Luke 12:40 - NASB).

Peter asked who Jesus was addressing. Jesus asked who "is the faithful and sensible steward, whom his master will put in charge of his servants ...?" (Luke 12:42a - NASB). Jesus explained that he will be blessed if he is doing what he is supposed to be doing when the master comes back. He will be handsomely rewarded, being placed in authority over all his master possesses. This sees believers as stewards or administrators.

But if the servant thinks the boss will be away for a long time (a hint that Jesus would not be returning real soon), and begins to mismanage those he supervises and gets drunk on the job, he will be surprised by his master's unannounced return and will be cut up and thrown in with the unbelievers (Luke 12:35-46 - NASB). John tells us what we are to do to prepare. He said that "everyone who has this hope in Him purifies himself just as He is pure" (1 John 3:3 - HCSB). Ready or not, here He comes!

### The *"much given, much required"* Kingdom Principle

This principle is a continuation of the *remaining watchful* principle, above. Jesus declares that the "slave who knew his master's will and did not get ready or act in accord with his will, will receive many lashes" while "the one who did not know it, and committed deeds worthy of a flogging, will receive but few" (Luke 12:47, 48a - NASB). This indicates there will be differing degrees of punishment in hell.

Jesus added: "From everyone who has been given much, much will be required; and to whom they entrusted much, of him they will ask all the more" (Luke 12:48b - NASB). God sees all. He knows fully what motivates people, what they know, what they are ignorant about. But even the ignorant are answerable for their actions. If you unknowingly drive with an expired driver's license and get pulled over, pleading ignorance won't help. You are responsible to know and obey the law.

It is astounding how some will spend hours on social media, wasting time on trivia and social gossip, and never pick up a Bible and investigate what it is God expects from them. Those of us who live in a free country—with churches on every other corner, with easy access to Christian books, Christian radio programs, and Christian websites—will be judged with much more severity than those who live in closed countries, where believers are marginalized and Christian resources are banned.

### [GK] Luke 13 - The narrow door into the Kingdom

As Jesus was on His preaching circuit, someone asked Him if only a few will be saved. Jesus answered, "keep on struggling to enter through the narrow door, because I tell you that many people will try to enter, but won't be able to do so."

Jesus explained there's a time when the opportunity will be gone, when it will be too late. The door will then be closed and no matter how much someone knocks, the door will not be open (Luke 13:24-25 - ISV).

What's worse, "in that place there will be crying and gnashing of teeth when you see Abraham, Isaac, Jacob, and all the prophets in the kingdom of God, and you yourselves being driven away on the outside." While those who should have known better seemed oblivious or uninterested, "people will come from east and west, and from north and south, and will eat in the kingdom of God" (Luke 13:28-29 - ISV; see "The *it's better to be an outsider with faith than a faithless insider* **Kingdom Principle**," under Matthew Chapter 8, above; see also Lazarus and the rich man in Luke 16:19-31).

Why will many try to enter the narrow door of heaven and fail? Perhaps because they're going about it in the wrong way. There seems to be a works-based, merit-based global mindset when it comes to getting into heaven. They do not realize the Law was *not* given as a means of salvation, but as a standard which shows us just how much we have fallen short. Shortly before this episode, Jesus had told a crowd that certain victims of recent tragedies were not more sinful than the rest of the population; to the contrary, "if you don't repent, then you, too, will all die" (Luke 13:1-5 - ISV).

The narrow door to salvation is entered only through repentance of sin and faith in the Lord Jesus.[5]

## [GK] Luke 14 - Humility; the parable of the great banquet

The *everyone who exalts himself will be humbled, and the one who humbles himself will be exalted* **Kingdom Principle** is found in Luke 14:11 - HCSB). This principle is connected to the **Kingdom Value** of humility.[6]

### The parable of the great banquet

This parable is similar to that of the wedding feast in Matthew 22:1-14, but comes in a different context, prompted by what was said by a participant at a meal offered by a prominent Pharisee (Luke 14:1, 15). Jesus had expressed that when giving a banquet, the underprivileged who cannot pay you back should be invited. He explained that "you will be blessed, because they cannot repay you; for you will be repaid at the resurrection of the righteous" (Luke 14:14 - HCSB). This confirms that rewards will be given shortly after the resurrection. The focus here, however, is that we ought to bless those who cannot return the favor. Hearing what Jesus said, the participant said, "the one who will eat bread in the kingdom of God is blessed!" (Luke 14:15 - HCSB).

Jesus replied to this statement with a parable, about a man who invited guests to his banquet but who, one by one, rejected the offer with the lamest of excuses (Luke 14:16-24). So, he tells his servants to go and invite the underprivileged in the streets and alleys, after which there was still room. Again he told them to go out and grab *anyone*, to fill the house. "For I tell you, not one of those men who were invited will enjoy my banquet!," the man said (Luke 14:24 - HCSB).

This parable ties in with what Jesus said before about the banquet frequented by the patriarchs and the prophets, where those who had originally been invited will not be able to get in, because of their sorry excuses and rejection of the Lord's initial invitation (see Luke 13:28-30). In the broader sense, this message is intended for Israel; more narrowly for all individuals who should know better and be receptive to the Lord's invitation, but reject it outright.

Yet God remains interested in the individual. The following chapter is a description of the Lord's compassionate heart, as He searches out and rescues the lost.

## [GK] Luke 15 - God rejoices when lost are found

### Rejoicing when lost individuals are found
The parable of the lost sheep, the parable of the lost coin, and the parable of the lost or prodigal son, are all designed to show how God cares about and seeks lost sinners, and how He rejoices when one is found and repents. Here, as in other passages, repenting presupposes faith and is equated with being saved.

Just as the one who has 100 sheep and loses one rejoices when he finds the stray animal (and the lost coins, or the lost son), and celebrates when that happens, "in the same way, I tell you, there is rejoicing in the presence of the angels of God over one sinner who repents" (Luke 15:10 - NIV).

## [GK] Luke chapter 16 - Faithfulness required and rewarded

### The *faithful over little, faithful over much Kingdom Principle*
This principle states that "whoever is faithful with very little is also faithful with a lot, and whoever is dishonest with very little is also dishonest with a lot" (Luke 16:10 - ISV). Jesus went on to say that those who have not been faithful with the wealth of this world cannot be trusted with the real deal; and those who haven't been faithful with someone else's property will not receive their own (Luke 16:11-12).

### The *you can't serve two masters Kingdom Principle*
Related to the previous principle, in this one Jesus states that "no servant can serve two masters, because either he will hate one and love the other, or be loyal to one and despise the other" (Luke 16:13a - ISV). In the immediate context,

Jesus applies this principle to money matters by declaring "you cannot serve both God and wealth!" (Luke 16:13b - ISV). The principle applies to anything else that would compete with God for sovereignty over our lives, like popularity, power, pleasure, and personal pursuits. These are not necessarily bad. But anything is bad if it takes first place—God's place—in our lives. Divided loyalty is no loyalty. And God expects us to prioritize loyalty to *Him*.

## *Kingdom Values* at odds with popular opinion

People like to justify themselves, but God knows their inner secrets and true motivation. The Pharisees were at it again and, because they "were lovers of money" (Luke 16:14 - ESV), this time they were scoffing at Jesus for what He had to say on the subject. Jesus said to them, "you are the ones who justify yourselves in the eyes of others, but God knows your hearts. What people value highly is detestable in God's sight" (Luke 16:15 - NIV).

The Lord had already told Samuel centuries before that "man does not see what the LORD sees, for man sees what is visible, but the LORD sees the heart" (1 Samuel 16:7 - HCSB). Furthermore, God is looking for something different from what people are looking for, because *Kingdom Values* have little or nothing to do with worldly values. While the Pharisees loved money and wanted to be adulated by onlookers, God was looking for humble and faithful hearts that were willing to serve.

## The Kingdom was being sought and attacked

"Until the time of John the Baptist, people had to obey the Law of Moses and the Books of the Prophets. But since God's kingdom has been preached, everyone is trying hard to get in" (Luke 16:16 - CEV). This verse is very similar to Matthew 11:12, already seen above. These verses are the only two places the Greek word *biázō* is used in the New Testament. The verb means "to use power to forcibly seize, laying hold of something with positive aggressiveness," as in "to advance forcefully."[7] The resulting effect can be positive or negative. So, how should we understand the meaning here?

There are almost as many ways to interpret the meaning of this verse as there are different English versions. Here's a sample: "everyone is pressing into it" (NKJV); "everyone is strongly urged to enter it" (HCSB); "everyone entering it is under attack" (ISV); and "everyone is forcing his way into it" (NIV). For the Matthew 11:12 verse, NIV has "violent people have been raiding it." It is hard to know exactly what Jesus meant with this statement. Perhaps both ideas are present, meaning many were seeking to enter the Kingdom with positive aggressiveness, while those opposed to it were attacking both the people trying to enter it and the Kingdom itself.

## [GK] Luke 17 - The arrival of the Kingdom of God

Pharisees were critical sorts, who seemed to enjoy giving those with competing views a hard time. They were used to being the ones in authority in religious matters, unquestioned by the populace. Now the people were flocking to Jesus, and the Pharisees were not happy. Some believe attacking is the best defense, and that is what they would do.

The Pharisees had heard Jesus constantly referring to the Kingdom, but now they confronted Him and wanted to know when this Kingdom was going to show up. "Jesus replied, 'The coming of the kingdom of God is not something that can be observed, nor will people say, 'Here it is,' or 'There it is,' because the kingdom of God is in your midst [or, is within you]'" (Luke 17:20-21 - NIV). Strictly limiting His answer to the intent of their question (they were not thinking about the eschaton, but about their present time), Jesus referred to the Global Kingdom in His answer. Except for the presence of the King in their midst during Jesus' earthly life and ministry, the manifestation of God's Kingdom on earth is largely limited to the spiritual realm, that is, to the heart or spirit of the redeemed. It happens on the inside, so that it is "not something that can be observed."

However, notice how Jesus then addresses His disciples and expands on His answer about the coming of the Kingdom which He refers to as the day or days of the Son of Man (Luke 17:24, 26, 30). If we were not to take the different aspects of the Kingdom into account, it would seem Jesus was contradicting Himself. Because He revealed that "the Son of Man in his day will be like the lightning, which flashes and lights up the sky from one end to the other" (Luke 17:24 - NIV). That is a highly visible manifestation. An eye-catcher. There will be no question when "the day the Son of Man is revealed" because of the evident ensuing tragedy, comparable to the days of Noah and the day Lot fled from Sodom (Luke 17:20-37).

Therefore, the Global Kingdom occurs mostly in the form of God's reign in the hearts of people and cannot be observed. The Millennial Kingdom will be observable and experienced outwardly, beginning with the day of the Son of Man, that is, the last portion of the Day of the Lord, the process of His return. These two aspects of God's Kingdom are very different in nature.

## [UK] [GK] Luke 19 - King will return after long absence, reward faithful

After Jesus defined His mission to Zacchaeus by revealing that "the Son of Man came to seek and save those who are lost" (Luke 19:10 - NLT), He told a crowd of people "a story to correct the impression that the Kingdom of God would begin right away" (Luke 19:11 - NLT). The parable He told was about Himself and reveals some extraordinary truths about the Kingdom. Jesus told of "a nobleman" who "was called away to a distant empire to be crowned king and then return" (Luke 19:12 - NLT).

This parable of the ten minas is similar to the parable of the talents, found in Matthew 25:14-30, also of a "man going on a journey," who called his servants and gave each a certain amount to invest while he was away and who, "after a long time," returned to settle accounts with them (Matthew 25:14, 19 - HCSB). But in this account, Jesus adds that "his people hated him and sent a delegation after him to say, 'We do not want him to be our king'" (Luke 19:14 - NLT).

Nonetheless, the nobleman left on his journey, was crowned king and returned, at which time he called his servants to settle up with him. The first two servants receive a "well done!," and the first is placed as governor over ten cities and the second over five, given their faithfulness. The third was afraid and hid his portion, being called a wicked servant by his master (see Revelation 21:8), who had his money taken and given to the one who had the most. The other servants protested but, in the form of a **Kingdom Principle**, the king told them that those who have will receive even more, and those who have nothing will see what little they have taken from them (Luke 19:26).

The second order of business is to deal those who didn't want this nobleman to become their king. He ordered them brought in and executed (Luke 19:27 - NLT).

We see clearly Jesus did not walk into a trap and lose His life unintentionally. The plan was to come, save the lost, return to the Kingdom's headquarters, be crowned king, return and rule. The fact that the faithful servants were given authority over entire cities may find a more literal fulfillment in the Millennial and Eternal Kingdom than one might suspect.

## [GK] Luke 21 When redemption draws near

In "The Greatness of the Kingdom," Alva McClain points out that there is a verse in Luke which has no parallel either in Matthew or in Mark. The verse says: "But when these things begin to take place, stand up and lift up your heads, because your redemption is near!" (Luke 21:28 - HCSB). This verse speaks of the *beginning* of the signs Jesus spoke about, at which time "your *redemption* is near." Three verses later, Jesus is speaking of their occurrence, at which point "the *kingdom of God* is near" (Luke 21:31 - HCSB).

"Now the 'redemption' of Luke 21:28 is not a synonym for the 'kingdom of God'" (...) "This means that our Lord, in the record of Luke, distinguishes in time between the redemption of the Christian's body and the arrival of the Kingdom of God."[8]

The great importance of this passage is that it is one of the few references to the redemption and Millennial Kingdom as separate events: The Rapture (redemption) could occur at any moment (since the signs, such as persecution, *began* during the time of the early Church), while the Kingdom would only come after these signs *come to pass*.

## [GK] [MK] Luke 22 - A Kingdom granted to Messiah's followers

Jesus had already told His disciples, "Don't be afraid, little flock, because your Father delights to give you the kingdom" (Luke 12:32 - HCSB). Now He reiterates the offer and explains it further when He tells them, "And I confer a kingdom on you, just as my Father has conferred a kingdom on me so that you may eat and drink at my table in my kingdom and sit down on thrones to govern the twelve tribes of Israel" (Luke 22:29-30 - ISV; see Matthew 19:28).

The King's subjects are not brainless order-takers. They are loved and respected by their Lord. There is a relationship that could not be closer and still maintain the Master-servant, King-subject relation. They are treated by the Son as the Son is treated by the Father. They receive authority in a way that mirrored the authority Jesus received from God. There is privileged fellowship—they get to sit at the Lord's table! And the delegated authority they received means they will sit on thrones and rule with Him over real people (the tribes of Israel) and real situations.

## [GK] Luke 23 - Entering Kingdom at the last moment

### The *it's never too late to enter the* Kingdom *Principle.*
Jesus was on the cross in excruciating pain, dying for the sins of humanity. He was busy saving the world, yet not too busy to focus on the need of a single person crying out to Him from another cross right beside His. This person was a criminal who deserved to be crucified, by his own admission. He "went on to plead, 'Jesus, remember me when you come into your kingdom!'" (Luke 23:42 - ISV). Jesus could have dismissed, lectured, or condemned him. Yet, "Jesus told him, 'I tell you with certainty, today you will be with me in Paradise'" (Luke 23:43 - ISV).

This forgiven criminal did not have time to do good works, go to church, get baptized, be discipled. This is unfortunate, but did not determine his eternal destiny. He was allowed in the Kingdom because it's never too late—as long as you're still alive.

## [GK] Luke 24 - Jesus conquers death, tells why Messiah had to suffer

Jesus had risen but none of His followers had yet seen Him. "Mary Magdalene, Joanna, Mary the mother of James, and the other women with them" saw two angels who told them Jesus had risen as promised. They hurried to tell the apostles (Luke 24:10 - HCSB).

On the same day, Jesus walked alongside two disciples on the road to Emmaus without identifying Himself. He addressed their bewilderment concerning the crucifixion: "'Didn't the Messiah have to suffer these things and enter into His glory?' Then beginning with Moses and all the Prophets, He interpreted for them the things concerning Himself in all the Scriptures" (Luke 24:26-27 - HCSB). Later, Jesus allowed them to see Who He was and then simply vanished. The disciples were so excited they ran all the way back to Jerusalem to tell the apostles.

When they got there and were telling them all that had happened, Jesus appeared to them and proved He was not a ghost. He ate with them and showed them what the Old Testament had predicted about Him. He told them Messiah was supposed to suffer all He did "and repentance for forgiveness of sins would be proclaimed in His name to all the nations, beginning at Jerusalem" (Luke 24:47 - HCSB).

Jesus led them to Bethany, just outside of Jerusalem, blessed them and was then taken up into heaven (Luke 24:51). The disciples worshiped Him and were full of joy. They went back to Jerusalem and spent time at the Temple, where they kept praising God.

# The Kingdom in John

John is the most unique of all the Gospels and focuses on Jesus' divine identity as the Son of God, which is fundamental in understanding His right to rule as King over all creation.

### [GK] John 1 - The King of Israel[9]
"Nathanael answered and said to Him, 'Rabbi, You are the Son of God! You are the King of Israel!'" (John 1:49 - NKJV). This precise title of "King of Israel" is rare in the New Testament, appearing only here, in Matthew 27:42, Mark 15:32, and John 12:13, always in relation to Jesus.

In the Old Testament the Lord is called "Israel's King and Redeemer" and "The King of Israel, the LORD" (Isaiah 44:6; Zephaniah 3:15 - NIV). In the New Testament the term "King of the Jews" was used by the wise men (Matthew 2:2). It would be used again several times during Jesus' trial. All four Gospels record Jesus being asked if He was the King of the Jews and the placard over His head on the cross being inscribed with the words "THE KING OF THE JEWS" (Mark 15:26). Jesus also receives the title "King of kings" in Revelation 19:16 and 1 Timothy 6:15.

Nathanael's confession was profound and demonstrated there was indeed the expectation of the arrival of a Messiah-King Who would be nothing less than "the Son of God."

## [GK] John 3 - Entering the Kingdom

### The *you must be born again to enter the* Kingdom *Principle*

A Pharisee named Nicodemus went to see Jesus. Unlike most other Pharisees we read about in Scripture, he was an honest seeker. He was "a ruler of the Jews" and addressed Jesus as "Rabbi," acknowledging that "we know that You have come from God as a teacher, for no one could perform these signs You do unless God were with him" (John 3:1-2 - HCSB). Jesus wasted no time, going directly to the point. He told him, "I assure you: Unless someone is born again, he cannot see the kingdom of God." Nicodemus didn't get it, so Jesus restated this **Kingdom Principle**: "I assure you: Unless someone is born of water and the Spirit, he cannot enter the kingdom of God" (John 3:3, 5 - HCSB).

Being born of water means being born physically (perhaps because babies are born shortly after the "water breaks"). Being born of the Holy Spirit is the same as "being born again" or being saved. Jesus was saying that to inherit or enter the Kingdom, you have to first be alive, plus you have to be regenerated by the Spirit of God. The next thing Jesus says confirms this: "Whatever is born of the flesh is flesh, and whatever is born of the Spirit is spirit (John 3:6 - HCSB).

Nicodemus still wasn't grasping what Jesus was telling him. Jesus told him that if he couldn't understand what was being said about earthly realities, what would happen if Jesus began to tell him about heavenly realities? Nicodemus was a teacher of Israel. He should have understood these concepts.

Jesus identifies His divine identity by telling Nicodemus that "no one has ascended into heaven except the One who descended from heaven—the Son of Man" (John 3:13 - HCSB). Jesus draws a parallel with the snake Moses lifted up in the desert, which required people who otherwise would die to look at it in order to be healed (Numbers 21:9). This required faith. Likewise, "the Son of Man must be lifted up, so that everyone who believes in Him will have eternal life" (John 3:14-15 - HCSB).

It was in this context that Jesus pronounced what has become the most quoted verse in the Bible, and which sums up the Good News of the Kingdom: "For God loved the world in this way: He gave His One and Only Son, so that everyone who believes in Him will not perish but have eternal life" (John 3:16 - HCSB).

## The *He must become greater and I must become less* Kingdom Principle

John was Jesus' forerunner and knew His ministry was limited to preparing the way for the Messiah. That was his calling, and he rejoiced in this mission. That's why he could humbly yet boldly state: "He must increase, but I must decrease" (John 3:27-30 - HCSB).

John the Baptist said Jesus was from above and this meant He was over everybody. The baptizer shed light on Jesus' baptism when he declared that "to him God gives the Spirit without limit." His baptism was His anointing as Priest, Prophet and King. Jesus wasn't anointed with oil, the symbol, but with the Spirit Himself. John also said "the Father loves the Son and has placed everything in his hands." Matthew and Luke, we have seen, said all power and authority was given to Jesus on Earth and in heaven. John, who administered a baptism of repentance, spoke also of the need for faith. He said, "Whoever believes in the Son has eternal life" but those who reject the Son can surely count on God's wrath (John 3:31-36 - NIV).

## [UK]-[GK] John 5 - The Father and Son's relationship

Jesus reveals details about His relationship with the Father, and the different roles they have. For instance, "The Father judges no one, but has entrusted all judgment to the Son" (John 5:22 - NIV). People have this image of God judging people, when this function has been entrusted to His Son. Another insight into the Father-Son relationship is that those who don't honor the Son don't honor the Father (John 5:23). On the flip side, those who believe the Son and the Father have eternal life, won't be condemned and have "crossed over from death to life" (John 5:24).

There is the revelation that the Son has life in Himself and the Father delegated authority to Him to judge "because he is the Son of Man" (John 5:27 - NIV). Jesus is the King, and it is the King's role to judge. He is the Son of Man Who received "authority to rule, and glory, and a kingdom so that those of every people, nation, and language should serve Him" (Daniel 7:14a - HCSB; see Isaiah 33:22). Jesus speaks further of His relationship with the Father, claiming to be the only One Who really knows Him, has heard His voice, has seen His form. He is the One sent from the Father, of Whom Scriptures testify, and of Whom Moses wrote (John 5:36-47).

## [GK] John 6 - Not a king by force; the Bread of Life from above

### Not that kind of king
After multiplying five loaves and two fish and feeding 5,000 men, a miracle so important it was reported in all four Gospels, the people figured He was the promised Prophet (Deuteronomy 18:18), and wanted to make Him king by force. But Jesus slipped away, as He was not called to be a temporal, earthly king, much less at that point. Jesus demonstrated His power to provide evidence of His identity as Messiah and, of course, to feed the hungry. But they wanted a king who would keep giving them free food on demand (John 6:1-15).

### Bread of life, sent from above
Jesus claimed to be "the bread of life" and spoke of satisfying spiritual hunger. He revealed that the Father gave Him those who come to Him: the Father attracts them to the Son and it is the Father's will that the Son not lose any of them, but that they have eternal life (John 6:35-40; see 43-51).

Many disciples deserted Jesus after hearing what and Who He had claimed to be. But Jesus already knew those who belonged to Him and those who did not. When He asked the Twelve if they also wanted to leave, Peter replied, "Lord, there is no one else that we can go to! Your words give eternal life. We have faith in you, and we are sure that you are God's Holy One" (John 6:68-69 - CEV).

## [GK] John 7 - Jesus as Messiah; the Feast of Tabernacles; the Holy Spirit

### Is Jesus really the Messiah?
The crowds and the religious authorities were asking themselves this question. The crowds were sincerely searching; the leaders wanted to deny and discredit. As the people discussed the issue, some said nobody would know where Messiah came from, yet they knew about Jesus' home town. Others wondered who could expect the Messiah to perform more miracles than Jesus.

### [MK] Feast of Tabernacles
It was the time to celebrate the Feast of Tabernacles and, taking advantage of the theme, Jesus got up on the last day of the Festival and announced: "Whoever is thirsty must come to me to drink. As Scripture says, 'Streams of living water will flow from deep within the person who believes in me'" (John 7:37-38 - GW). This Feast is related to the inauguration of the Millennial Kingdom, when "living water will flow out from Jerusalem" (Zechariah 14:8-9, 16). This stream represents the Holy Spirit, Who believers in Jesus would one day receive, but only after He had ascended and been glorified (John 7:39).

## The Holy Spirit

While the Holy Spirit came over a select few during the era of the kingdom of Israel, and while His indwelling or manifestation was usually temporary and sporadic (see Psalm 51:11), from Pentecost forward, the Holy Spirit was given to all believers on a permanent basis. A righteous man called Simeon (Luke 2:25-35) had the Holy Spirit "upon him." The Holy Spirit also "moved" him and revealed to him that he would not die until he had personally seen the promised Messiah, which he did when Jesus was presented at the Temple, shortly after being born. But Simeon belonged to the "old school," to the time that antedated the Church.

During Messiah's earthly life and ministry God gave Jesus "the Spirit without limit" (John 3:34 - NLT). Jesus told His closest disciples, "It is for your benefit that I go away, because if I don't go away the Counselor will not come to you. If I go, I will send Him to you" (John 16:7b - HCSB). When Jesus appeared to His disciples, after His resurrection, "he breathed on them and said to them, 'Receive the Holy Spirit'" (John 20:22 - ESV). And, of course, Jesus then sent the Holy Spirit to inaugurate the Church, on Pentecost (Acts 2:1-4).

Back to the Feast of Tabernacles, after Jesus' public proclamation, some believed He was indeed "the Prophet" (Deuteronomy 18:15-19), some that "He is the Christ." Others were confused, thinking He had been born in Galilee, not Bethlehem. But nobody could claim Jesus wasn't an excellent and convincing speaker, as the guards, who had been sent to arrest Him but came back empty-handed. When pressed, they replied, "no one ever spoke the way this man does" (John 7:46 - NIV).

## [GK] John 8 - The One and only: No doubt about identity, mission

Jesus was not the least bit confused about His identity, as some critics have suggested. He said, "I know where I came from and where I am going" (John 8:14, 42). And that was from and to God, the One Who sent Him. As He defended Himself against His accusers, we learn more about Jesus' character and attributes.

### Good Judge, exclusive Savior

Jesus claimed to be a good, well-informed Judge (John 8:16). He made it clear that "if you do not believe that I am the one I claim to be, you will die in your sins" (John 8:24 - NIV). Jesus warning is echoed in Peter's proclamation that "there is salvation in no one else! God has given no other name under heaven by which we must be saved" (Acts 4:12 - NLT). Ironically, Peter too was speaking to the religious leaders of the day, after Jesus' resurrection and ascension. Jesus told His disciples that "I am the way and the truth and the life. No one comes to the Father except through me" (John 14:6 - NIV). Jesus was an exclusivist. He was not an "all roads lead to Rome" kind of Savior. If there were any other way to obtain our salvation, He would not have died on the cross. God would have spared His Son.

He was courteous, gentle, and respectful. When unjustly and aggressively accused, He stood His ground, being firm but nice, as He told His accusers that "I am not possessed by a demon ... but I honor my Father and you dishonor me" (John 8:48-49 - NIV). Jesus informed the religious leaders His Father was the One they called their God, though they didn't know Him. And His Father was the One Who glorified Him. Jesus told them their father Abraham saw His day and rejoiced (John 8:54-56).

## [GK] John 9 - The Son of Man

This whole chapter is about a man who had been born blind. Jesus told His disciples this happened so God's work could be shown in the blind man's life. He gave him back his sight and a controversy arose because this happened on the Sabbath. The Pharisees got involved and questioned the former blind man, then his parents, then the man again. Exasperated, the man said "it's well known that God isn't at the beck and call of sinners, but listens carefully to anyone who lives in reverence and does his will. That someone opened the eyes of a man born blind has never been heard of—ever. If this man didn't come from God, he wouldn't be able to do anything" (John 9:31-33 - MSG).

The Pharisees kicked him out. When Jesus heard what had happened, He found him and asked him, "Do you believe in the Son of Man?" The man asked Who that was. Jesus told him, "You have both seen Him, and He is the one who is talking with you." The man responded, "Lord, I believe" and then "he worshiped Him" (John 9:35-38 - NASB). Jesus defined another aspect of His mission while on earth: To make the blind see and those who see to become blind. This was what Jesus began to do when He was blasphemed by the religious leaders, who claimed He was demon-possessed. He then began teaching through parables, so that only the initiated would be able to understand (see Matthew chapter 12, above).

## [GK] John 10 - The Good Shepherd

Jesus separates Himself from the hired hands who tended the flock for money. He declared Himself to be the Good Shepherd because He knew His sheep and was willing to die in their defense (John 10:11-14). Jesus also claimed to be the access to salvation. He said, "Yes, I am the Gate. Those who come in by way of the Gate will be saved and will go in and out and find green pastures" (John 10: 9 - TLB). The paradigm model for this Kingdom study is based on this truth. Jesus is at the center of the paradigm as the doorway to the Kingdom.[10]

Jesus' mission is not just to get you into the Kingdom, His "purpose is to give life in all its fullness" (John 10:10 - TLB). Many search for happiness in the wrong place and as an end in itself. But we were made for fellowship with God, and as Pascal put it, "there is a God-shaped vacuum in the heart of every person which cannot be filled by any created thing, but only by God, the Creator."[11] Happiness comes **as the result** of finding God and enjoying a good relationship with Him.

The religious leaders tried to stone Jesus, claiming He had blasphemed against God for identifying Himself with the Father. Jesus invited them to take His great miracles into account so that they could "understand that the Father is in me, and I in the Father" (John 10:38 - NIV). Despite the controversy, many there came to faith in Jesus.

## [GK] John 11 - The King's power over death

Lazarus, Jesus' friend from Bethany, had died. When Lazarus was still alive, the message of his illness reached Jesus, but the Lord decided to wait a couple of days before going. When Jesus and His disciples arrived, Lazarus had already been dead for four days. Lazarus' sister, Martha, went out to meet Jesus and lamented He had not gotten there in time to heal her brother. Jesus told Martha, "I am the resurrection and the life. He who believes in me will live, even though he dies" (John 11:25 - NIV).

When Mary, Lazarus's other sister, saw Jesus, she threw herself at His feet and, weeping, said she wished He'd been there so her brother would not have died. Jesus was moved by her tears and went to the tomb where Lazarus was. "You will recall that Jesus' arrival was perfectly timed for the resurrection to take place on the 4th day, when it was believed that resurrection was no longer possible."[12] That was because Jews held the belief that the soul remains close to the body for three days and then leaves. Jesus wanted them to understand He had power and authority over death. He told them to roll the stone away. Jesus prayed and then called in a loud voice: "Lazarus, come out!" He did, and Jesus told them to unwrap his grave strips of linen and let him go. There are no other examples in Scripture of anyone being raised from the dead after four days.

## Religious leaders reject Jesus, plot His death

Many of the Jews who had been there to visit Mary were convinced by this miracle and believed in Jesus. Others, however, went to the Pharisees and told them what happened. A meeting of the Sanhedrin was called and their response was beyond disappointing. It is shocking to see just how calloused their hearts had become. At no time did they doubt Jesus had raised his friend to life. There is no sign they questioned the testimony of the witnesses who had broken the news to them. They understood Lazarus was living proof of Jesus' unprecedented power and authority. But instead of praising God and placing their faith in Jesus, Who had given more than enough proof of His identity as Messiah, they met to plot His death. They came to the point of confessing to each other that "here is the man performing miraculous signs. If we let him go on like this, everyone will believe in him" (John 11:47-48 - NIV).

There is no other way to understand this: theirs was a full-blown rejection, made with an absolutely clear understanding of Jesus' power and authority, as well as proof positive of His Messianic claims. It was not based on lack of evidence. It was not even based on lack of "belief," since they confessed the facts freely to each other. And it was not a lack of understanding of messianic prophecies, for they were the best equipped and most educated in the nation when it came to the Holy Scriptures. As many today, they simply did not desire to submit to God, repent of their sins, and open their hearts to Him.

These religious leaders claimed their concern was fear the Roman authorities would interfere with their religious activities and take away their nation. But hadn't the Romans already done so? And was it worth throwing away all hope in Messiah in order to try to appease a political foe and guard their little turf? Had they not thought of the eternal implications of their decision? (See John 12:25).

From an unlikely source, the high priest Caiaphas, during this infamous meeting, came a surprising statement, which is a foundational *Kingdom Principle*: "*it is better for you that one man die for the people than that the whole nation perish*" (John 11:50 - NIV). And so it was that Jesus died as our substitute, taking upon Himself our sin, condemnation, and the punishment due to each of us and applying it those who repent and believe.

## [GK] John chapter 12 - Messiah to be glorified; *Kingdom Principles* and mysteries revealed

### A time to die
Jesus announces His imminent death by stating the outcome: He said it was time for the Son of Man to be glorified. Then He provided three *Kingdom Principles* as an explanation of why it was necessary for Him to die, as well as for His disciples to be willing to do so.

### The *worth more dead than alive Kingdom Principle*
"*Unless a kernel of wheat falls to the grown and dies, it remains only a single seed. But if it dies, it produces many seeds*" (John 12:24 - NIV). There are many laws of nature which are similar and apply to the Kingdom as well. If a seed is not planted

in the ground, if it does not "die," it cannot sprout and give life to a bush or tree which will, in turn, produce much more fruit and more seeds. If we place ourselves on a shelf and do not allow ourselves to be planted in God's world, and if we do not die to self and allow God to take control, we will not bear fruit. Our lives may be on display, but there will be no fruit for the glory of God and the benefit of others.

Being what God designed us to be and doing what He planned for us to do brings glory to Him. After proclaiming these **Kingdom Principles,** Jesus said His heart was troubled, but that He had come for this very reason—to die. He then exclaimed, "Father, glorify your name!" To which the Father responded, "I have glorified it, and will glorify it again" (John 12:27-28).

## The *you love it, you lose it* Kingdom Principle
"*The Man who loves his life will lose it, while the man who hates his life in this world will keep it for eternal life*" (John 12:25 - NIV). The Pharisees in the preceding chapter are a perfect example of those who love their position and ambition in life more than God and His purpose. They refused to let go and let God.

## The *to serve Jesus you got to follow Him* Kingdom Principle
"*Whoever serves me must follow me; and where I am, my servant also will be. My Father will honor the one who serves me*" (John 12:26 - NIV). Jesus may have been referring to those who serve Him when it's convenient, on their own terms, if and when they feel like it. On the other hand, a disciple follows and shadows his Master. It is impossible to do that if you don't show up and go where Jesus goes. The implication is that serving has to be a full-time job. Jesus promises that the Father will honor those who serve Him. Having the Father's recognition is a great reward in and of itself. The world's recognition may seem more immediate and tangible, but it pales in comparison.

## Kingdom Mysteries
Jesus proclaims what we could call Kingdom mysteries when He declares that the time had come for the world to be judged; that "now the prince of this world will be driven out;" that Jesus would be "lifted up" (crucified), and this would attract many people to Him (John 12:31-33 - NIV).

The Lord's death and resurrection would accomplish all that was needed to open the way to the Kingdom for fallen humanity. It would mean the offering of atonement. It would signal the defeat of evil and the evil one. But it would also mean that now, more than ever, there would be no excuse and each individual would be required to pick a side: to submit to the King or to remain in rebellion; to enter or not to enter the Kingdom.

"'Judgment' does not imply that the final day of judgment has come (...) Jesus conveyed the meaning that God, having now made his final revelation, must hold men responsible for their obedience or disobedience (...) The revelation of God in Christ is itself a disclosure of sin and a judgment on it" (see parallel in Acts 17:30-31).[13]

Satan, the prince of this world, would be driven out by what Jesus was about to accomplish on the cross. His death and resurrection would seal Satan's defeat, demonstrating that all the enemy's efforts did not gain anything of lasting value for him—much to the contrary. "Though Satan is still active, his action is only the desperation of futility (cf. Rev 12:12)."[14]

## Messiah: if He is to reign forever, why would He be crucified?

The crowd reacted to Jesus' news that He—the Son of Man—would be "lifted up" by saying, "We have heard from the scripture that the Messiah will remain forever. So how can You say, 'The Son of Man must be lifted up'? Who is this Son of Man?" (John 12:34 - HCSB). The crowd did not have immediate access to the Scriptures as we do today. In the time of Jesus there was a generalized misconception about Messiah. The prophecies about His identity as king were known, but those that spoke of Him as a Servant and referred to His suffering and death, were largely ignored (see "The King's Anointing" under Matthew chapter 3, above).

The questions the crowd raised are legitimate. First, would the Messiah not remain? Yes. And no. He would not remain at that time because His mission was "to serve, and to give his life as a ransom for many" (Mark 10:45b - NIV). And yes, He would return and establish His Kingdom and remain forever.

The second question was, "Who is this Son of Man?" Jesus prefers not to answer that question directly, but identifies Himself as "the light." He tells them the light will be with them only a little while longer and that they should take advantage of that while He is still among them (John 12:34).

As with Nicodemus, Jesus is in control of what is communicated. He doesn't always answer questions directly, but addresses what matters most. He doesn't tell people what they want to hear, He tells them what they *need* to hear.

## [GK] John 13 - Kingly power used to... serve!

Jesus knew it was about time to leave the world and go back to the Father. He loved His own here and was going to show them the full extent of His love very soon. Jesus knew the Father had placed all things under His power, so He dresses down like a servant and washes His disciples' feet! He did this as an example of servant leadership that His disciples should follow. If the Teacher and Master could wash His followers' feet, how much more should they wash each other's feet, so to speak. "Serving one another" is a *Kingdom Value* (John 13:1-17).[15]

## [GK] John 14 - The King's promise to return; the only way to God; and, to love is to obey

### *Kingdom Promise*: "I will be back and take you to be with Me"

In John 14:1-4 our Lord speaks about the Rapture of the Church. Before we address this powerful passage, some background information will help us get a better picture of the imagery Jesus employs.

### The wedding imagery of ancient Israel

In "A Christian Love Story," Zola Levitt explains that the language Jesus uses is clearly one of a Jewish wedding. The tradition was that a young man would find a young woman he wished to marry. He would speak to her father, enter into an agreement with him, and pay a price—a dowry—for marrying his daughter. He would then turn to the daughter, his future bride, and tell her something like, "I'm going to prepare a place for you, and when it is complete, I will come back for you, to take you with me."

He would go back home and, with his father's consent, build a chamber on to the family house and prepare it for the honeymoon. Only the father could determine when the son was finished with the room, after which he could go after his bride. This would usually happen late at night, perhaps at midnight, when the bridegroom would come with his party, unannounced, to surprise the bride and her bridesmaids. The bride, for her part, had to do a lot of waiting and, at the same time, be prepared to be surprised at any moment.

She had no doubt the bridegroom was coming because of the high price he had paid for her. Just before arriving at her house, one of his companions would shout, "the groom is coming!" The groom would whisk her away and off they would go, with the bridesmaids, to the big banquet at the father's house. There they would enter the chamber and shut the door behind them. They would stay in there for seven days while the wedding party was taking place in the father's house, with his guests. At the end of the seven days the couple would emerge, to the cheers of all the guests, and partake of a marriage supper with all present. At that point the couple would leave and go to their own house, which had also been prepared by the bridegroom.[16]

## Jesus as the Bridegroom, the Church as the bride
Does this story sound familiar? Do you see the parallels? "I am going to prepare a place for you ... in my Father's house," Jesus promises. The Church is the bride of Christ (Ephesians 5:25-27). And when He comes back for the Church, "the Lord himself will come down from heaven, with a loud command, with the voice of the archangel and with the trumpet call of God, and the dead in Christ will rise first" (1 Thessalonians 4:16 - NIV).

Now, Jesus says "and if I go and prepare a place for you, I will come back and take you to be with me that you also may be where I am." Jesus promised His disciples and the Church they represented that He would come back and take them to be with Him. And He told them He was going to be in His Father's house, that is, in heaven. This is important because it tells us the raptured Church will be taken to heaven first, before coming back to Earth, the Son's "new home," with the conquering King Messiah (see Revelation 19:11-21).

## The *Jesus is the only way to the Father Kingdom Principle*
When Jesus told His disciples He was going to His Father's house to prepare a place for them, Thomas said He didn't know where the Lord was going or how to get there. Jesus explained "I am the way, the truth, and the life. No one comes to the Father except through Me" (John 14:6 - NKJV). How do you get to the Father's house? How do you enter the King's palace? Jesus is the one and only way.

I like to point this out when I get a chance, when witnessing to someone. Because Jesus didn't say "all roads lead to Rome." He didn't say, "I can lead you there, but so can so many others." He didn't claim to be *a* way or one of many truths. He told His disciples in no uncertain terms He was *the* way, *the* truth, and *the* life. Jesus would elaborate on His identification with the Father in the following verses, but here He is already doing so by stating that "no one *comes* to the Father..." And, last of all, Jesus would make His claim to exclusivity, when He declared that "*no one*" gets in "*except* through Me."

## The *if you love Jesus, you obey Him Kingdom Principle*
"If you love Me, keep My commandments," Jesus told His disciples (John 14:15 - NKJV). Jesus also said, "If anyone loves Me, he will keep My word," and adds, "My Father will love him, and We will come to him and make Our home with him" (John 14:23 - NKJV). Jesus says we prove our love through our obedience. And one of the greatest benefits is that He takes up residence in us by giving us His Holy Spirit. "I shall ask the Father to give you someone else to stand by you, to be with you always. I mean the Spirit of truth" (John 14:16-17a - PHILLIPS).

## [GK] John 15 - Messiah shares Kingdom mysteries with disciples

### The *without Me you can do nothing Kingdom Principle*

Jesus uses the imagery of the grape vine to illustrate the vital relationship of the Father and Son to Jesus' disciples. Jesus is the true vine, the Father is the gardener, and the disciples are the branches. If you look closely at a grape vine, you will notice that just about everything you see, aside from the leaves, are the vines. The branches are those little, skinny stems that connect the vine to the fruit. It is easy to see the vines are doing all the work and the stems are simply the conduits that take the vine's nutrients and life to form and feed the grapes. By themselves, the branches are worthless, just as extension cords that aren't plugged into the electrical outlet. Jesus taught: "I am the Vine and you are the branches. Get your life from Me. Then I will live in you and you will give much fruit. You can do nothing without Me" (John 15:5 - NLV). If you've tried to live the Christian life in your own power, you know just what Jesus means!

### The *bearing a lot of fruit brings glory to the Father Kingdom Principle*

"My Father is glorified by this: that you produce much fruit and prove to be My disciples" (John 15:8 - HCSB). God expects us to be productive. To take the time, talents, and treasures He has given us and use them to serve others, do good, spread the Word, bring others into the Kingdom, disciple them, plant and grow churches, bless society, be salt and light in the world and, through all of this, to glorify the Father (see Matthew 25:14-30; Luke 19:11-27).

### *Kingdom Secrets*

These are "mysteries," the surprising facts related to the Kingdom and to how the King relates to His subjects. They are not exactly principles but stated truths. Following are a few from John, chapter 15.

### *Kingdom Secret* about the extent of the Father's love

"I have loved you even as the Father has loved me. Live within my love" (John 15:9 - TLB). We cannot comprehend just how much the Father loves His Son. But we know it is a boundless, infinite love. Yet, Jesus tells His disciples that the Father also loves them in the same way He loves His Son!

### *Kingdom Secret* about the importance of obedience

Our relationship to Jesus depends on our obedience to Him. Imagine a kingdom where the king has no authority over his subjects, where everyone does what they please and ignore the repeated commands from the throne. There must be obedience and respect for the chain of command. Jesus said, "If you keep My commands you will remain in My love, just as I have kept My Father's commands and remain in His love" (John 15:10 - HCSB). As seen above, obeying the Lord willingly is proof that we love Him. Jesus said that "you are my friends if you obey me" (John 15:14 - TLB). And, being in this special status affords us certain privileges: "I no longer call you slaves, for a master doesn't confide in his slaves; now you are my friends, proved by the fact that I have told you everything the Father told me" (John 15:15 - TLB).

## Three *Kingdom Secrets* in John 15:16: chosen; must be fruitful; requirement for having requests granted

1) We usually speak in terms of "accepting Jesus as our Savior," and the like. However, Jesus said, "You did not choose Me, but I chose you." To know our Creator loves us and desires to have us in His company is both comforting and exhilarating. To be chosen means to be accepted and welcomed into the Kingdom, if we respond in obedience.

2) And this is why He chose us: "I appointed you that you should go out and produce fruit and that your fruit should remain." The result of our work for the Lord remains when it comes about and is done according to His will and plan. Jesus explained to His disciples that "every plant that my heavenly Father has not planted will be pulled up by the roots" (Matthew 15:13 - NIV).

3) If we are fruitful, "Whatever you ask the Father in My name, He will give you" (John 15:16 - TLB). Prayer, someone said, is not so much about getting our will done in heaven as it is getting the King's will done on earth.

## Kingdom command to love
"This is My command: Love one another as I have loved you" (John 15:12 - HCSB). Love is not optional. It is the motivation behind everything done in the Kingdom. Love is a **Kingdom Value**.[17] We are to love each other as Jesus loved us! This is what is implied: "No one has greater love than this, that someone would lay down his life for his friends" (John 15:13 - HCSB). And who are His friends? Those who obey His commands (John 15:14). Jesus reiterated: "This is what I command you: Love one another" (John 15:17 - HCSB).

## [GK] John 16 - Holy Spirit Kingdom mysteries revealed

### *Kingdom Secret*: Jesus had to go so the Holy Spirit would come
"But the fact of the matter is that it is best for you that I go away, for if I don't, the Comforter won't come. If I do, he will—for I will send him to you" (John 16: 7 - TLB). This confirms what was said earlier, about the different roles played by each of the three Persons of the Holy Trinity. For the Holy Spirit to come in His new role as a permanent dweller in the lives of believers who make up the universal Church, Jesus would have to return to the Father.

## *Kingdom Secret*: The role of the Holy Spirit in conviction

The Holy Spirit "will convict the world of **sin** and of **righteousness** and of **judgment**" (John 16:8 - MEV). The **sin** is unbelief. Unbelief is an attitude problem, not a lack of evidence problem. Ultimately, people believe in what they *want* to believe. Therefore, believing is a decision. Christianity is based on historical facts and there is enough proof to convince the serious seeker who will investigate and discover that the Bible presents a consistent message from start to finish. God's not afraid of our questions. In fact, He invites us to "come now, let us reason together, says the LORD" (Isaiah 1:18 - ESV). Only the dishonest critic will continue to give excuses, look the other way, and ignore the evidence. Like the Pharisees, they see the evidence all around them; they just prefer to stay as they are.

The Holy Spirit would begin His ministry of convincing people concerning the need for **righteousness** because that was what Jesus did and taught throughout His whole ministry. But now He was leaving them. Righteousness, being the standard of the Kingdom, is essential to understanding God, His will, and the *Kingdom Values* that follow.

The Holy Spirit will also convict the world of **judgment**, "because the ruler of this world stands condemned" (John 16:11 - MEV). We must understand the Kingdom program is advancing, and the ruler of this world *and his followers* will be dealt with severely. The world prefers to focus on God's love, claiming He does not judge anybody. "All we need to do is to be nice to each other and we will be fine in the end," my neighbor once told me. But when people are convicted by the Holy Spirit, they feel the weight of their guilt and understand there must be judgment for those who do not repent and believe the Good News.

## [UK]-[GK] John 17 - Messiah's priestly prayer

### Jesus reports His ministry to His Father (John 17:1-5)

In His priestly prayer for His disciples, Jesus allows them to hear Him speaking openly and plainly with the Father. In the first part of the prayer, from verses 1 to 5, Jesus first prays about His mission and how He glorifies the Father and the Father glorifies the Son. The main points are:

- Jesus had received authority from the Father over all of humanity;
- This authority included giving eternal life to those people the Father had given the Son;
- This eternal life is defined as knowing the one and only true God, and the One He sent, Messiah Jesus;
- Jesus glorified the Father by completing the task the Father had given Him to do;
- Jesus asks the Father: "Glorify me in your presence with the glory I had with

you before the world existed" (John 17:5 - ISV). Not the glory He had before His incarnation; the glory He had before *creation*. Apparently His humbled state (Philippians 2:6-8) began much earlier than when He came in flesh (John 1:14); it took place in the beginning, right "before the world existed."

## Jesus prays to Father for His followers (John 17:6-26)

In the remainder of His prayer, Jesus intercedes for His disciples. Here are the main points:

- Jesus introduced the Father to "these men whom you gave me from the world," who had belonged to the Father and now had been given to the Son (v. 6);
- They received Jesus' words, believing He indeed was sent by the Father;
- Jesus prayed for His own, not for the world;
- All Jesus has belongs to the Father, and vice versa;
- He intercedes for their protection, since He would no longer be there to do so Himself;
- His followers received joy and His word, but the world hated them because they belonged to the world no more than He did;
- Jesus prayed: "Sanctify them by the truth. Your word is truth" (John 17:17 - ISV);
- He commissions them to go to the world, just as He, and sets Himself apart to sanctify them in the truth;
- Jesus also intercedes for all believers, present and future, that they will all be one—with each other and with the Lord—so the world will believe;
- He prays "that the world may know that you have loved them as you loved me" (John 17:23 - ISV);
- Jesus requests that His own may always be with Him and see the glory God gave Him, knowing that the Father loved Him before creation;
- He calls God "Righteous Father" and says the world never knew Him; but His followers did come to know Him. He requests the Father's love for the Son be in followers as well.

## [GK] John 18 - Messiah mistreated by high priest

### Is that the way to treat ...?

When the high priest questioned Jesus about His teaching, Jesus told him He had preached openly in the Temple and synagogues. He had said nothing in secret, so why the interrogation? At this, "one of the officers standing by struck Jesus with his hand, saying, 'Is that how you answer the high priest?'" (John 18:22, 23 - ESV). The irony could not be greater. Jesus was being accused by a mere mortal, to whom He was responding with integrity and civility. For no reason at all, the Son of God is struck by one of those present, who reprimands Him for providing a truthful answer to the high priest. The office of high priest, at the time a tainted and politicized position, was supposed to be occupied by a representative of God. If he were, it would have been clear that standing before him *was* God.

Looking back at this event with the knowledge of Jesus' identity, as One entrusted with "authority over all people" (John 17:2), it is shocking and inconceivable that an official of the high priest would have struck Jesus, probably in the face! How tragic that the highest religious office in Israel had become mostly self-serving, and that it was used, not to glorify the Lord, but to condemn His Son to death. (See Acts 23:1-5 for a parallel).

## [GK] John 20 - Returning to the Father

Jesus' resurrection was the fulfillment of prophecy, the proof that what He foretold had came to pass. It was a shout of victory that demonstrated Jesus successfully not only died vicariously for our sins, but was victorious over death itself. It reversed all perception of failure by the disciples—once they finally grasped the stunning fact that Jesus was alive and glorified. It confirmed His identity as Messiah, Son of God and King over all creation.

Mary Magdalene was by the Lord's tomb when she looked inside and saw two angels there, who asked her why she was crying. She told them it was because they had taken her Lord away. Just then she turned around and saw Jesus, but thought He was the gardener. She asked if He had removed "Him" (she didn't say "the body"). "'Don't cling to Me,' Jesus told her, 'for I have not yet ascended to the Father. But go to My brothers and tell them that I am ascending to My Father and your Father—to My God and your God'" (John 20:17 - HCSB).

Jesus did not say "our Father" and "our God." "The reason for the distinction in his word to Mary was not, of course, that there were two gods but rather that her relationship with God was different from his. He is the eternal Son of the Father; she, as well as all the disciples, had become a member of the family by receiving him (cf. John 1:12). Both relationships concerned only one God."[18]

Jesus told her, "Go to My brothers and tell them." "The news that the crucified Jesus has been raised from the dead and is now Lord of the world" is foundational to Christian faith and ministry. And entrusting this message to Mary was "almost as huge a revolution as the resurrection itself," says N.T. Wright. Because Jesus chose a woman to go and proclaim this message to His (male) disciples.[19]

## [GK] John 21 - Restoring a much loved leader

Peter had denied Jesus three times. Now, Jesus gives Peter an opportunity to confess Him three times (John 21:15-19).

The risen Lord appeared on the shores of the Sea of Galilee to find His disciples frustrated after a night of fruitless fishing. He told them to throw their nets to the other side of the boat and, to their surprise, the nets were so full they had a hard time getting them to shore. When they arrived, they discovered it was Jesus. And He had fish and bread ready for them, for breakfast. Jesus then asked Peter, "Do you love Me more than these?" Peter answered "yes." Jesus asked this two more times. At the end of each positive answer, Jesus told Peter, "Feed My lambs," "Shepherd My sheep," and "Feed My sheep," simultaneously.

What was the point in all of this? Jesus restored Peter by giving him the opportunity to confess his love for Him the same number of times he had denied Him. Each time, Jesus gave and reiterated the important role He was giving Peter in His Kingdom (he was to become the first leader of the early Church). Mercy would have been to forgive and restore him. Grace went a step further and offered him a meaningful place at the table. Notice also that Jesus was demonstrating they could do nothing without Him, not even in their fishing profession. As future leaders they would need to keep that in mind.

There is a sense in which the Church is to the New Testament what Israel is to the Old Testament—mainly, the representative and conduit of the Kingdom of God on Earth. The Church, having the Apostles and their teaching as its foundation, has been called to continue Christ's ministry here until He returns.

*Chapter*

# 8

# History: Acts of [the Holy Spirit through] the Apostles

## The Kingdom in the book of Acts

### [GK] Acts 1 - The 40-day Kingdom emphasis

Jesus had promised to send the Holy Spirit to continue His work through His followers. The book of Acts is a collection of stories about how the Holy Spirit worked through the apostles and Christians in general to spread the gospel of the Kingdom, plant churches, do missions, and strengthen the fellowship.

**Jesus appears to the apostles, discusses the Kingdom**
After His death and resurrection, Jesus appeared to the apostles many times, proving over and over that He was alive. "He appeared to them over a period of forty days and spoke about the kingdom of God" (Acts 1:3 - NIV). He had told them before His crucifixion: "I still have a lot to say to you, but you cannot bear it now" (John 16:12 - ISV). It was probably during these days that He told them about things they would not have been able to grasp before.

But if Jesus was talking to them about the Kingdom during that time, what specifically would He be speaking about? He had already explained why He had to suffer and die. He had already restored Peter. What lay before the apostles at that point? What was the mission Jesus had in store for them? It seems obvious, given that the whole book of Acts is devoted to the subject of the Church, that this was the specific aspect of the Kingdom Jesus was instructing His apostles about. Israel would no longer be the main representative of the Kingdom on earth (Matthew 21:43). This responsibility and privilege had now fallen to the Body of Christ. And the apostles needed to be prepared and empowered for what was coming their way, in terms of the outpouring of the Holy Spirit, the opportunities and the persecution they would face.

On one of those occasions when they were meeting with the glorified Jesus, the apostles asked Him if the time had now come for Him to restore the Kingdom to Israel. Some have found this to be naïve on the part of the apostles, as though they should have known the Lord was never to restore the Kingdom to Israel again. But Jesus did not correct them. In fact, did not the Lord tell Peter that "at the renewal of all things, when the Son of Man sits on his glorious throne, you who have followed me will also sit on twelve thrones, judging the twelve tribes of Israel" (Matthew 19:28 - NIV)? The apostles just wanted to know about the timing, since they had been told that one day the Kingdom would be restored and Israel would play a central part.

And it was precisely about the chronology that Jesus spoke. He told them that "it is not for you to know times or seasons that the Father has fixed by his own authority" (Acts 1:7 - ESV). He didn't deny the restoration, He simply said that was the Father's business.

Then Jesus refocused their attention on what God was about to do with and through them, there and then. He told them they were about to "receive power when the Holy Spirit comes upon you. And you will be my witnesses, telling people about me everywhere—in Jerusalem, throughout Judea, in Samaria, and to the ends of the earth" (Acts 1:8 - NLT). Having restated their commission (see Matthew 28:18-20), Jesus ascends before their very eyes. Two "men" dressed in white appeared beside them and informed them Jesus would be coming back in the same way He left (Acts 1:6-11).

## [GK] Acts 2 - The Church is inaugurated: the new Kingdom agency begins to impact the world

With the sound of blowing wind, the Holy Spirit is poured out, those present are filled with the Holy Spirit, and they begin to speak in other tongues. Godly Jews from several countries who are in Jerusalem are attracted to the sound they hear. When they arrive on the scene, they hear Galileans speaking and yet they all could understand them in their own native language! Onlookers were amazed, but some thought the disciples were drunk. Peter took advantage of their presence and began to preach, explaining they were fulfilling prophecy!

In Peter's Kingdom message that followed, he quotes prophecy about the outpouring of the Holy Spirit (Joel 2:28-32), explains what happened to Jesus and why; quotes David's messianic psalm which refers to the resurrection, declaring God had promised David He would place one of his descendants on his throne (Acts 2:30). Peter proclaimed that God took Jesus, Whom they had crucified, and made Him Lord and Messiah (Acts 2:36). The people were impacted and asked what they should do. Peter told them they should repent so that their sins would be forgiven. Then he told them they would receive the Holy Spirit as a gift. Those who accepted the message were baptized and close to 3 thousand were added to the Church that day!

## [GK] [MK] Acts 3 - Repentance and restoration preached

Peter's second sermon was also very bold, as he told the crowd that formed around him that "you disowned the Holy and Righteous One and asked for a murderer to be granted to you" (Acts 3:14 - NASB). He affirmed Christ's resurrection, and told them, "Therefore repent and return, so that your sins may be wiped away, in order that times of refreshing may come from the presence of the Lord" (Acts 3:19 - NASB). Jesus had foretold that "repentance for forgiveness of sins would be proclaimed in His name to all the nations, beginning from Jerusalem" (Luke 24:47 - NASB).

If they would repent, Peter preached, God "may send Jesus, the Christ appointed for you, whom heaven must receive until the period of restoration of all things about which God spoke by the mouth of His holy prophets from ancient time" (Acts 3:20-21 - NASB). Alva McClain sees here an "official *reoffer* of the Messiah and His Kingdom... to the nation of Israel" (see Acts 3:12; about the restoration or renewal of all things, see Matthew 19:28; Acts 1:6). "And the nation of Israel must understand that while the exact time of this grand event is unrevealed, its arrival at this particular stage of history is morally conditioned upon the repentance of the nation."[1] That period of restoration will take place at the onset of the Millennial Kingdom. Until then, Jesus will await in heaven, where He intercedes for His followers (Romans 8:34; Hebrews 7:25).

## [GK] Acts 4 - The Kingdom's exclusive message; boldness

### The *no other name Kingdom Principle*:
"There is salvation in no one else! God has given no other name under heaven

by which we must be saved" (Acts 4:12 - NLT). The exclusive message Jesus had brought (John 14:6) is now proclaimed by His apostles. The world sees this as narrow-minded. How could the way be so steep, the gate so narrow, the solution so exclusive? But if there were any other way—let alone many other ways—why, pray tell, would the Father allow His Son to go through such humiliation, suffering and then death? Hadn't Jesus Himself asked the Father to pass that cup from Him if it were possible? But there was and is no other way.

## Kingdom boldness

Peter healed a crippled beggar in the Temple area and this gave him an opportunity to proclaim Jesus. The authorities later arrested Peter and John for preaching about the resurrection. When they were taken before the religious leaders the next day, they were threatened and warned not to preach about Jesus any longer. "But Peter and John answered them, 'Whether it is right in God's sight to listen to you rather than to God, you must judge; for we cannot keep from speaking about what we have seen and heard'" (Acts 4:19-20 - NRSV). They were further threatened yet released.

Their boldness caused the other believers, who heard their story firsthand, to praise the Lord and quote Psalm 2 concerning the ruling King Messiah. They understood everything was under God's control. Then they prayed for boldness and courage to stand up against all the threats they were receiving. The whole place was shaken "and they were all filled with the Holy Spirit and spoke the word of God with boldness" (Acts 4:31b - NRSV). Boldness is a component of courage, **Kingdom Value #64.**[2]

## [GK] Acts 5 - Kingdom power; strict beginnings; rejoicing when persecuted

### *Kingdom Secret: Kingdom power and authority comes through the Holy Spirit*

Barnabas had sold a field he owned and brought the money to the apostles for the general church fund (Acts 4:36-37). Ananias and Sapphira may have been seeking recognition, favor or status for doing the same (Acts 5:1-11). But they conspired to withhold part of the money received from the sale of their possession, then offer the rest as though it were the whole amount.

They didn't have to offer everything; they didn't even have to offer *anything*. The problem was the lie they were telling the Church. With spiritual discernment, Peter understood just how serious a precedent this could be. He said, "Ananias, why has Satan filled your heart to lie to the Holy Spirit?" And, "you haven't lied to men, but to God" (Acts 5:3-4 - WEB). Ananias immediately fell down and died, which brought fear to those who heard about it. Sapphira came in three hours later, kept up the lie, and also fell to her death.

After Pentecost we see a completely different Peter. He is bold, courageous, wise, and has the spiritual gifts of prophecy (preaching), discernment, and healing. He has become a strong leader with great authority and power. Peter's Kingdom authority can be seen in the case of Ananias and Sapphira's untimely death.

## The *strict beginnings Kingdom Principle*
Why was God so strict with Ananias and Sapphira? Why does this typically not happen in the Church today? Usually God is stricter at the onset of something new, because everything else grows out of that beginning and carries its DNA, so to speak. If the Church had lost its integrity and had become corrupt in the beginning, then all other churches stemming from it would have carried that germ. The whole spiritual organism of the Church would have been contaminated. Later on, with churches being planted and growing in many places, if one or some of them become corrupt, the problem is localized and will not necessarily affect all the other churches.

## The *rejoicing for suffering for Jesus Kingdom Principle*
"Then they went out from the presence of the Sanhedrin, rejoicing that they were counted worthy to be dishonored on behalf of the Name" (Acts 5:41 - HCSB). Not only were the apostles and disciples bold, they were so full of faith and enthusiasm they felt blessed to be persecuted. Jesus had taught: "Blessed are those who are persecuted for righteousness' sake, for theirs is the kingdom of heaven. Blessed are you when others revile you and persecute you and utter all kinds of evil against you falsely on my account" (Matthew 5:10-11 - ESV).

This beatitude looks nice on paper but when others insult us for following Jesus and our blood starts to boil, we all too soon start complaining about how unfair the accusers are. Or, we complain against God for allowing us to be treated like that. There is so much we can learn by going back to our roots as the Church and emulating the early Christians' attitude and lifestyle!

Why the rejoicing? Because being persecuted and suffering for Jesus meant they were being counted worthy of Him.[3]

## [GK] Acts 6 - Full of faith, grace, power, wisdom, and the Holy Spirit
"Stephen, a man full of faith and the Holy Spirit" (Acts 6:5 - HCSB), was selected by the congregation to become one of the first deacons in the Church. He was a man of wisdom (Acts 6:10) and was "full of grace and power." This power was

related to "performing great wonders and signs among the people" (Acts 6:8 - HCSB). Stephen clearly demonstrated the Values of the Kingdom. His whole life was a testimony that glorified God. As was his death.

## [GK] Acts 7 - First Christian martyr sees Son of Man in vision

Stephen had just finished giving a thorough summary of the Old Testament, referred to Jesus as "the Righteous One," and now, shortly before being stoned by the religious leaders of the Sanhedrin, had a glorious vision. Filled with the Holy Spirit, Stephen "saw God's glory, with Jesus standing at the right hand of God, and he said, 'Look! I see the heavens opened and the Son of Man standing at the right hand of God!'" (Acts 7:55-56 - HCSB). Instead of deterring his accusers, this only made matters worse. They covered their ears, shouted as loud as they could, took him outside of the Jerusalem city limits, and began to stone him.

As they were stoning him, Stephen cried out "Lord Jesus, receive my spirit!" and prayed, "Lord, do not charge them with this sin!" (Acts 7:59-60 - HCSB). Truly he had the Spirit of Jesus, the same attitude and reaction our Lord had while laying down His life on the cross. Stephen is a great example of love, forgiveness, and compassion. He is indeed a Kingdom hero.

During His interrogation, Jesus had told the Sanhedrin that "from now on the Son of Man shall be seated at the right hand of the power of God" (Luke 22:69 - ESV). Yet Stephen saw Him *standing* at God's right hand. It seems Jesus was standing in order to welcome Stephen home—with honor.

## [GK] Acts 8 - Proclaiming the Good News of the Kingdom

### Philip preaches the Good News of the Kingdom

It's the Good News about Jesus, the King Who came as a Servant to give His life for the salvation of all who would accept His gift. After Stephen had been stoned to death, Saul began vigorously persecuting the Church. This caused the believers to scatter, yet in so doing, to take the Good News with them and share it wherever they went.

Philip the evangelist, one of the deacons (Acts 6:5), went to the city of Samaria, where he preached Jesus as Messiah. "But when they believed Philip preaching good news concerning God's Kingdom and the name of Jesus Christ, they were baptized, both men and women" (Acts 8:12- WEB). Many people were physically healed and delivered from demons who had been tormenting and possessing them. "As a result, there was great rejoicing in that city" (Acts 8:8 - ISV). That's what the Good News does: it brings joy!

Then an angel of the Lord told Philip to go south to a road that connected Jerusalem to Gaza. He went and saw an Ethiopian eunuch reading Isaiah (what we now have as Isaiah 53, one of the most profound prophecies about Messiah's vicarious death). The Spirit told Philip to go and talk to him. He asked him if he understood the passage. The eunuch indicated he needed help, "so Philip proceeded to tell him the good news about Jesus, beginning from that Scripture" (Acts 8:35 - HCSB). The eunuch accepted the message and was baptized on the side of the road! When they came up from the water, "the Spirit of the Lord snatched Philip away" (Acts 8:39 - ISV).

In this story we can see how believers, using the Holy Scriptures, are aided by angels and the Holy Spirit to proclaim the Good News about Jesus and His Kingdom to those who are being prepared to receive it. No wonder Isaiah exclaimed, "How lovely on the mountains are the feet of him who brings good news, who announces peace and brings good news of happiness, who announces salvation, and says to Zion, 'Your God reigns!'" (Isaiah 52:7 - NASB, quoted by Paul in Romans 10:15; see also Isaiah 40:9).

## The Good News (of the Kingdom) in the New Testament

Jesus' earthly ministry focused on proclaiming the Good News about the Kingdom (Matthew 4:23). Jesus claimed, "I must preach the kingdom of God to the other cities also, for I was sent for this purpose" (Luke 4:43 - NASB). The Gospel of Mark opens with the statement, "The beginning of the good news about Jesus the Messiah, the Son of God" (Mark 1:1 - NIV).

In the book of Acts, the Good News, or Gospel, is said to be "the good news that Jesus is the Messiah" (Acts 5:42 - HCSB)p "the good news of peace through Jesus Christ–He is Lord of all (Acts 10:36 - HCSB)p and "the good news about Jesus and the resurrection" (Acts 17:18 - NIV). Paul called it "the gospel of your salvation" (Ephesians 1:13 - HCSB), and claimed that "by this gospel you are saved" (1 Corinthians 15:2 - NIV).

## [GK] Acts 10 - The Kingdom: exclusive *and* inclusive

### The *all-inclusive* Kingdom Principle

God has no favorites. All are invited. All are accepted on the same terms (fearing Him and doing what is righteous). This, based on Peter's experience with Cornelius, a Gentile centurion who lived with his family in Caesarea. He was a God-fearing man, as was his whole family. God directed Peter to go and tell them about Jesus. When Peter saw how they readily accepted the Gospel message he said, "Now I really understand that God doesn't show favoritism, but in every nation the person who fears Him and does righteousness is acceptable to Him" (Acts 10:34-35 - HCSB).

Peter proclaimed Jesus, Who is Lord of all (Acts 10:36), Judge of living and dead (Acts 10:42), of Whom all prophets testified. "Everyone who believes in Him will receive forgiveness of sins" (Acts 10:43 - HCSB). Notice this last statement. It says that while the Gospel is exclusive about the *means* of salvation (one must believe in Jesus), it is inclusive in terms of *who can follow that means* of salvation ("everyone").

## [GK] Acts 12 - Kingdom powerful prayer

### The *powerful prayer Kingdom Principle*

Peter was in prison and set to be executed. The church was in earnest prayer for him because "the apostle James (John's brother)" had already been ordered killed. The night before his execution, Peter was fast asleep, "under the guard of sixteen soldiers," and "double-chained between two soldiers with others standing guard before the prison gate." But an angel appeared, woke him up, and ordered him to get up quickly, get dressed and follow him out of the prison.

The chains fell off and Peter did what he was told, all the while thinking it was a dream. The prison gate opened on its own and Peter finally realized what had happened. He went to John Mark's mother's house and knocked. Rhoda, one of the believers, came to the door. She was so excited to hear Peter's voice, she went back in "where many were gathered for a prayer meeting" to tell them who was at the door. They didn't believe her. But Peter kept knocking so they went and when they saw it truly was Peter, "their surprise knew no bounds" (Acts 12:1-19 - NLT).

Prayer is a **Kingdom Value**.[4] It is an instrument the Lord has given His followers to use in conformity to His will. Many times intense, caring, prayer is required, in Jesus' name and according to God's will (John 14:12, 13; 15:16; 16-23; 1 John 5:14, 15). Notice that "earnest prayer was going up to God from the church for his safety all the time he was in prison" (Acts 12:5 - NLT). And yet, when Rhoda told them Peter was at the door, "they didn't believe her. "'You're out of your mind,' they said. When she insisted they decided, 'It must be his angel. They must have killed him'" (Acts 12:15 - NLT). That is not exactly solid faith. But their prayers had been sincere and "constant" (Acts 12:5 - NKJV).

There is a lot of mystery surrounding prayer. Prayer can go either way: it can be answered in a wonderful and sometimes miraculous way; or, it we can have our request denied. A few months ago I read a book titled "Prayer: Not my Will but your Will; Lessons Learned when God gave Undesirable Answers to my Prayers."

Jackson Day, the author and a friend, is a retired missionary who lost his wife to a terrible sickness, though he had cried out for her healing. More recently I read "Unlocking the Mystery of Divine Healing," by Tony Myers. This author had suffered a progressively debilitating disease that left him crippled and in pain. One day God answered his prayer, and he was instantaneously and completely healed!

Why are some healed or delivered while others are not? We saw, above, that "King Herod moved against some believers and killed the apostle James (John's brother)" (Acts 12:1-2 - TLB). It is doubtful believers had not been praying for James with the same intensity they prayed for Peter. Yet, in God's sovereignty, He allowed James to be executed. (For Paul's unanswered prayer, see 2 Corinthians 12:8-9). God had other plans for Peter and, at that point, he was delivered. This is a complex matter which cannot adequately be covered here. There are many contributing factors, but two truths must be taken into account: God's sovereign will, and the fact that He still performs unexplainable miracles today.

## [GK] Acts 14 - Hardships on the way in

### The *many hardships on the way in to the* Kingdom *Principle*

Paul and Barnabas were on their first official missionary journey, planting and strengthening churches. They had been in Iconium where many Jews and Gentiles believed. Some of the Jews who didn't believe started stirring up trouble. So they left and went to Lystra where they healed a man. The people were so excited they thought Paul and Barnabas were gods in human form: Hermes and Zeus. They were having a hard time convincing the people they were mere mortals, when the unbelieving Jews from Antioch and Iconium arrived and easily persuaded the crowd to stone Paul. They drug him outside of the town and left him for dead. But when the disciples came around he got up, went back into town and then left the next day with Barnabas, to the city of Derbe. There they also made many disciples.

It was at that point that they turned around and went back through the cities they had been to before, "strengthening the disciples by encouraging them to continue in the faith and by telling them, 'It is necessary to pass through many troubles on our way into the kingdom of God'" (Acts 14:22 - HCSB). This was no prosperity Gospel. They shared with the authority of those who had personally faced "many troubles" while proclaiming the Gospel of the Kingdom, and as they made their way to their inheritance in the Eternal Kingdom.

## [GK] Acts 15 - The message of grace

### The *by grace alone Kingdom Principle*

Paul and Barnabas had gone back to Antioch, "where they had been entrusted to the grace of God for the work they had now completed" (Acts 14:26 - HCSB). They were commissioned and sent out by God's grace, and they preached this grace wherever they went. How ironic to come back and discover that "some men came down from Judea and began to teach the brothers: 'Unless you are circumcised according to the custom prescribed by Moses, you cannot be saved!'" (Acts 15:1 - HCSB).

Paul and Barnabas debated the issue with them. It was decided they should go to Jerusalem to take the matter to the apostles and elders there. After they debated the issue among themselves, Peter got up and insisted, "On the contrary, we believe we are saved through the grace of the Lord Jesus in the same way they are" (Acts 15:11 - HCSB). Grace is a **Kingdom Value**.[5] It is by grace that believing and repentant Jews and non-Jews alike are accepted into the Kingdom.

## [GK] Acts 17 - The message of the Kingdom summarized

When Paul was in Thessalonica, he spent three Sabbaths in the local synagogue explaining why the Messiah had to suffer, after which He rose from the dead. Some Jews got it and joined Paul, Silas and several non-Jews. But some Jews opposed the message, organized a mob and went after Paul. Their accusation before the city officials was that, "They are all guilty of treason against Caesar, for they profess allegiance to another king, named Jesus" (Acts 17:7 - NLT). They had understood the message loud and clear: Jesus was the awaited Messiah, the only true King to Whom we all owe allegiance, over and above anyone else.

Later, Paul went to Athens and became distressed when he noticed there were idols all over town. He went to the synagogue, the market place, and finally the Areopagus to share the Gospel. The philosophers and debaters, some who loved to discuss the latest ideas, wanted to hear more. So they asked Paul to explain what this new teaching was all about.

Paul presents the message of the Kingdom in a nutshell in Acts 17:24-31. The message of the *Gospel* concentrates on repentance, faith, and the atonement offered through the sacrifice of Messiah, as well as His resurrection. But the people of Athens needed some background. So Paul went all the way back to the beginning, proclaiming "the God who made the world and everything in it—He is Lord of heaven and earth" (Acts 17: 24 - HCSB). Inspired by a statue to "An Unknown God," Paul went from creation to the resurrection in eight short verses!

## [GK] Acts 19 - What evil spirits know

## *Kingdom Secret: the spirit world knows who's who*

Before we get to the subject of evil spirits, it is important to mention that in Ephesus "Paul went into the synagogue and spoke boldly there for three months, arguing persuasively about the kingdom of God" (Acts 19:8 - BSB). I would love to have been in those classes! He did not shy away from teaching new Christians (who had not even heard of the Holy Spirit until he got there) about the Kingdom of God. And his teaching was not superficial, as he kept at it for three months.

Now about evil spirits. They know Who Jesus is and who His followers are (Acts 19:13-15). When some exorcists tried using the "we exorcise you by the Jesus whom Paul preaches" line, "the evil spirit answered and said, 'Jesus I know, and Paul I know; but who are you?'" (Acts 19:15 - NKJV). At which point the possessed man beat them so badly they "ran out of that house naked and wounded" (Acts 19:16 - HCSB).

Most—if not all—evil spirits are demons, who are fallen angels. It would only make sense that they know Who Jesus is (see Mark 5:1-13). James said: "'You say you have faith, for you believe that there is one God. Good for you! Even the demons believe this, and they tremble in terror" (James 2:19 - NLT).

## [GK] Acts 20 - Be a giver, not a taker

When we love someone, we want to bless them. We are blessed just knowing they are blessed. This is why, in a **Kingdom Principle**, Jesus states **"it is more blessed to give than to receive"** (Acts 20:35 - NLT). That's what parents feel when they see their kids opening their Christmas presents. Or, when they grow up and get better grades or jobs than they ever did.

## [GK] Acts 28 - Declaring the Kingdom of God

Paul had appealed to Caesar and was in Rome when he decided to invite the leaders of the Jews to hear him out. They told him they had not received any word about—or against—him, but had heard that "people everywhere are talking against this sect" (Acts 28:22 - NIV). A meeting was arranged and several Jews came to the place Paul was staying. "He explained and testified about the Kingdom of God and tried to persuade them about Jesus from the Scriptures. Using the law of Moses and the books of the prophets, he spoke to them from morning until evening" (Acts 28:23 - NLT). Some were convinced but others refused to believe. Paul quoted Isaiah's prophecy about hard hearts to them (Isaiah 6:9-10), which made some of them leave. Paul told them the Gentiles *were* listening and receiving God's offer of salvation.

The book of Acts ends on a very positive note. Luke signs off by informing his readers that "for the next two years, Paul lived in Rome at his own expense. He welcomed all who visited him, boldly proclaiming the Kingdom of God and teaching about the Lord Jesus Christ. And no one tried to stop him" (Acts 28:30-31 - NLT). What did Paul teach about the Kingdom to the Romans? His letter to them, no doubt, contains much of what he preached during those two years there.

Paul was already beginning to fulfill prophecy, as Jesus had foretold that "this gospel of the kingdom will be proclaimed in the whole earth, for a testimony to all the nations; and then the end will come" (Matthew 24:14 - BLB). Our task is to keep preaching the Kingdom until His Millennial Kingdom comes.

*Chapter*

# 9

# The Letters of Paul

## The Kingdom in Romans

**[GK] Romans 1 - 7 - An emphasis on righteousness**

The essence of the Gospel is this: We repent and believe, and God credits us with His righteousness. Righteousness is the standard of the Kingdom. Repentance and faith are the keys for entering the Kingdom's Gate. And Jesus is that Gate. Romans explains these concepts in detail, which are briefly mentioned below.

Paul begins by explaining that Jesus is a descendant of David, the Son of God, Who was resurrected from the dead, and Who is Messiah and Lord (Romans 1:1-4). Paul said the Gospel "is the power of God that brings salvation to everyone who believes," and revealed that "in the gospel the righteousness of God is revealed—a righteousness that is by faith from first to last, just as it is written: 'The righteous will live by faith'" (Romans 1:16-17 - NIV; see Habakkuk 2:4).

Righteousness (more specifically justification) by faith is the central theme of the first eleven chapters of this letter. In the second half of chapter one Paul tells why God's wrath has come upon humanity, as people have suppressed the truth and exchanged it for lies. Because rebellious people were unrepentant, God gave them over to sinful desires.

In chapters two and three, Paul makes a case for the fact that all have sinned, are without excuse, are deserving of God's wrath, but may freely be justified (declared without guilt) before God by faith, apart from keeping all the Law. Chapter four gives the example of Abraham, the one who discovered this ***Kingdom Principle***, and who "believed God, and it was credited to him for righteousness" (Romans 4:3 - HCSB; see Genesis 15:6).

Chapter five states that this justification by faith leads to peace with God and access to His grace, which leads us to rejoice in hope, even when we suffer (Romans 5:1-3). Paul then speaks about how sin entered humanity through Adam and grace and God's gift of salvation through Jesus (Romans 5:12-21). Chapters six, seven and eight speak about sanctification or the struggle with—and victory over—sin.

## [UK] [GK] [MK] [EK] Romans 8 - Kingdom heirs of glory

"The Spirit Himself testifies together with our spirit that we are God's children, and if children, also heirs—heirs of God and coheirs with Christ—seeing that we suffer with Him so that we may also be glorified with Him" (Romans 8:16-17 - HCSB). Our present suffering pales in comparison with the future glory we are going to experience (v. 18).

What is the nature of this glory? Now we only "have the Spirit as the firstfruits," the down payment of our salvation. We live in this fallen world which has been locked in a state of degeneration and groans as if in labor pains. But when our salvation comes to fruition, then we will be gloriously free as God's children, our adoption will be complete, and our bodies will be redeemed. This gives us hope for the present and helps us to be patient as we wait for the future.

**The *things favor those who love God Kingdom Principle*:**
"We know that all things work together for the good of those who love God: those who are called according to His purpose" (Romans 8:28 - HCSB). God's universe *conspires* in favor of those who seek and love God. We all live in a fallen world where there is real pain and suffering and bad things happen to good people. Still, those who love God follow His directives and live out His **Kingdom Values**. If everyone practiced these values, laws would be taken seriously, authorities respected, people could trust each other, businesses would look out for the greater good, and families would live in harmony. Things would just work better for everybody.

But when there is greed, when people try to take advantage of others, and nobody can trust anybody, and there is no love, respect or harmony, then everything is more complicated. The risks are bigger, the crime rate is higher, families are divided, the government is corrupt, and things just don't function like we know they should. Even so, when Jesus' followers do what's right, they contribute to everyone's well-being. The God's universal laws, plus His special blessings and guidance, mean that ultimately all things work for the good of the righteous.

Joseph is the perfect example (Genesis 37, 39-50). Bad things happened to him for a long time. He was caught and sold into slavery by his own brothers in Canaan, lied about by his master's wife in Egypt, thrown in prison and forgotten there for two whole years. He never complained. He never wavered. He kept trusting the Lord and doing what was right. And he was greatly used to bless the whole nation of Egypt and his family clan.

*Kingdom Secret: God already knew those He was one day going to save; and He had already destined them to be like His Son. He then invited them, declared them not guilty, and took them to glory.*
That is a loose version of Romans 8:29-30. The important *Kingdom Mystery* revealed here is that bringing us into the Kingdom was not an afterthought or a last-minute decision. It was planned. *We* were planned. Way ahead of time.

*Kingdom Secret: Paul's victory song says God is always for us!*
This majestic song appears in Romans 8:31-39. The main idea is that God is for us no matter what. God didn't even spare His Son; and is willing to give us everything else, with Him. No one can accuse God's elect, since God justifies them; nor condemn them, since Jesus died for them and intercedes for them at God's right hand. Nobody can separate them from Christ's love, not even anguish, persecution, famine, danger or the threat of death. Though the followers of Jesus are like sheep to be slaughtered, in Him they are more than victorious. Not even life or death, angels or rulers, the present or the future, or any created thing can separate us from the love of God through Jesus our Lord!

## [GK] Romans 9, 10 - Representatives in the Global Kingdom

In Romans nine, ten and eleven Paul addresses the issue of Israel and the Church. (Though Paul does not use the term "church" in theses passages, he speaks of "Gentiles" who have been justified by faith). This is a critical issue for the Kingdom, since Israel was the Kingdom representative in the Old Testament and the Church has had this role from the New Testament days until the present day.

## [GK] Romans 11 - Israel and the Kingdom

We are in the Church age. But does that mean Israel is out of the picture? Paul answers emphatically: "By no means!" and "not at all!" (Romans 11:1, 11). The two *Kingdom Secrets* below explain why.

*Kingdom Secret: The hearts of Jews have been hardened for a season*
"So that you will not be conceited, brothers, I do not want you to be unaware of this mystery: A partial hardening has come to Israel until the full number of the

Gentiles has come in" (Romans 11:25 - HCSB). This **Kingdom Secret** sheds light on why Jewish people have remained so closed to the Gospel. It also reveals there is a known amount of Gentiles who will "come in" to the Kingdom. When that number is complete, then Israel's hardened heart problem will be over.

## *Kingdom Secret: One day all Israel will be saved*

At the end, when the season of Israel's hardened heart is over, all Israel will be saved. "And in this way all Israel will be saved, as it is written: 'The Liberator will come from Zion; He will turn away godlessness from Jacob. And this will be My covenant with them when I take away their sins'" (Romans 11:26-27 - HCSB).

## The *it's all about God Kingdom Principle*

"For from Him and through Him and to Him are all things. To Him be the glory forever. Amen" (Romans 11:36 - HCSB). Everything that is, came from God; all that exists, exists for God. He is the originator, conceptualizer, creator, and sustainer. This being the case, why should anyone else receive the ultimate glory?

## Romans 12 - A list of *Kingdom Values*

Romans 12 is a very practical passage, with a long list of **Kingdom Values**. These are some that can be found there (see chapters 4 and 5 about **Kingdom Values** for further details on each value):

- Verse 1: **Holiness** (being holy), **worship** (your spiritual worship);
- Verse 2: **Goodness** (good… will of God);
- Verse 3: **Grace**, **humility** (not thinking more highly of oneself than one should); **faith** (measure of faith);
- Verse 5: **Mutuality** (one body in Christ, members of one another);
- Verse 6: **Grace** (the grace given to us);
- Verse 7: **Service** (as a spiritual gift);
- Verse 8: **Benevolence** / giving (with generosity), **encouraging** (exhorting), **mercy** (showing mercy);
- Verse 9: **Love**, **exposing evil** (detest evil), **goodness** (cling to what is good);
- Verse 10: **Brotherly affection** (family affection …brotherly love), **honoring** (outdo one another in showing honor);
- Verse 11: **Service** (serve the Lord);
- Verse 12: **Rejoicing in the Lord** (Rejoice in hope), **patience** (be patient in affliction), **prayer** (be persistent in prayer);
- Verse 13: **Preferring other believers** (share with the saints in their needs); **hospitality** (pursue hospitality);
- Verse 14: **Being persecuted** (bless those who persecute you);
- Verse 15: **Rejoicing in the Lord** (rejoice with those who rejoice);

- Verse 16: **Harmony** (be in agreement with one another), **humility** (do not be proud; associate with the humble; not wise in your own estimation);
- Verse 17: **Forgiving** (do not repay anyone evil for evil); **witnessing** (try to do what is honorable in everyone's eyes);
- Verse 18: **Reconciliation** (live at peace with everyone);
- Verse 19: **Enduring suffering** (do not avenge yourselves);
- Verse 20: **Grace** (if your enemy is hungry, feed him);
- Verse 21: **Goodness** (conquer evil with good).

## [GK] Romans 13 - The *Kingdom Principle* of authority

Paul lays out the principles in these statements, found in verses 1-7:

1) All authority comes from God;
2) Positions of authority have been assigned by God;
3) Rebelling against authorities means rebelling against what God has established;
4) Rebelling against authority brings punishment;
5) Authorities don't bring fear to those who do right, but to wrongdoers;
6) Authorities are God's servants, there for your good and to punish wrongdoers;
7) You must submit to authority (to avoid punishment and maintain a clear conscience);
8) Give respect and honor to those in authority;
9) Pay your taxes (government workers need to be paid); and pay your debts.

We could say this is the ideal we hope for in a fallen world. It is based on authorities who truly do go after the bad guys, not the good guys. We are not called to interpret the laws of the land, nor to try to manipulate them in our favor, or use "religious" excuses. But when there is sincere doubt, or following human law would go against our Christian conscience, we must revert to item one on the list: "all authority comes from God."

Let's remember a very real and practical situation. "The apostles were brought in and made to appear before the Sanhedrin to be questioned by the high priest. 'We gave you strict orders not to teach in this name,' he said. 'Yet you have filled Jerusalem with your teaching and are determined to make us guilty of this man's blood' (Acts 5:27-28 - NIV). "But Peter and the apostles replied, 'We must obey God rather than any human authority'" (Acts 5:29 - NLT). They had been told to stop preaching about Jesus. So they reverted back to item one and told the human religious authorities that their ultimate allegiance was with God, His will and His command. The use of the term "rather" doesn't imply they did not obey human authority, but carries the idea of "more than."

## [GK] Romans 14 - Don't judge; every knee will bow; accountability; righteousness

### The *don't judge your brother or sister* Kingdom Principle
Christ is the Lord to Whom we and our brothers and sisters will answer. Since they do not answer to us, we have no business judging them.

Paul addresses the ultimate issue of life and death when he declares that whether we live or die, we live or die for the Lord, because we belong to Him. And Christ died and rose again to be Lord over both the dead and living. For this reason we should abstain from judging our brothers and sisters, thinking we are better than they, because we will all stand before God and be judged by *Him* (Romans 14:7-10). That is why "you cannot judge another person's servant. The master decides if the servant is doing well or not. And the Lord's servant will do well because the Lord helps him do well" (Romans 14:4 - NCV).

There are mutuality **Kingdom Values**, the "one another" actions which build each other up. "Judging one another" is not one of them. Judging is not a spiritual gift, but has at its root bitterness, envy, anger, or a desire for revenge. Hardly edification values. No Kingdom citizen should be on a mission to humiliate, denigrate, destroy, and tear down other people. Paul insists with the Romans that "for that reason we should stop judging each other" or "no longer criticize one another" (Romans 14:13 - NCV and HCSB respectively). Instead, "we must pursue what promotes peace and what builds up one another" (v. 19 - HCSB).

### The *every knee shall bow* Kingdom Principle
"As I live, says the Lord, every knee will bow to Me, and every tongue will give praise to God" (Romans 14:11 - HCSB; Paul, quoting Isaiah 45:23). By some estimates, only close to 10% of the Earth's population is saved. That means there are millions—or potentially billions—of people who are on their way to eternity who have never acknowledged the lordship of Jesus or the sovereignty of God. But one day they will. One day, "at the name of Jesus every knee should bow, in heaven and on earth and under the earth, and every tongue confess that Jesus Christ is Lord, to the glory of God the Father" (Philippians 2:10-11 - ESV). Every living and dead soul will confess God is King. Unfortunately, for most it will be too late to make a difference in their eternal destiny.

### The *everybody is accountable to God* Kingdom Principle
"So then, each of us will give an account of himself to God" (Romans 14:12 - HCSB; see also Ecclesiastes 12:7). Those who refuse to bow down and acknowledge God as Lord and King in this life will still have to appear before Him on judgment day and answer for all they have done in life. Christ followers are not

exempt. Paul explains elsewhere, however, that ours will be more like an evaluation, not for eternal condemnation, but for rewards (see "**Kingdom Secret**: We must all appear before Christ to be evaluated," under 2 Corinthians 5:10, below). Knowing we are accountable to God should motivate us to live each day responsibly and intentionally. It's God's Kingdom, He's the final authority, and He deserves our best.

### The *righteousness Kingdom Principle*

"For the kingdom of God is not eating and drinking, but righteousness, peace, and joy in the Holy Spirit" (Romans 14:17 - HCSB). This whole chapter deals with controversies related to eating and drinking. But the Kingdom is not about "dos" and "don'ts" or legalistic rules. It's about righteousness, the standard of the Kingdom which sums up all of God's will, all the good He wants *for* us and *from* us. This inevitably leads to peace—with God and with one another. Peace, not strife. Or nit-picking.

Peace results in joy in the Holy Spirit, because joy is a fruit of the Spirit (Galatians 5:22). And "whoever serves Christ in this way is acceptable to God and approved by men" (Romans 14:18 - HCSB).

### [GK] Romans 16 - God's Kingdom defeats kingdom of darkness

***Kingdom Secret**: "And the God of peace will crush Satan under your feet shortly" (Romans 16:20a - NKJV).*
Prophecies have several functions, one of the main being to encourage. And how encouraging to know our archenemy is going to be irreversibly defeated in the end. How good to know our King is sovereign and by His power and authority has declared Satan is going down. In Paris there is a large statue of "Saint Michael" stepping on an ugly and angry diabolical figure. It is a reminder that God will one day crush Satan under our feet (see Revelation 12:7-9; see Psalm 108:13).

While we wait for this to happen, Paul wishes "the grace of our Lord Jesus Christ be with you. Amen" (Romans 16:20b - NKJV). Paul ends his letter to the Roman believers exclaiming, "to God, alone wise, be glory through Jesus Christ forever. Amen" (Romans 16:27 - NKJV).

# The Kingdom in 1ˢᵗ and 2ⁿᵈ Corinthians

**[GK] [EK] 1 Corinthians 2 - Mystery of the Kingdom seen by few; revealed by the Holy Spirit**

### The Secret Wisdom of the Kingdom:
The secret of Kingdom wisdom is including God and eternity in the equation of life. This secret wisdom has nothing to do with the "wisdom" of the rulers of this age. "On the contrary, we speak God's hidden wisdom in a mystery, a wisdom God predestined before the ages for our glory" (1 Corinthians 2:7 - HCSB). Paul says that if the rulers of this age had understood this wisdom "they would not have crucified the Lord of glory" (1 Corinthians 2:8 - NIV). Paul then exclaims:

> No eye has seen, no ear has heard, and no mind has imagined the things that God has prepared for those who love him. But God has revealed those things to us by his Spirit. For the Spirit searches everything, even the deep things of God. (1 Corinthians 2:9-10 - ISV)

Before creating us, God had already planned extraordinary things for those who were to inherit the Kingdom. Although the Scriptures allude to some of what awaits us on the other side, the human mind cannot comprehend what eternity holds in store for the saved. We learn by observation and are limited by our experience. Even the most creative minds have trouble imagining that which is not part of our reality. For instance: try to imagine a new color, one you have never seen before. Were you successful? All that comes to mind are colors from our visible spectrum of light with their hues, tints, tones and shades, all of which we have seen before.

### The secret knowledge of the Kingdom
It's like we, Kingdom citizens, have been given a pair of glasses through which we can see another dimension. We see and feel fundamental spiritual matters so clearly. Yet when we point to them and try to show others, they don't see what we see. They don't want it anyway, they imply. They don't feel a need for it. They just don't get it. "But the unbeliever does not welcome what comes from God's Spirit, because it is foolishness to him; he is not able to understand it since it is evaluated spiritually" (1 Corinthians 2:14 - HCSB). To "get it" we must have the Holy Spirit (1 Corinthians 2:12). We must have the mind of Christ. His followers do (1 Corinthians 2:16).

**[GK] [EK] 1 Corinthians 3 - Worldly wisdom; God has given us everything**

## Worldly wisdom is foolishness to God

Paul again addresses the issue of wisdom, this time stressing that "the wisdom of this world is foolishness with God" and that "the Lord knows that the reasonings of the wise are meaningless" (1 Corinthians 3:19-20 - HCSB). How could a tiny brain, trapped in a physical body, limited to time and space, try to outsmart God? Atheists try every day. But others—atheists or not—deep down, believe their way is better than God's way. Otherwise they would have come to Him and aligned their life with His Kingdom standard and values. Whether outright rebellious or subtly placing God on the margin of their lives, they rely on worldly wisdom to maneuver through the ups and downs of life.

## "Everything is yours"

An inheritance. A hidden treasure. The Kingdom the Father is pleased to give us (Luke 12:32 - NLT). Paul had asked the Roman Christians, "If God didn't hesitate to put everything on the line for us, embracing our condition and exposing himself to the worst by sending his own Son, is there anything else he wouldn't gladly and freely do for us?" (Romans 8:32 - MSG). Here he tells the Christians in Corinth they should not boast about their leaders, choosing one famous name over the other, "for everything is yours," whether "the world or life or death or things present or things to come—everything is yours, and you belong to Christ, and Christ belongs to God" (1 Corinthians 3:21-23 - HCSB).

We have been sealed with the Holy Spirit as proof that we belong to Christ and have eternal life; we are "in Christ" and Christ is in us; our loving Father takes care of us (Matthew 6:11, 32-33); God has taken us into His family, as His children (Ephesians 3:14). He has indeed given us all we need here and in the hereafter.

## [GK] [EK] 1 Corinthians 6 - Redeemed to judge the world; unrighteous denied access

*Kingdom Secret: We will judge the world. We will judge the angels.*
Paul scolds the church in Corinth because believers were suing each other. Instead of resolving issues among themselves, they were taking matters to the courts. So Paul asks them, "Do you not know that the holy ones will judge the world? If the world is to be judged by you, are you unqualified for the lowest law courts? Do you not know that we will judge angels? Then why not everyday matters?" (1 Corinthians 6:2-3 - NABRE).

Paul said to find someone in the church who is able to settle their cases instead of resorting to the secular court system. And if there is not, then it is preferable to suffer injustice and loss than to drag each other to court (1 Corinthians 6:4-8).

**Kingdom warning:** *The unrighteous will not inherit God's kingdom*
"Don't you realize that those who do wrong [the unrighteous] will not inherit the Kingdom of God? Don't fool yourselves. Those who indulge in sexual sin, or who worship idols, or commit adultery, or are male prostitutes, or practice homosexuality, or are thieves, or greedy people, or drunkards, or are abusive, or cheat people—none of these will inherit the Kingdom of God" (1 Corinthians 6:9-10 - NLT). Despite this warning, many today are being deceived. God's standard of righteousness and His **Kingdom Values** do not and cannot change. If we attempt to declare *any* one of these sins on the list as acceptable before the Lord (even something as "harmless" as greed), we are only deceiving ourselves.

If your favorite sin is on this list (or any other list in Scripture), you need the antidote for unrighteousness given in 1 John 1:9. Following these instructions, you can go from being unrighteous to righteous. And this is not a "one time only" remedy. Don't abuse it, but use it as often as necessary: "If we confess our sins, He is faithful and righteous to forgive us our sins and to cleanse us from all unrighteousness" (HCSB).

Who will ultimately inherit the Kingdom and who will be denied entrance?[1] We are not called to judge, much less make that decision. That is up to the Lord. One thing is for sure, "God's solid foundation stands firm, having this inscription: The Lord knows those who are His, and everyone who names the name of the Lord must turn away from unrighteousness" (2 Timothy 2:19 - HCSB).

Some members of the church in Corinth could identify with what Paul was saying because, as he told them, "Such were some of you; but you were washed, but you were sanctified, but you were justified in the name of the Lord Jesus Christ and in the Spirit of our God" (1 Corinthians 6:11 - NASB; see also Titus 3:3-7).

## [UK] [GK] [MK] 1 Corinthians 15 - Kingdom returned to Father; these bodies don't get in

***Kingdom Secret:*** *Jesus will defeat all His enemies, then turn the Kingdom back over to the Father.*
This is precious inside information. Paul writes about the resurrection: Jesus' which came first, then of those who belong to Him, when Christ comes back. "After that the end will come when he will turn the Kingdom over to God the Father, having put down all enemies of every kind. For Christ will be King until he has defeated all his enemies" (1 Corinthians 15:24-25 - TLB). This will happen at the end of the Millennial Kingdom. The final enemy is death, which will be done away with at the end. After Messiah has vanquished all enemies, He "will put himself

also under his Father's orders, so that God who has given him the victory over everything else will be utterly supreme" (1 Corinthians 15:28 - TLB).

### *Kingdom Secret: These old bodies cannot inherit the Kingdom. So, we're getting new ones!*

"What I am saying, dear brothers and sisters, is that our physical bodies cannot inherit the Kingdom of God. These dying bodies cannot inherit what will last forever" (1 Corinthians 15:50 - NLT). The operative word here is "inherit." To inherit the Kingdom is to receive or enter eternal life. We can't take our bodies with us when we go to heaven (neither would we want to!). There are no physical flesh and blood individuals in the eternal state, nor can there be.

Therefore, Paul unveils a mystery, a new revelation: not all believers are going to die. Some will be transformed in the blinking of an eye, when the last trumpet sounds. That's when those who have already died will be resurrected and those alive instantaneously transformed, receiving an incorruptible and immortal body. Death is going to lose and instead there will be eternal life and victory through Jesus! This describes the Rapture, which is when the resurrection—the redemption of the body—takes place.

At the end of this revelation, Paul encourages believers: "So then, dear brothers and sisters, be firm. Do not be moved! Always be outstanding in the work of the Lord, knowing that your labor is not in vain in the Lord." (1 Corinthians 15:58 - NET Bible). This is a very practical verse, but how does it relate to what was just said? It is shortly after the Rapture and resurrection that rewards are awarded, based on fruitfulness and faithfulness (1 Corinthians 3:14; Colossians 3:23, 24; Revelation 22:12). That is almost certainly why Paul said our labor in the Lord is not in vain. Working for the Lord and seeing no immediate results can be extremely discouraging. "William Carey spent seven years in India before seeing his first convert."[2] Yet his efforts sparked the modern-day missions movement, and he and his team succeeded in translating the Bible into several languages. He also left behind many contributions to the Indian society. More importantly, Carey did what he did for the Lord. Current marketing techniques tell us to change strategies quickly if we don't see results. But in the Kingdom, if we are under God's orders to do something, we stay the course and leave the results to God.

## [GK] [UK] 2 Corinthians 5 - faith vs. sight; final evaluation

### The *walking by faith not by sight Kingdom Principle*

The way God's Kingdom operates makes it necessary to take Him at His word; to believe God each day, even though we don't "see" Him; and to trust Him for all He promised will be coming after this life. "So we are always confident, knowing that while we are at home in the body, we are absent from the Lord. For we walk by faith, not by sight" (2 Corinthians 5:6-7 - NKJV).

We must remember life is a test, and part of the test is learning to trust God even when it doesn't seem to make sense. We can learn to do so by reminding ourselves of God's track record and His character. We know "it is impossible for God to lie" (Hebrews 6:18). Still, when the crises come, when our emotions are out of whack, when the desires of our lower nature flare up, walking by faith and not by what we see, feel and perceive to be reality, is a very challenging thing indeed.

### *Kingdom Secret: We must all appear before Christ to be evaluated*

What was Paul's aim in life? He had several goals: spread the Gospel, plant churches, and strengthen disciples, to name a few. But what was the motivating factor behind all of this? In management by objective terms, we could ask: what is the Key Objective that defined the Critical Performance Areas and drove the Specific Objectives? It was quite simple: "To be pleasing to God." To be pleasing to God implied obedience, surrender, self-denial, and faithfulness to God. Jesus called it seeking the Kingdom first. Paul put it this way: "Therefore we make it our aim, whether present or absent, to be well pleasing to Him" (2 Corinthians 5:9 - NKJV).

To be pleasing to God is to keep in mind we will stand before our Lord and give an account of everything we have done. This helps keep the believer focused and in check. This is the *bema* or "judgment seat" judgment, which will be the believer's final evaluation. To ignore this future event is foolish. The *bema* judgment will probably take place right before the promised rewards are awarded. Paul explained: "We must all appear before the judgment seat of Christ, that each one may receive the things done in the body, according to what he has done, whether good or bad" (2 Corinthians 5:10 - NKJV).

I have in my office a handwritten poem on yellowed paper, held by a simple wooden frame. It was composed in 1939, by my father, William Alvin Hatton, when he was 18 years old. It expresses his aim in life.

> *My Heart's Desire*
>
> *My heart's desire*
> *Is to be on fire*
> *For those who are lost in sin.*
>
> *My heart's desire*
> *Is to help from mire*
> *Condemned and dying men.*

*My heart's desire*
*Is to never tire*
*In doing what God wants me to.*

*My heart's desire*
*Is to inspire*
*All that I can to live anew.*

And this he did till the day he died. He and my mother served as missionaries in Brazil for 40 years. My father began an organization called Royal Ambassadors there and is to this day remembered by thousands of youth in that country as an inspiration to represent the King on Earth in a manner worthy of His name and calling.

# The Kingdom in Galatians

[GK] **Galatians 3 - A Kingdom Promise: sonship**

*Kingdom Secret: We are sons of God, through faith in Jesus*
"For in Christ Jesus you are all sons of God through faith. For as many [of you] as were baptized into Christ [into a spiritual union and communion with Christ, the Anointed One, the Messiah] have put on (clothed yourselves with) Christ" (Galatians 3:26-27 - AMP). Because the Son of God became our Savior when He died in our place, we can now be adopted as sons and daughters into God's family—if we repent and believe. This is clear: "But to all who believed him and accepted him, he gave the right to become children of God" (John 1:12 - NLT).

[GK] **Galatians 5 - A Kingdom Warning; the fruit of the Spirit**

*Kingdom Secret: Those who are continually ruled by the sinful nature will not inherit God's kingdom.*
This is similar to the list already seen in 1 Corinthians 6:9-10, but names a few more sins. Paul enumerates the ugly consequences of the "works of the flesh," which is what happens when people are ruled by their fallen human nature.

> It is obvious what kind of life develops out of trying to get your own way all the time: repetitive, loveless, cheap sex; a stinking accumulation of mental and emotional garbage; frenzied and joyless grabs for happiness; trinket gods; magic-show religion; paranoid loneliness; cutthroat competition; all-consuming-yet-never-satisfied wants; a brutal temper; an impotence to love or be loved; divided homes and divided lives; small-minded and lop-

sided pursuits; the vicious habit of depersonalizing everyone into a rival; uncontrolled and uncontrollable addictions; ugly parodies of community. I could go on. This isn't the first time I have warned you, you know. If you use your freedom this way, you will not inherit God's kingdom.
(Galatians 5:19-21 - MSG)

This is a serious warning. As my former boss and good friend George Foster once said, "whatever your theological position [such as the perseverance of the saints, falling from grace, or the believer's eternal security], one thing is for sure: there is no safety in sin."

**Each aspect of the fruit of the Spirit is a *Kingdom Value***
Paul told the Galatian believers to "walk by the Spirit." Being controlled by the Holy Spirit demands denying the flesh and allowing God to have free rein in our lives. Only then will the Holy Spirit produce the results or fruit enumerated in this list: love, joy, peace, patience, kindness, goodness, faithfulness, gentleness, and self-control.[3]

While the works of the flesh are all lawless and sinful activities and attitudes, when it comes to the fruit of the Spirit, "there is no law against things like this. Those who belong to Christ Jesus have crucified the self with its passions and its desires" (Galatians 5:23b, 24 - CEB). Kingdom citizens should consistently walk in the Spirit, "crucify" their "self" and evil desires (see Galatians 2:20), and manifest the fruit of the Spirit in their daily lives, inside and outside of church.

# The Kingdom in Ephesians

[UK] [GK] **Ephesians 1 - Kingdom destiny**

***Kingdom Secret: the mystery of His will–destined to be blameless, heirs***
When we search the Bible for deeper truths about God's Kingdom, we won't always find the term "kingdom" being used. A good example is Ephesians chapter 1. Here Paul speaks of being blessed in the heavenly realms by God. God's Kingdom was already populated with celestial beings, but He wanted more subjects, so He set in motion His plan to create... *us*! He started out with an ideal in mind: we were to be holy and blameless. In order to accomplish this, He decided beforehand to adopt us through Jesus, showing His favor to us (see Ephesians 1:3-6). He chose, predestined, adopted, redeemed, forgave and lavished us with His grace.

God knew we would have to be bought back from sin, so He offered His Son through Whom we would "have redemption in Him through His blood, the forgiveness of our trespasses, according to the riches of His grace that He lavished on us" (Ephesians 1:7-8 - HCSB).

God revealed "the mystery of His will" which was to unite everything in heaven and Earth through Messiah Jesus. With this, we were given an inheritance and sealed with the Holy Spirit as "the down payment" (Ephesians 1:14 - HCSB; see also verses 9-13). All of this would be for God's praise and glory. Jesus said all authority had been given to Him in both heaven and Earth, and one day Jesus will bring these two realms of the Kingdom together. (At the end, all aspects will fuse into one Eternal Kingdom).

This may sound complicated, but if the Ephesians could get it, we can too. But not without God's Holy Spirit to guide us. That's why Paul asked the Lord to give them "the Spirit of wisdom and revelation," and prayed they would understand the hope and rich inheritance to which we've been called.

This chapter ends by speaking of King Jesus, Who was raised, seated at God's right hand in heaven, and had everything placed under His authority, power and dominion. Can you see how many references are made to Kingdom features in this passage? God wants us to be enlightened. He wants us to connect the dots and to be Kingdom-minded. He wants us to place our hope in the inheritance we have in His Kingdom!

## [UK]-[EK] Ephesians 2 - Raised and seated with Christ

### *Kingdom Secret: in Christ we have a position in the heavenly realm*
"For he raised us from the dead along with Christ and seated us with him in the heavenly realms because we are united with Christ Jesus" (Ephesians 2:6 - NLT). We were raised and seated. Both of these are in the past tense. Something has already taken place, or is so sure that it's as though it has already occurred. For all intents and purposes, it's a done deal. Those who are "in Christ" share in His death, resurrection, and life. God has raised us up *with* Jesus. Paul said, "I want to know Christ and experience the mighty power that raised him from the dead" (Philippians 3:1a - NLT).

To be seated with Christ is a privilege which entails more than we could know at this point. Yet we know it is a privilege of cosmic proportions. To be seated with Christ means we enjoy His presence and fellowship. And, "if we endure" here and now, "we will also reign with Him" in the hereafter (Revelation 2:26-27; 2 Timothy 2:12).

"Being caused to sit down with" (Greek **synekathisen**)[4] with Christ in the heavenly realm means being "enthroned with him in heaven," according to Charles Hodge.[5] The clear implication is "that we have part (see on 1 Corinthians 6:2) in the dominion of the Exalted One (2 Timothy 2:12); which Paul likewise sees as already accomplished with the installing of Christ at the right hand of God"[6]. Many commentators agree that our close association and identification with Christ leads to partaking in the honors and glory ascribed to Him because of His victory over sin and death. This is another consequence of being "in Christ," an important theme in this letter. This would include reigning with Him in His Millennial and Eternal Kingdom. Although we are here in the Global Kingdom, things have already been influenced, prepared and set in motion for us, by God's favor and grace, in eternity.

## [GK] Ephesians 5 - Darkness vs. Light; and another warning

*Kingdom Secret: those in darkness will not inherit the Kingdom*
"For of this you can be sure: No immoral, impure or greedy person—such a person is an idolater—has any inheritance in the kingdom of Christ and of God" (Ephesians 5:5 - NIV). God's word is emphatic: "no," "has any," and "let no one deceive you with empty words, for because of such things God's wrath comes on those who are disobedient" (Ephesians 5:6 - NIV). There are no exceptions given, no excuses provided. It's all or nothing. (See *Kingdom warning: The unrighteous will not inherit God's kingdom,* above, concerning 1 Corinthians 6:9-10, to see what Scripture says about how to deal with these and other sins).

Paul had been more specific prior to the statement above, providing a list that includes sexual immorality (of which, he said, there should not even be a hint), impurity, greed, obscenity, foolish talk and coarse joking. He called practicing these things "darkness." He told the believers in Ephesus, "For you were once darkness, but now you are light in the Lord. Live as children of light" (Ephesians 5:8 - NIV). And, the "fruit of the light consists in all goodness, righteousness and truth" (Ephesians 5:9 - NIV). Righteousness is the standard of the Kingdom; goodness and truth are **Kingdom Values**.

Believers *are* light, are *in* the light, and must live as children *of* the light. They belong to God, Who "has qualified you to share in the inheritance of his holy people in the kingdom of light" (Colossians 1:12 - NIV). They have been rescued "from the kingdom of darkness," from Satan's dominion (Colossians 1:13 - NLT), a domain characterized by evil, unrighteousness and lies, just the opposite of the fruit of light.

Whereas giving a lot of fruit glorifies God the Father (John 15:8), we are to "have nothing to do with the fruitless deeds of darkness, but rather expose them" (Ephesians 5:11, 13 - NIV). Did you catch that? The deeds of darkness, like the ones stated above, produce no fruit! They are selfish, they don't build up or serve anybody, and contribute nothing to the family, the church or society. Much to the contrary: they are detrimental, corruptive, and destructive. They are the antithesis of everything God's Kingdom stands for. Which is why they provoke God's wrath.

# The Kingdom in Philippians

### [L&K] [GK] Philippians 2 - Hyper exalted, with a name above all

Jesus is the King and, as such, is not only our supreme commander, He is our most excellent example of how to conduct ourselves in His Kingdom. Paul, therefore, tells his brothers and sisters in Philippi to have the same attitude Jesus did because, although He was God, He did not grab onto His divine prerogatives but left His glory behind, was born like a human being, lived like a servant, and humbled Himself to the point of dying the worst kind of death, that is, death by crucifixion (Philippians 2:5-8).

"Therefore God also highly exalted him and gave him the name that is above every name, so that at the name of Jesus every knee should bend, in heaven and on earth and under the earth, and every tongue should confess that Jesus Christ is Lord, to the glory of God the Father" (Philippians 2:9-11 - NRSV). "Highly exalted," from the Greek verb *hyperypsōsen*, means to "exalt to the highest place,"[7] that is, to be "hyper exalted"!

The author of Hebrews says something very similar: "Looking to Jesus the pioneer and perfecter of our faith." This implies observing and following His example. He explains that Jesus "endured the cross, disregarding its shame" because of "the joy that was set before him." We can only deduce this was the joy of saving us so He could have us by His side forever. Finally, at the end of His sacrifice for us, He "has taken his seat at the right hand of the throne of God" (Hebrews 12:2 - NRSV). That is, He was glorified again and took His rightful place of authority over all creation.

What a wonderful King we have! He was willing to leave Heaven behind in order to come down to Earth disguised as a simple human being, suffer and die in our place and save us. That is why the Father exalted Him and why we owe Him an eternal debt of gratitude, our very lives, and everything we've got.

# The Kingdom in Colossians

**[L&K] [GK] [UK] Colossians 1 - Kingdom of darkness vs. Kingdom of light; Christ the Creator**

*Kingdom Secret: we've been transferred from the kingdom of darkness to the Kingdom of God's Son!*
We are "always thankful to the Father who has made us fit to share all the wonderful things that belong to those who live in the Kingdom of light. For he has rescued us out of the darkness and gloom of Satan's kingdom and brought us into the Kingdom of his dear Son, who bought our freedom with his blood and forgave us all our sins" (Colossians 1:12-14 - TLB).

We have just seen, in Ephesians 5, what it means to be in the Kingdom of light and the kingdom of darkness. Here we have the full picture, painted majestically to portray the wonderful rescue operation from which we benefited so much. Before we "saw the light," we were under Satan's influence, beneath a constant cloud of doom and gloom. We had no hope, no prospects in life, nothing really to live for. But Satan's domain was invaded by our rightful King, and we were delivered from our former bondage and transported over to the Kingdom of light, the Kingdom of God's dear Son, Who bought us back with His blood. He then gave us a fresh start, forgiving not some, not most, but *all* of our sins!

*Kingdom Secret: Christ created everything, including the spirit world with its kings and kingdoms, over which He is supreme.*
There are several Christological mysteries which are revealed and explained in this passage. First, "Christ is the exact likeness of the unseen God" (Colossians 1:15a - TLB). For us in the digital era, it may be easier to exemplify this truth. Because it would be like making a digital copy of a file on the computer. The copy is exactly the same as the original. Not that Jesus is a copy, but the idea is that of being of the exact same essence.

Second, there was a point in eternity before which God had not yet created anything. And yet Christ was there, because "He existed before God made anything at all" (Colossians 1:15b - TLB). We understand Jesus to be uncreated, ever existing, one with, and of the same essence as, God the Father.

Third, when the creation process began, Christ was directly involved. "In fact, Christ himself is the Creator who made everything in heaven and earth, the things we can see and the things we can't; the spirit world with its kings and kingdoms, its rulers and authorities; all were made by Christ for his own use and glory" (Colossians 1:15b, 16 - TLB). And it is He Who "holds everything together" (Colossians 1:17 - TLB). During the final weeks of His ministry, Jesus shared with His disciples that the Father had placed everything under His authority, in heaven and on earth. He has this authority because He "made everything in heaven and earth," the material, physical, and spiritual. Jesus is the One Who created positions of authority and placed beings there to be in charge, all answerable to Him, as He is supreme over all.

Which brings us to our fourth mystery revealed: Jesus "is the Head of the body made up of his people—that is, his Church—which he began" (Colossians 1:18a - TLB). In fact, "he is first in everything; for God wanted all of himself to be in his Son" (Colossians 1:18b, 19 - TLB).

As Creator, He made everything. As King, He structured a hierarchical system and placed rulers in their appropriate places, under His leadership. And as for the Church, He became its Head, and the Church became His "body."

# The Kingdom in 1st and 2nd Thessalonians

### [GK] 1 Thessalonians 2 - Behavior befitting the Kingdom

***Kingdom Fact:** Those called into the Kingdom must live in a manner that is worthy of their calling.*
When I was in my late teens, I went to downtown Rio de Janeiro to apply for a job teaching English. The director asked me what I was doing in Rio. I explained my parents had been missionaries there for close to 40 years. His demeanor changed abruptly, and he began to rant and rave about how the Church had been founded in order to exploit people financially and make its leaders rich. I told him I knew plenty of people who had given their life for the cause, serving others sacrificially and honestly—my parents included. But his mind was made up and that was the end of the interview since neither of us wanted me to work there after that.

Unfortunately, there has been so much exploitation, dishonest gain, and unacceptable behavior in the Church over the years. This is shameful and turns people away in droves. Paul, on the other hand, had a servant heart and a real desire to make a difference. He was a giver, not a taker.

Paul told the Thessalonians, "You and God are witnesses of how pure, honest, and blameless our conduct was among you who believe. You know very well that we treated each of you the way a father treats his children. We comforted and encouraged you, urging you to live in a manner worthy of God, who calls you into his kingdom and glory" (1 Thessalonians 2:10-12 - ISV).

All Kingdom citizens should conduct themselves in a way that is honoring to God and worthy of their calling.

## [GK] 1 Thessalonians 4 - The Rapture

***Kingdom Secret: believers who are alive at that time, will be raptured.***
(This **Kingdom Mystery** ties in with 1 Corinthians 15, above, subtitled **Kingdom Secret**: *These old bodies cannot inherit the Kingdom. So we're getting new ones!* )

Paul was concerned about the Thessalonians being ready to meet the Lord. At the end of a prayer for them, he expresses his hope that the Lord will keep them blameless and holy "before our God and Father at the coming of our Lord Jesus Christ with all His saints" (1 Thessalonians 3:13b - NKJV). He goes on to warn them to avoid sin and to remain holy. Then he gives them some of the best insight we have in Scripture pertaining to the Lord's return.

He tells them clearly that Jesus will come down from heaven with a loud command, the voice of the archangel (Michael?), and a trumpet blast, and with all the redeemed (their spirits) who have died. They will wait in the air while the glorified bodies of the "dead" are raised up and joined to them. Then those who are still alive will "all be changed in a moment, in the twinkling of an eye" and be snatched up. All the redeemed will then be together with the Lord "in the air" and forever (1 Corinthians 15:51-52 - NRSV).

Now let's see the verses themselves, as there remains so much controversy around this passage. It is from 1 Thessalonians 4 that we get our word "Rapture." First, "through Jesus God will bring those who have died with him" because, the Lord revealed to Paul, "we who are alive and remain until the coming of the Lord will by no means precede those who have died" (1 Thessalonians 4:14-15 - ISV).

Then there will be "a shout of command, with the archangel's call" and "the sound of God's trumpet" which is when "the Lord himself will come down from heaven, and the dead who belong to the Messiah will rise first" (1 Thessalonians 4:16 - ISV). At that point, "we who are alive and remain will be caught up in the clouds together with them to meet the Lord in the air. And so we will be with the Lord forever" (1 Thessalonians 4:17 - ISV).

"Rapture" comes from "caught up," and "came into use by way of the Latin *rapio* used to translate the Greek term of 1 Thessalonians 4:17, *harpagēsometha*."[8] The original meaning was to "seize by force; snatch up, suddenly and decisively—like someone seizing bounty (spoil, a prize); to take by an open display of force (i.e. not covertly or secretly)."[9]

There are mainly two areas of controversy surrounding this passage: 1) Is this the same as the Second Coming or a different event? 2) If not the same, when does the Rapture occur in relation to the Tribulation period? The first issue has more Biblical information to support the idea that this is not the same as the Second Coming, when Jesus will come back, bring the war of Armageddon to a close, and establish His Millennial Kingdom (Revelation 19 and 20). None of these factors are mentioned in 1 Thessalonians 4, which is a passage about the resurrection and when the living redeemed will meet the Lord in the air—*not* come down to Earth with Him. The second issue is much more difficult to solve, as Scripture is silent concerning the timing of the Rapture (there are no specific or conclusive verses about this). Many believe it will be just prior to the Tribulation period (pretribulationists). Others, that it will occur close to the middle of the Tribulation (midtribulationists or pre-wrath). And a few, that it will take place at the end of the Tribulation period (post-tribulationists). Bible students should study this issue carefully, yet we cannot do this here as it is outside of the scope of this book.

The Rapture is encouraging news (1 Thessalonians 4:18), and demonstrates the Lord's care for those who belong to Him. Jesus promised: "I am with you always, to the end of the age" (Matthew 28:20 - HCSB). As vital and wonderful as this is, it is limited to His spiritual presence, via the Holy Spirit, while we are in this physical realm, the Global Kingdom. But come the Rapture and "we will be with the Lord forever." We could say that now He is always with us; then we will always be with Him!

## [GK] 1 Thessalonians 5 - Wrath-free

***Kingdom Secret: believers are not destined to undergo the wrath of the Day of the Lord.***
Although "the Day of the Lord will come like a thief in the night," the truth is "you are not in the darkness, in order that the Day of the Lord might surprise you like a thief." But we must "stay awake and be sober," because "we belong to the day" (1 Thessalonians 5:2, 4, 6, 8 - ISV).

What is the Day of the Lord? As you look at the highlights of the Kingdom in the Old Testament, you will see many passages concerning the Day of the Lord included in the text. The Day of the Lord disrupts the Great Tribulation with God pouring down His wrath on an unrepentant, unbelieving, and rebellious world population. Although referred to as a "day," it is most likely the period required to exact God's vengeance on Earth, begin the process of our Lord's return, and bring the Battle of Armageddon to its conclusion. Immediately after these events He will inaugurate His Millennial Kingdom.

Although there is a great deal of controversy surrounding the timing of the Rapture of the Church, most agree the Church will not have to endure the Day of the Lord. First, because God's wrath is for the unrepentant; and second, because of Paul's very clear statement on the subject, which follows his reference of the Day of the Lord: "For God has not destined us to receive wrath but to obtain salvation through our Lord Jesus, the Messiah, who died for us in order that, whether we are awake or asleep, we may live together with him" (1 Thessalonians 5:9-10 - ISV).

### [GK] 2 Thessalonians 1 - Persecutors vs. persecuted

**The** *persecution brings about opposite results for persecuted and persecutors* **Kingdom Principle**
The persecuted who stand firm in the faith become worthy of the Kingdom, while the persecutors will be punished severely at the coming of the Lord. Paul commends the believers in Thessalonica for enduring persecution and remaining faithful through it all. "All of this proves that God's judgment is just and as a result you will become worthy of his Kingdom, for which you are suffering" (2 Thessalonians 1:5 - GNT). Enduring suffering is a **Kingdom Value**.

While God was using this persecution to strengthen their resolve and develop their faith, making them all the more worthy of the Kingdom, because God is just "he will bring suffering on those who make you suffer" and finally "give relief to you who suffer ... when the Lord Jesus appears from heaven with his mighty angels, with a flaming fire." He will "punish those who reject God and who do not obey the Good News about our Lord Jesus." Their punishment will be "eternal destruction" and separation from the Lord (2 Thessalonians 1:6-9 - GNT).

# The Kingdom in 1st and 2nd Timothy

### [L&K] 1 Timothy 1 - Grace leads to praise

***Kingdom Fact**: God's grace leads to praising the eternal King.*
Paul's testimony is that he used to be a blasphemer, persecute Jesus' followers, and was very prideful. But he was reached by God's grace so Christ's patience could be demonstrated to those who were going to be saved (1 Timothy 1:13-14, 16 - HCSB). And it was for this reason Paul said, "I give thanks to Christ Jesus our

Lord who has strengthened me, because He considered me faithful, appointing me to the ministry" (1 Timothy 1:12 - HCSB). This led him to express his gratefulness in a Kingdom doxology, declaring, "Now to the King eternal, immortal, invisible, the only God, be honor and glory forever and ever. Amen" (1 Timothy 1:17 - HCSB). God is the one and only King, Who is without beginning or end, cannot be seen by mortals, and deserves all honor and glory throughout eternity.

## [L&K] 1 Timothy 6 - Pursuing righteousness, fighting the good fight

***Kingdom fact*: Jesus is the King of kings and Lord of lords.**
Timothy is reminded to run from the temptations that come with the desire to become rich, and instead to "pursue righteousness" (the Kingdom's standard) and "godliness, faith, love, endurance, and gentleness" (all of which are **Kingdom Values**). He is to "fight the good fight for the faith," claim the eternal life he was called to, and be faithful to the commands he received, "without fault or failure until the appearing of our Lord Jesus Christ" which will happen in God's timing (1 Timothy 6:10-15 - HCSB).

Exultant, Paul declares that God is:

> The blessed and only Sovereign, the King of kings, and the Lord of lords, the only One who has immortality, dwelling in unapproachable light; no one has seen or can see Him, to Him be honor and eternal might. Amen. (1 Timothy 6:15-16 - HCSB).

## [GK] 2 Timothy 2 - Enduring and reigning

**The *if we endure for Him, we will reign with Him* Kingdom Principle**
If while on earth, our testing grounds, we remain faithful, if we deny and die to self, then "we will also live with Him; if we endure, we will also reign with Him" (2 Timothy 2:11-12 - HCSB). Although He remains faithful to Himself, He will deny those who deny Him, according to this trustworthy saying.

Jesus Himself warned His listeners, "And I say to you, everyone who confesses Me before men, the Son of Man will confess him also before the angels of God; but he who denies Me before men will be denied before the angels of God" (Luke 12:8-9 - NASB; see also Matthew 10:32 and Revelation 3:5).

## [GK] [MK] 2 Timothy 4 - Preach! For the Judge is coming; safe arrival to the heavenly kingdom

**The Kingdom as motivation to keep on preaching and teaching**
Paul solemnly charges Timothy, his disciple and son in the faith, to be prepared to

preach the message at any time, to "correct, rebuke and encourage," since the time was coming when people would not accept sound doctrine but would crave hearing what resonated with their own desires. All of this Timothy was to do "in the presence of God and of Christ Jesus, who will judge the living and the dead, and in view of his appearing and his kingdom" (2 Timothy 4:1-3 - NIV; see 1 Timothy 6:14-15). When Jesus comes back, it will no longer be as the Suffering Servant, but as the Reigning King. He first came as the Lamb of God then; He will come again as the Lion of Judah. As King, He will also exercise His authority as Judge.

By placing the Lord's "appearing" (*epiphany*, as in a visible manifestation) next to "and his kingdom," it is very likely Paul has in mind the establishment of the Millennial Kingdom right after His return.

The next verse says those who reject sound doctrine "will turn their ears away from the truth and turn aside to myths" (2 Timothy 4:4 - NIV). Have you noticed that those who refuse to believe in God—because they deem faith to be "unscientific," "irrational," "incompatible with higher reasoning," and "illogical"—will then open themselves to mystical religions, mythological fantasies, or the most illogical and nonsensical concepts, for which they demand no proof? If they don't allow the Holy Spirit to convince them, the enemy certainly will. Even so, the charge is given to "do the work of an evangelist" (2 Timothy 4:5 - NIV), a challenge we too must accept because we know many *will* believe.

## Paul confident of safe arrival to heavenly Kingdom
Paul had risked it all for the sake of his call, enduring hardships, persecution, attempts on his life, and the threat of execution. But during his whole ministry he could say "the Lord stood by me and gave me strength" and "I was rescued from the lion's mouth" (2 Timothy 4:17 - NIV). Paul was certain the Lord would continue to protect him to the end. He declared, "The Lord will rescue me from every evil attack and will bring me safely to his heavenly kingdom. To him be glory for ever and ever. Amen" (2 Timothy 4:18 - NIV).

The "heavenly Kingdom" refers to heaven. Heaven is the headquarters of God's Universal Kingdom. Those who are now in heaven will come back with Jesus to establish the Millennial Kingdom. After the Millennial Kingdom draws to a close, we can say the Universal, Global and Millennial aspects will have run their course and that, from that point forward, there will only be the Eternal Kingdom. This is similar to the fact that the old covenants (the Noahic, Abrahamic, Mosaic, and Davidic) were superseded by the New Covenant. They all had their importance in their time, but were stepping stones to God's ultimate goal.

It is true those who are in heaven are in an eternal state, as they will never again die. And it could be said that heaven can presently be called "the Eternal Kingdom." And that would be Biblical (2 Peter 1:11) and accurate. Yet, this study prefers to reserve that term for the final phase, as explained in the previous paragraph, in order not to confuse the Kingdom aspects.

# Chapter 10

# The General Letters

## The Kingdom in the book of Hebrews

**[L&K] [UK] [GK] Hebrews 1 - The Son reflects the Father**

God's highest revelation of Himself to humanity came through His Son, "to whom he has given everything and through whom he made the world and everything there is" (Hebrews 1:2 - TLB). There could be no better revelation than the one received through Jesus, because "the Son is the radiance of God's glory and the exact expression of His nature" (Hebrews 1:3a - HCSB). Besides, He sustains all creation with His power, made purification for our sins, and then "sat down at the right hand of the Majesty on high" (Hebrews 1:3b - HCSB).

*Kingdom Secret: the Son is to be worshipped, He is called "God," His Kingdom is forever, He is Creator, Lord, will reign with a scepter of justice, and loves righteousness.*

God never told angels what He told Jesus: "You are My Son; today I have become Your Father" (Hebrews 1:5 - HCSB). This verse states the supremacy of Jesus over the angels and His identification with God the Father. It identifies the Royal Son of Psalm 2, which is being quoted with the Lord Jesus (see Psalm 2:7). "Today I have become Your Father" refers to Jesus' incarnation, the day He also became human, when God brought "his firstborn into the world" (Hebrews 1:6 - HCSB). It does *not* refer to a *time* in eternity past when the Father decided to beget or create the Second Person of the Trinity. Jesus is without beginning.

God ordered all angels to worship the Son. While the angels are messengers, God calls the Son "God" and declares His throne to be forever. God says of Him, "the scepter of Your kingdom is a scepter of justice. You have loved righteousness and hated lawlessness" (Hebrews 1: 8-9 - HCSB). Similar to what we have seen above, Jesus is said to have established the earth and that the heavens are His own creation.

The confirmation that Jesus is Creator, Lord, God, the Son and is to be worshiped even by the angels is an important reminder. The reaffirmation that His is a Kingdom of justice and righteousness is fundamental to understanding the King's character and the Kingdom's characteristics.

*Kingdom Secret: The Earth and the heavens will perish.*
They will wear out like clothing, God will roll them up and they will be changed like a robe, while God will remain the same and never cease to exist (Hebrews 1: 11-12 - HCSB). The universe being "changed" points to the New Heavens and New Earth (see below, under *2 Peter 3*, "**Kingdom Secret: God will create New Heavens and New Earth**").

*Kingdom Secret* (**agents**): *Angels are messengers, sent to serve those who will be saved.*
While God invited the Son to "sit at My right hand until I make Your enemies Your footstool," angels are "ministering spirits sent out to serve those who are going to inherit salvation" (Hebrews 1: 13-14 - HCSB). Angels have a vital role in the Kingdom as they are God's secret agents who, among other assignments, are sent to serve those who will inherit the Kingdom. They are created beings. They are not God—not even gods—and are not to be worshiped or venerated. Jesus, on the other hand, has a special relationship with the Father, sitting on His right hand of His throne, and having the promise of complete victory over His foes.

## [UK] [GK] Hebrews 2 - The position of humans; bringing people to glory; our Older Brother

*Kingdom Mystery: humans given a special place of authority over creation*
David writes, "You made him little less than God..." (Psalm 8:5a - HCSB). The LXX (the Septuagint) has "angels" but the Hebrew *Elohim* can mean "God," "gods," or "heavenly beings" (Holman Christian Standard Bible's footnote). The author of Hebrews is quoting from Psalm 8 and that passage relates to humans. In that Psalm, David wonders, as he observed God's handiwork—the heavens with the moon and stars, how God could take puny little human beings into account. Looking up towards the Milky Way on a cloudless night, before the invention of electricity, was sure to have been breathtaking. I remember doing this many times, when all lights were out, up at the camp site my parents ran. It does make one feel tiny. It is awe-inspiring and speaks volumes of the glory of God.

David continues his psalm: "and crowned him with glory and honor. You made him lord over the works of Your hands; You put everything under his feet" (Hebrews 2:5-6 - HCSB). But when David describes the "everything" that is "under his feet," he lists domestic and wild animals, birds and fish (Psalm 8:7-8). This is consistent with Genesis 1:26-28, when God initially placed the earth and its animals under humanity's rule.

Before quoting this psalm, the author of Hebrews says that God "has not subjected to angels the world to come that we are talking about" (Hebrews 2:5 - HCSB). It would seem superfluous to say that the eternal state will be subject to Jesus after all that was said about the Son in chapter one. The logical interpretation would be that redeemed human beings, who have elsewhere been promised to reign with Christ, are the ones to whom the world to come will be subjected, which would include having authority over angels.

> In that God put all things in subjection to man, he left nothing unsubjected. It is a picture of a divinely instituted order in which man is sovereign over all creation. A few commentators see 'him' as referring in this place to Christ, to whom alone all things are rightly subjected. But grammatically there is no reason for this. The passage is describing the place of mankind in God's order, and we do not come to Christ's place until v.9. While there is a sense in which it is only Christ everything is subject to, there is another sense in which man has his rightful place of supremacy over the other created things. It is this latter sense that is in view here.[1]

### *Kingdom Secret: God is bringing many sons to glory.*
God used His Son to bring "many sons to glory" (Hebrews 2:10) by becoming their Savior, and He achieved this through much suffering. These will inherit not only the Kingdom, but its glory. Science today shows us the majestic beauty and complexity of nature, the vastness of the cosmos, the microscopic size of subatomic particles and we are blown away. Imagine what our reaction will be when the Creator reveals to us what He has in store for His Kingdom people! No wonder Paul said, "No eye has seen, no ear has heard, and no mind has imagined what God has prepared for those who love him" (1 Corinthians 2:9 - NLT).

### *Kingdom Secret: Older Brother and younger brothers share same Father.*
Jesus is both savior and sanctifier. He and the ones He sanctifies have the same Father, so "Jesus is not ashamed to call them brothers" (Hebrews 2:11 - HCSB; see John 20:17). A portion of the psalm that begins with the Lord's words on the cross is quoted in this passage. Jesus is saying "I will proclaim Your name to My brothers; I will sing hymns to You in the congregation" as well as "Here I am with the children God gave Me" (Psalm 22:22; Hebrews 2:12-13 - HCSB; read John 17:2,

6). While people ponder the meaning of life and wonder about their place in the grand scheme of things, God's Word says He is seeking "godly offspring" (Malachi 2:15 - NIV). He wants children who are set apart. He desires to bring many sons to glory. He plans to populate His Kingdom—with **us**!

## [UK] [GK] Hebrews 4 - Nothing hidden: The King sees all

***Kingdom Secret: The King sees all; all must give an account.***
"Nothing in all creation is hidden from God's sight. Everything is uncovered and laid bare before the eyes of him to whom we must give account" (Hebrews 4:13 - NIV). The Lord sees everything: every hidden thought, every warped motivation, every mischievous plan, every secretive action. This can be a scary thought. Or not. It can be a tremendous relief not to feel we have to hide something from God, because He already knows everything about us.

Knowing He sees all also helps us when we are being treated unfairly. We know God is just, that He sees what we are going through, and that at the right time, *His* time, He will deal with the injustice we are enduring. And there is the positive aspect of God's protection and desire to bless those who live out His **Kingdom Values**. "For the eyes of the Lord are on the righteous, and his ears are open to their prayer" (1 Peter 3:12a - ESV). He would be unable to do so if He did not see everything and have ultimate control.

## [GK] Hebrews 6, 7 - Jesus as High Priest and King of Righteousness

The Messiah is the Anointed One because He occupies the offices of priest, prophet and king. Regular priests are descendants of Aaron, himself a Levite. Messiah Jesus, on the other hand, is "a high priest forever in the order of Melchizedek" (Hebrews 6:20 - HCSB; see Genesis 14:1 and Psalm 110:4).

Now, Melchizedek was more than a priest. He was also a king. The Hebrew name Melchizedek is made up of two words: **Malki**, which signifies "king" and **tsedeq** which means "righteousness." And since He was the King of Salem (Jeru-Salem), which means peace, He is both the King of Righteousness and the King of Peace.

The author of Hebrews explains it this way: "For this Melchizedek—King of Salem, priest of the Most High God, who met Abraham and blessed him as he returned from defeating the kings, and Abraham gave him a tenth of everything; first, his name means king of righteousness, then also, king of Salem, meaning king of peace; without father, mother, or genealogy, having neither beginning of days nor end of life, but resembling the Son of God" (Hebrews 7:1-3 - HCSB).

## [GK] Hebrews 9 - Messiah establishes new and better covenant

Jesus wasn't just a special priest with a special connection back to Melchizedek. He was a "high priest, who sat down at the right hand of the throne of the Majesty in the heavens" (Hebrews 9:1 - NABRE). In this position, "Jesus has now obtained a superior ministry, and to that degree He is the mediator of a better covenant" (Hebrews 9:6 - NABRE).

The "better covenant" is the "new covenant," which God promised He would establish with Israel (Jeremiah 31:33). The earlier covenant had its shortcomings (Hebrews 9:7), possibly because it depended too much on human effort. It was limited because it was preparatory, laying the groundwork for the permanent and better covenant to be inaugurated by Messiah. It was during the last Passover meal that Jesus shared with His disciples: "This cup is the new covenant in my blood" (Luke 22:20 - NIV), "which is poured out for many for the forgiveness of sins" (Matthew 26:28 - NIV; see also Mark 14:24; 1 Corinthians 11:25).

This time God did not establish His covenant through a human representative. No, "Christ is the mediator of a new covenant" (Hebrews 9:15 - NIV). That is why it can decisively deal with our sin problem. In this covenant God promises: "For I will be merciful to their wrongdoing, and I will never again remember their sins" (Hebrews 9:12 - NABRE). The new covenant is superior because Jesus is superior. He is the perfect High Priest *and* Lamb without blemish, Who offered up His own blood so that He could be King over many.

## [KiG] Hebrews chapter 12 - Thankful for an unshakable Kingdom

On Thanksgiving Day my wife Monica and I joined our ministry colleagues in Rio de Janeiro, where we came together to share a meal and express our gratitude to the Lord. One of our colleagues reminded the rest of us that when Paul wrote the Romans about God's wrath towards human sin, even before he got to the list that shows the downward spiral of wickedness, he wrote: "For although they knew God, they neither glorified him as God nor gave thanks to him" (Romans 1:21a - ISV).

Ignoring God and demonstrating indifference while receiving His blessings is a sign of ingratitude. On an infinitely smaller scale, if you are a parent, have you ever sacrificed your budget, gone out of your way, or lavished one of your kids with special gifts, only to receive total silence in return? Gratitude is an important attitude. "Therefore, since we are receiving a kingdom that cannot be shaken, let us be thankful, and so worship God acceptably with reverence and awe, for our 'God is a consuming fire'" (Hebrews 12:28 - NIV).

God's Eternal Kingdom is unshakable because it is immune to the attacks of the enemy or the wear and tear of time. It is unshakable because there will never be a turnover in its leadership, as is the case with human governments and institutions. And it is unshakable because God cannot be defeated, deposed, or destroyed. What a privilege it is to belong to God's unshakable Kingdom! Thank You, Lord!

## [UK]-[EK] Hebrews 13 - Waiting for the heavenly city, our home

The unshakable Kingdom has an eternal capital city. Now we call it "heaven." One day we will know it as "the New Jerusalem" (Revelation 3:12; Revelation 21:2). What will it mean? No more tears. No more goodbyes. No more moving around from place to place or the sinking feeling that comes from missing family and friends. "Here we do not have a lasting city, but we are seeking the city which is to come" (Hebrews 13:14 - NASB). That nagging emptiness we often have is a sign that we crave a better world. We are longing for our eternal home where we will finally *feel* at home, in the Eternal Kingdom where our permanent residency and citizenship belong.

# The Kingdom in James

## [GK] James 1 - Enduring testing; rewarded with a crown of life

### The *pass the test, get the crown* Kingdom Principle

We just talked about receiving God's unshakable Kingdom and seeking the lasting city which is to come. But we're not there yet, so it's time for a reality check. What must we face while still here, before being transferred to our eternal home? We must be tested through trials and temptations. Life is a test: How are you doing?

You probably don't like being tested any more than going to the doctor and getting a shot. But remember: "God blesses those who patiently endure testing and temptation. Afterward they will receive the crown of life that God has promised to those who love him" (James 1:12 - NLT).

The crown of life is synonymous with eternal life. Jesus, in His glorified state, told the church members in Smyrna they were going to be tested. However, He said: "Be faithful until death, and I will give you the crown of life" (Revelation 2:10 - NKJV). If you pass your tests in life, God will reward you with the crown of life. Crowns are for champions! A promise was made to the overcomers in the church in Thyatira—to those who were faithful to the end: They would rule with Christ over the nations (Revelation 2:26-27).

**[GK] James 2 - Poor materially, rich in faith, heirs of Kingdom**

*Kingdom Secret*: **Poor in this world, rich in the next**
"Listen, my beloved brothers, has not God chosen those who are poor in the world to be rich in faith and heirs of the kingdom, which he has promised to those who love him?" (James 2:5 - ESV). I have seen a lot of poor people in my life, most of them in Brazil, where I grew up. They have a much easier time trusting in God than the wealthy, though one would think it would be quite the opposite.

It usually comes down to learning to depend on the Lord for survival. The rich must be careful not to fall into a false sense of security and independence. The poor, on the other hand, see the hard evidence of their need for God's help and His intervention on their behalf, on a daily basis. Plus, they are not usually well-connected. They rarely have friends they can count on. So they must depend on God. And that is a blessing in disguise. Because when they learn to place their trust in God, they become "rich in faith," which leads to inheriting the Kingdom.

# The Kingdom in 1st and 2nd Peter

**[GK] 1 Peter 2 - A chosen race, a royal priesthood, a holy nation; the rejected Stone becomes the Cornerstone**

### Chosen, a priesthood, a nation, a people, and a Kingdom
"But you are a chosen race, a royal priesthood, a holy nation, a people for his own possession, that you may proclaim the excellencies of him who called you out of darkness into his marvelous light" (1 Peter 2:9 - ESV). This passage is reminiscent of the promise God made to Israel, when He first mentioned the Kingdom and invited those who kept His covenant to be His treasured possession, a kingdom of priests and a holy nation (Exodus 19: 5, 6). Once again we are exposed to the concept of abandoning darkness and entering God's "marvelous light" (see Colossians 1:12-14 and "*Kingdom Secret: we've been transferred from the kingdom of darkness to the Kingdom of God's Son!*," above).

### Rejected Stone became Cornerstone of a building of living stones
Jesus, the Stone that humans rejected, was chosen and considered a precious Stone by God. The builders (Israel) may have rejected Him, but He became the Cornerstone of the spiritual house that is being built with living stones, which are His chosen people. But for those who do not wish to obey God's revelation, Jesus

has become a stumbling stone and an offensive rock. "They stumble because they disobey the word, as they were destined to do" (1 Peter 2:8b - ESV).

The cornerstone was the central piece and most important stone in a construction in Bible times. All other stones had to fit around the cornerstone. If they did not, they had to be chiseled and adapted, while the cornerstone remained intact, for it was the reference point for the whole building. Likewise, we are called to follow Jesus as our supreme standard and leader. If there is something that we don't agree with or isn't working, guess who needs to change: the Master or the disciple? The King or the subject? The Leader or the follower?

## [GK] [UK]-[EK] 2 Peter 1 - Preparing for the Eternal Kingdom

### The *living out Kingdom Values ["virtues"] leads to a rich welcome into the Eternal* Kingdom *Principle.*

A constant theme in the New Testament is our present struggle and need to be tested during our pilgrimage through the Global Kingdom (on Earth), while we await the time when we will be transferred to the Eternal Kingdom (heaven). The goal is to avoid sinning. The problem is that even born-again Christians still have a fallen human nature. This fallen nature naturally craves selfish pleasure, power, and popularity. The Bible calls this "the lust of the flesh, the lust of the eyes, and the pride in one's lifestyle" (1 John 2:16 - HCSB).

The question arises: How can we avoid following these evil desires? Peter reveals that all we need for godly living has already been provided and that we have been given promises that allow us to share in God's divine nature. With this we may "escape the world's corruption caused by human desires" (2 Peter 1:3-4 - NLT). Peter then teaches that we need to supplement our faith with "moral excellence ... self-control ... patient endurance ... godliness ... brotherly affection ... love for everyone" (2 Peter 1:5-7 - NLT), each step leading to the next. These virtues are **Kingdom Values** which result from righteousness. Failing to grow in this manner means we are "shortsighted or blind" and have forgotten that we have been cleansed from old sins (2 Peter 1:9 - NLT).

Lastly, Peter warns us to "make every effort to confirm" that God has called and chosen us (2 Peter 1:10), which we do by following the steps mentioned above. Then "you will receive a rich welcome into the eternal kingdom of our Lord and Savior Jesus Christ" (2 Peter 1:11 - NIV). While some will barely make it to heaven (1 Corinthians 3:15), how awesome it will be for those who arrive to a warm reception and receive a heartfelt welcome home!

## [EK] 2 Peter 3 - **New heaven and New Earth**

*Kingdom Secret: God will create a New Heaven and a New Earth.*
"We are waiting for new heavens and a new earth" (2 Peter 3:13 - ESV). They will not be duplicates, but substitutes. That's why the Bible speaks of the future destruction of the heavens and the Earth, which must come first. "Look up to the heavens, and look at the earth beneath; for the heavens will vanish like smoke, the earth will wear out like a garment, and its inhabitants will die like gnats. But My salvation will last forever, and My righteousness will never be shattered" (Isaiah 51:6 - HCSB). Jesus said, "Heaven and earth will disappear, but my words will never disappear" (Matthew 24:35 - ISV).

God's creation will suffer a demise and rebirth, while His salvation, righteousness and Word will firmly persist without a skipping a beat. Even during the time it will take to switch over from the old to the new, righteousness will continue to be the core value and standard of the Kingdom. And God's Word, which proclaims God's glory and His **Kingdom Values**, will never change or undergo reform. It is what it is. God never changes and neither do His word or His values.

The old heaven and Earth, in contrast, must be discarded so that the new may take its place. Earth will wear out as an old garment and must be switched out for the new, clean, and permanent, "a world filled with God's righteousness" (2 Peter 3:13 - NLT). Scripture speaks of the New Heaven and New Earth in 2 Peter 3:13 and three other passages.[2]

The fact that God will get rid of the old heaven and Earth demonstrates how devastating sin is to God's creation and how offensive it is to God. The creation of the New Heaven and New Earth prove just how profound God's love is for those He has brought into His Kingdom, via the redemptive work of His Son. The new creation also helps us to better understand His ultimate plan and eternal purpose for redeemed humanity.

# The Kingdom in 1st John

### [GK] 1 John 1 - Confession as a principle

### The *confession Kingdom Principle*
"If we confess our sins, He is faithful and just to forgive us our sins and cleanse us from all unrighteousness" (1 John 1:9 - MEV). I cannot remember who, but someone preached a good sermon on this passage and I wrote these notes in my Bible:
- *Tell God your sins;*
- *Turn from them;*

- *Trust* God to forgive you;
- *Deal* with them and move on.

This passage states a fundamental **Kingdom Principle** for dealing with the problem of unrighteousness. We are promised more than forgiveness. We are guaranteed we will be cleansed from all unrighteousness when we confess our sins to God. We are made righteous and once again placed in a favorable position before the Lord.

### [UK] [GK] 1 John 3 - Kingdom transformation

***Kingdom Secret**: We will become like Him.*
Through the years this has been one of my favorite verses: "See what kind of love the Father has given to us, that we should be called children of God; and so we are" (1 John 3:1a - ESV). We belong. We are cared for. We were created for fellowship with our Father. He loves us and is coming back for us. We don't know what we will become once we are transformed, but we know that we'll be like Him when we see Him as He really is (1 John 3:2).

We were created in His image and likeness, we share in His nature, and once He comes back, we will be like Him. Sin will be a thing of the past (no more evil inclinations or desires to struggle with); and righteousness and **Kingdom Values** will come "naturally" (now they must come "supernaturally"). We understand that here John is also speaking about the resurrection, the redemption of our bodies. We will see Him in His resurrected and glorified body and will, at that time, be given our own.

Because of this certain hope, we need to start—or continue—purifying ourselves... now!

# The Kingdom in the letter of Jude

### [UK] [GK] Jude 1 - Eternal punishment vs. sweet reunion

***Kingdom Secret**: Judgment, eternal fire, and blackest darkness forever reserved for unbelievers.*
The contrast in the Bible could not be starker. While God's loving arms are open to those who heed His warnings and accept the invitation to join His Kingdom, the door is shut closed to those who refuse to repent, believe and surrender. This

means that, in life, the stakes could not be higher—both for the winners and for the losers.

Jude compares stubborn unbelievers with fallen angels, Sodom and Gomorrah, several Old Testament villains, and "wandering stars, for whom the deepest darkness has been reserved forever" (Jude 13 - NRSV).

***Kingdom Secret:*** *Jesus is able to present you before God's glory without fault and with unspeakable joy.*
I was at *The Holy Land Experience, a* Bible-based theme park in Orlando. An actor was playing the role of Jesus, moving through the crowd, picking up little children and blessing them, standing up and saying some things Jesus had proclaimed to His audience. I got caught up in the moment, so when "Jesus" started coming in my direction I froze. I kind of shifted away and hid. He went elsewhere. I was relieved as somehow I felt unworthy. Part of my reaction is understandable since I am an introvert. Whatever the deeper causes of my strange reaction, Jude assures us there is no need to fear: The Lord can prepare us for this ultimate encounter with our Creator and Savior. It will be the sweetest of reunions. One our soul aches for. One we can hardly wait for.

"Now to him who is able to keep you from falling and to present you before his glory without fault and with unspeakable joy, to the only God, our saviour, be glory and majesty, power and authority, through Jesus Christ our Lord, before time was, now, and in all ages to come, amen" (Jude 1:24-25 - PHILLIPS).

While Scripture insists we must prepare for this appearing before Christ (1 John 3:3), it also clarifies the determining factor will be God's mercy and grace. Jude had just written: "Keep yourselves in the love of God while you are waiting for the mercy of our Lord Jesus Christ, which leads to eternal life" (Jude 1:21 - MEV). That's the perfect balance: Staying close to God and His love while we wait. Then, he describes the Lord's return as "the mercy of our Lord." Peter maintained the same balance between preparation on the one hand, and not depending on our performance but on God's grace, on the other. He said, "Therefore, with minds that are alert and fully sober, set your hope on the grace to be brought to you when Jesus Christ is revealed at his coming" (1 Peter 1:13 - NIV).

# Chapter 11

# The Revelation of Jesus Christ

## The Kingdom in Revelation

If Daniel is a Kingdom book, and Matthew is the Gospel of the Kingdom, then Revelation is the story of the final victory of God's Kingdom. Therefore, we could say Revelation's key verse is, "The kingdom of the world has become the kingdom of our Lord and of His Christ; and He will reign forever and ever" (Revelation 11:15b - NASB). All four aspects of the Kingdom are present in the pages of this cryptic book, from the Universal Kingdom, seen in God's sovereign control over all the spiritual and physical creation; to the horrible events on Earth, in the Global Kingdom; to the setting up of the Millennial Kingdom; followed by the Eternal Kingdom with its New Heaven and New Earth.

**[L&K] [GK] [MK] Revelation 1 - The Ruler of the kings of the earth; to the partners in the Kingdom**

John identifies Jesus as "the ruler of the kings of the earth" (Revelation 1:5 - HCSB), the One Who "made us a kingdom, priests to His God and Father," to Whom belong "the glory and dominion ... forever and ever" (Revelation 1:6 - HCSB). We have now come full circle because the first mention of the Kingdom of God, found in Exodus 19:5 and 6, speaks of a covenant people being God's special possession and becoming "My kingdom of priests and My holy nation" (HCSB). This has now been accomplished by "Him who loves us and has set us free from our sins by His blood" (Revelation 1:5 - HCSB).

The promise is made of Christ's return with the clouds, which will be seen by everybody everywhere, leading all peoples on Earth to mourn. This could only mean that when Jesus returns, many of those left here will be in a state of open rebellion and unbelief (Revelation 1:7).

John identifies himself as "your ... partner in the ... kingdom" (Revelation 1:9). He describes Jesus as "One like the Son of Man, dressed in a long robe and with a gold sash wrapped around His chest" (Revelation 1:13 - HCSB). The Son of Man is the One Who has authority to rule, possesses glory, and owns the Kingdom—the One Whose dominion will last forever (Daniel 7:13-14).

## [MK] Revelation 2 - Reigning with Christ

The promise of the risen Lord is striking: His faithful will reign with Him! Their influence in the world will no longer be limited to being salt and light. Power and authority will be delegated to them. The resurrected Lord promises the overcomer: "To him I will give power over the nations—'He shall rule them with a rod of iron; They shall be dashed to pieces like the potter's vessels,'" and be awarded the morning star (Revelation 2:26-28 - NKJV).

Ruling the nations with an iron rod or scepter is associated with Messiah's Millennial rule. If it were related to the Eternal Kingdom or state, would there be any need to dash the nations? Overcoming is **Kingdom Value #62.**[1]

## [L&K] [GK] Revelation 5 - The Lamb is worthy; made us kings and priests to reign on Earth

The Lamb is the only One worthy of opening the scroll presented in heaven, which represents the title deed to planet earth. The four living creatures and the twenty-four elders bowed before the Lamb and sang this new song: "You are worthy to take the scroll, and to open its seals; for You were slain, and have redeemed us to God by Your blood out of every tribe and tongue and people and nation, and have made us kings and priests to our God; and we shall reign on the earth" (Revelation 5:9-10 - NKJV).

John said he "heard the voices of thousands and millions of angels around the throne and of the living beings and the elders. And they sang in a mighty chorus" (Revelation 5:11-12 - NLT). They worshiped the Lamb, saying, "Blessing and honor and glory and power be to Him who sits on the throne, and to the Lamb, forever and ever!" (Revelation 5:13 - NKJV). The Lamb will reign for all eternity and those He redeemed will reign with Him on Earth.

## [GK] [MK] Revelation 11 - The kingdom of the world becomes the Kingdom of Messiah

An angel announces that "the kingdom of the world has become the kingdom of our Lord and of His Messiah, and He will reign forever and ever!" This is the central theme of this Revelation. Jesus is worthy, He has the authority, He is the rightful owner, and He has the power to take over the government of the Earth when the time comes. And when He does, it will be forever. It will start with a 1,000-year reign, but that will then extend throughout eternity.

The 24 elders who were seated on thrones worshiped God and thanked Him because He had taken His great power and had begun to reign. The nations were angry (see Psalm 2), but God's wrath had come and it was time to judge the dead and reward God's servants, and to destroy those who were destroying the earth (Revelation 11:15-18 - HCSB).

## [GK] Revelation 12 - Satan attacks Son Who will rule nations

A woman is seen who gives "birth to a son, a boy, who is to rule all the nations with an iron scepter," and Who "was snatched away and taken to God and to his throne." The woman flees to the desert seeking protection. A war breaks out in heaven and Michael and his army of angels fight the dragon, that is, the "ancient serpent, called the Devil and Satan, the deceiver of the whole world" and defeat them, hurling them down to Earth. Then a loud voice says, "Now the salvation, the power, the kingdom of our God, and the authority of his Messiah have come" (Revelation 12:5-10 - ISV). Satan tries to devour the Child, then goes after the woman and her descendants (Revelation 12:4, 13, 17). Satan ultimately fails and the Son, the Messiah, receives authority and begins ruling with an iron scepter, a code for the Millennial Kingdom.

## [KiG] Revelation 16 - The beast's throne plunged into darkness

"The fifth angel poured his bowl on the throne of the beast. Its kingdom was plunged into darkness. People gnawed on their tongues in anguish and cursed the God of heaven because of their pain-filled sores. But they did not repent of their behavior" (Revelation 16:10-11 - ISV). It is ironic that the kingdom of darkness was plunged into darkness.

Satan's kingdom is recognized in the Bible (Revelation 2:13). It is a parasite kingdom which feeds off of God's creation. Look at the Kingdom paradigm model of this study and see how the kingdom of darkness casts its long shadow over the Global Kingdom. It has been a stain on human history. Its purpose is the perdition of humanity and the exaltation of Satan over God and His Kingdom (Isaiah 14:12-14).

Notice that even after all the suffering, the world's population refuses to repent. Instead, they curse the Almighty.

## [L&K] Revelation 17 - Earthly kings receive authority, join the beast, battle the Lamb, fail miserably

Ten kings (seen as horns in the vision) receive authority, are in agreement with the beast (Antichrist), and together "these will make war with the Lamb, and the Lamb will conquer them, because he is Lord of lords and King of kings, and those with him are called and chosen and faithful" (Revelation 17:14 - LEB).

There is a consensus among God's enemies that leads them to join forces. They oppose the King and His Kingdom and one day will seek to make war with Him. They will be utterly defeated. This will take place in the battle of Armageddon, as seen in Revelation 19:17-21, when the beast and the false prophet will be captured and "thrown alive into the fiery lake of burning sulfur" (Revelation 19:20 - NIV).

## [L&K] [UK] Revelation 19 - God is in control; marriage supper; King of kings; Armageddon

The throne of God and of the Lamb is a reoccurring theme in Revelation (Revelation 5:6, 13; 6:16; 7:10, 17; 22:1, 3).

The atmosphere of God's headquarters is filled with the incense of praise and adoration; His throne room echoes with the sounds of worship. From there the Lord God Almighty commands everything everywhere. Nothing escapes His control. From there His plans are set in motion and no force can deter Him. God is sovereign. He is supreme. He is on His throne.

"And the twenty-four elders and the four living creatures fell down and worshiped God who was seated on the throne, saying, 'Amen. Hallelujah!' And from the throne came a voice saying, 'Praise our God, all you his servants, you who fear him, small and great'" (Revelation 19:4-5 - ESV).

## "Hallelujah! For the Lord our God the Almighty reigns;" the Marriage Supper of the Lamb

There are only four times the term "Hallelujah!" (meaning "praise God!") is used in the New Testament, and they all occur right here in Revelation 19. The first and second come from what sounded like a big multitude, which shouted, "Hallelujah! Salvation and glory and power belong to our God, for his judgments are true and just" (Revelation 19:1-3 - ESV). This, because the Lord had condemned the great prostitute (the false religious system), and avenged the blood of those she martyred.

The third "Hallelujah!" came from the 24 elders and four living creatures. The fourth "Hallelujah!" came from what sounded like a multitude, rushing water and peals of thunder, motivated by the fact that "the Lord our God the Almighty reigns" (Revelation 19:6 - ESV). And, because it was time to celebrate and give God glory for "the marriage of the Lamb" and "the marriage supper of the Lamb" which had come (Revelation 19:7, 9 - ESV). The Lamb's wife—specifically representing the Church and generically the saints of all ages—was prepared by wearing fine, bright and pure linen which "represents the righteous acts of the saints" (Revelation 19:7-8 - HCSB).

What a contrast between the prostitute, symbolizing the false world religion of the end-times, and the Bride of Christ, the true Church! In the last and most intense world crisis, loyalties are put to the test like never before, and it becomes clear who belongs to the beast and who belongs to the Lamb.

## King of kings rules with a rod of iron

While the war of Armageddon is raging on Earth, heaven opens up and the Rider of a white horse Who "judges and makes war in righteousness," and Who wears "on His thigh" the title "KING OF KINGS AND LORD OF LORDS," leads the charge against the beast, the false prophet and their followers. He comes with the armies of heaven, defeats His enemy with a verbal command ("a sharp sword came from His mouth"), brings "the fierce anger of God" related to the Day of the Lord to its conclusion, and will soon rule over the whole Earth "with an iron scepter," in His Millennial Kingdom (Revelation 19:13-16 - HCSB).

## [MK] Revelation 20 - The one thousand-year reign of Messiah

Nobody disputes that apocalyptic language is highly symbolic and numbers have special meanings. But isn't it interesting that "1,000 years" is repeated not twice, but a total of six times in the first seven verses of Revelation 20? All of these references are to the period when Satan will be bound, at the end of which he will be let loose, and during which Messiah will reign over the earth with the raised tribulation martyrs and all the others who will participate in the first resurrection (Revelation 20:4, 6). Because of the way it is presented in this chapter, it is highly likely that the 1,000 years refers to a literal amount of time.

Although these are the only references to the duration of the Millennial Kingdom (from where it gets its name), this third aspect of the Kingdom of God is also referred to as the Messianic Age or Messianic Kingdom. For a more thorough discussion on the subject, please refer to chapter 6, "The Millennial Kingdom," in **The Secret of the Kingdom of God**, first volume in this series. Suffice to say this will be a time of unprecedented prosperity, peace, goodwill among nations, great physical health and everything Earth was meant to be before the fall. Jesus will be physically reigning from Jerusalem, which will be the capital of the world, and multitudes will stream to the King's city to worship Him.

## [EK] Revelation 21 - New Heaven, New Earth, New Jerusalem

"Then I saw a new heaven and a new earth, for the first heaven and the first earth had passed away" and "the Holy City, new Jerusalem, coming down out of heaven from God" (Revelation 21:1-2 - HCSB). In the Lord's prayer, Jesus refers to God as "our Father in heaven" (Matthew 6:9). The word He used for heaven (*ouranos*), is the same used in "new heaven" in this passage. This would not be referring to our visible heavens or the universe in general, but to God's abode, the location of His throne. This is confirmed by the fact that John saw "the holy city, Jerusalem, coming down out of heaven from God" (Revelation 21:10 - NASB).

The creation of the new heaven and the new earth marks the beginning of the Eternal Kingdom proper. We may, in one sense, refer to heaven as belonging to the Eternal Kingdom aspect because of its eternal quality. However, technically the present or heaven belongs to the Universal Kingdom aspect.

Once the New Heaven, the New Earth, and the New Jerusalem are in place, their eternal status will never change, but will go on forever. From that moment forward, God will live among His people. There will never again be pain, death or sadness. These are things of the past—things to be forgotten. This will be a completely new beginning of a permanent state and a Kingdom with no end, as foreseen by the Old Testament prophets.

For more details concerning the New Heaven and New Earth, see chapter 7, on the Eternal Kingdom, in *The Secret of the Kingdom of God*, first volume in this series.

## [EK] Revelation 21, 22 - The New Jerusalem and the Eternal Kingdom

An angel invited John: "Come, I will show you the bride, the wife of the Lamb." Instead, and surprisingly, the angel showed John "the holy city, Jerusalem, coming down out of heaven from God" (Revelation 21:9-10 - HCSB). We can understand from this that the holy city is where God's people live. The Old Testament saints are represented by the fact that "the names of the 12 tribes of Israel's sons were inscribed on the gates." The New Testament saints, or the Church, are represented by the fact that "the 12 names of the Lamb's 12 apostles were on the foundations" (Revelation 21:12, 14 - HCSB).

The New Jerusalem is a beautiful megacity, displaying God's glory, shining like a multi-colored precious stone. John did not see a sanctuary in the city, "because the Lord God the Almighty and the Lamb are its sanctuary" (Revelation 21:22 - HCSB). Although it has massive high walls, its gates are always open and the whole city is illuminated by God's glory. "The nations will walk in its light, and the kings of the earth will bring their glory into it. Nothing profane will ever enter it: no one who does what is vile or false, but only those written in the Lamb's book of life" (Revelation 21:24, 27 - HCSB).

Inside of the city there is a river flowing from God and the Lamb's throne with the crystal clear water of life, reminiscent of the river of life in the Millennial Kingdom (Zechariah 14:8). "On each side of the river grew Trees of Life, bearing twelve crops of fruit, with a fresh crop each month; the leaves were used for medicine to heal the nations" (Revelation 22:2 - TLB). God's ideal (Ephesians 1:3-12), which He purposed from the beginning, is realized at last! Those made holy will be before the throne of God and of the Lamb "and his servants will worship him. And they shall see his face; and his name shall be written on their foreheads" and "they shall reign forever and ever" (Revelation 22: 3-5 - TLB).

**Yes, the Lamb wins in the end, but don't let your guard down just yet.**
Even after the Lamb's definitive victory over the beast and false prophet—even after the presentation of the Millennial Kingdom, the New Heaven and the New Earth—there is a warning. This has been a consistent pattern throughout the Kingdom highlights in New Testament: On the one side, the offering of God's grace, forgiveness, calling, and acceptance of His people. On the other, the warning not to take sin lightly and the list of consequences for those who want nothing to do with **Kingdom Values** and God's invitation.

In this passage we are told that Jesus will soon be coming back with His reward and we receive the reassurance that "those who wash their robes" are blessed and will be granted access into the Kingdom's capital city. On the other hand, "outside the city are the dogs—the sorcerers, the sexually immoral, the murderers, the idol worshipers, and all who love to live a lie" (Revelation 22:14, 15 - NLT). They are forever excluded from the Kingdom and from God's presence.

## Grace with the last word
But the Bible does not close on a gloomy note. How fitting that the last verse in the Bible wishes "the grace of the Lord Jesus be with God's holy people" (Revelation 22:21 - NLT), since grace is so central to the Good News of the Kingdom and is itself a **Kingdom Value**.[2]

# End Notes

**Acknowledgments**
1. https://www.bizjournals.com/orlando/stories/2002/01/14/newscolumn1.html; cited July 17, 2019
2. Ibid
3. http://christiannewswire.com/news/606909311.html; cited July 17, 2019

**Introduction**
1. See https://answersingenesis.org/the-word-of-god/3-unity-of-the-bible

**Chapter 1 – Books of the Pentateuch**

1. See *Rediscovering the Holy Spirit* by Michael Horton.

2. For a scholarly view on this subject, see *Reversing Hermon: Enoch, the Watchers & the Forgotten Mission of Jesus Christ*; Dr. Michael S. Heiser.

3. See "God Works through Kingdom Covenants" in Chapter 5, The Global Kingdom, of *The Secret of the Kingdom of God*, volume 1 in this series.

4. For more information, read *The Feasts of the Lord, God's Prophetic Calendar from Calvary to the Kingdom*, by Kevin Howard and Marvin Rosenthal, from Thomas Nelson publishers.

5. *The Temple: Its Ministry and Services*; by Alfred Edersheim, Hendrickson Publishers; by Hendrickson Publishers, Peabody, Massachusetts. All rights reserved ©1994; p. 231. Used by permission.

6. *The Expositor's Bible Commentary*; Ronald B. Allen; on Numbers 24:17; Zondervan Publishing House, 5300 Patterson Avenue SE, Grand Rapids, Michigan 49530; electronic version from CD.

**Chapter 2 – Books of History**

1. See Jericho, Israel on Google Earth and look over at the Jordan River, or go to https://earth.google.com/web/@31.83705485,35.5329287,-360.62511146a,16212.96586573d,35y,4.64736634h,0t,0r/data=ChUaEwoLL2cvMTIxNmY0M24YAiABKAI

2. Taken from *A Survey of the Old Testament* by Andrew E Hill and John H. Walton Copyright © 1991. p. 190. Use by permission of Zondervan. www.zondervan.com.

3. Notes from "The Kingdom within the Hebrew Bible;" by Dr. Brian Stephens; an unpublished study.

4. See more on the Davidic Covenant in *The Secret of the Kingdom of God*, volume one in this series, p.p. 112-116.

5. For the importance of righteousness in relation to the Kingdom, see Chapters 1 and 2 of *The Values of the Kingdom of God*, volume 2 in this series.

6. *Wycliffe Bible Dictionary;* by Charles F. Pfeiffer, Howard F. Vos, John Rea; Theocracy; copyright 1999 by Hendrickson Publishers, Peabody, Massachusetts. Used by permission. All rights reserved; p.1690.

**Chapter 3 – Books of Wisdom**

1. See Chapter 6 concerning "The Millennial Kingdom," in *The Secret of the Kingdom of God*, volume 1 of this series.

2. See more under "The Davidic Covenant in Psalm 89" in Chapter 5, "The Global Kindom," in *The Secret of the Kingdom of God*, volume one in this series.

3. *The Expositor's Bible Commentary*; Willem A. VanGemeren; Psalms; Zondervan Publishing House, 5300 Patterson Avenue SE, Grand Rapids, Michigan 49530; ISBN 0-310-2301-8; electronic version from CD.

*End Notes*

4. See "The Heavenly Council" in Chapter 4, "The Universal Kingdom," in *The Secret of the Kingdom of God*, volume 1 in this series.

5. *The Expositor's Bible Commentary*; Willem A. VanGemeren; Psalms; Zondervan Publishing House, 5300 Patterson Avenue SE, Grand Rapids, Michigan 49530, ISBN 0-310-2301-8; electronic version from CD.

6. www.statisticbrain.com/bibles-printed; Source: Gideon; Research Date: 4.28.2013.

7. Righteousness and *Kingdom Values* are extensively covered in *The Values of the Kingdom of God*, the second volume in this series

**Chapter 4 – Major Prophets**

1. See *The Values of the Kingdom*, volume two in this series.

2. Taken from *The MacArthur Study Bible* by John MacArthur Copyright © 1997 Word Publishing / John MacArthur. Used by permission of Thomas Nelson. www.thomasnelson.com.

3. http://en.wikipedia.org/wiki/Israel; cited December 14, 2019.

4. *Epicenter—Why the current rumblings in the Middle East Will Change your Future*; Joel C. Rosenberg; Tyndale; © 2006, 2008 p. 85.

5. *The Expositor's Bible Commentary* on Ezekiel 40; Ralph H. Alexander, author of the Ezekiel commentary; Zondervan Publishing House, 5300 Patterson Avenue SE, Grand Rapids, Michigan 49530; electronic version from CD.

6. Ibid

7. *A Survey of the Old Testament*; Andrew E. Hill and John H. Walton; Zondervan Publishing House, Grand Rapids, Michigan, 1991; p.p. 354-5.

8. Fox News online; https://www.foxnews.com/faith-values/isis-christian-burned-survived; cited October 15, 2019.

9. Ibid, p. 26

10. *The Expositor's Bible Commentary*; Frank E. Gaebelein, General Editor, J.D. Douglas, Associate Editor; Zondervan Publishing House, 5300 Patterson Avenue SE, Grand Rapids, Michigan 49530; electronic version from CD.

11. *The Coming Prince*; Sir Robert Anderson; p. 52; public domain

12. Ibid, p. 53

13. *Daniel's Prophecy of the 70 Weeks*; Dr. Alva J. McClain; BMH Books; ©2007 by BMH Books; Winona Lake, Indiana; www.bmhbooks.com; p. 25

14. Ibid, p. 26

15. *The Expositor's Bible Commentary*; Frank E. Gaebelein, General Editor, J.D. Douglas, Associate Editor; Zondervan Publishing House, 5300 Patterson Avenue SE, Grand Rapids, Michigan 49530; electronic version from CD; on Daniel 11.

16. Taken from *The MacArthur Study Bible* by John MacArthur Copyright © 1997 Word Publishing / John MacArthur. Used by permission of Thomas Nelson. www.thomasnelson.com.; Commentary on Daniel 11:36-45; p. 1248.

**Chapter 5 – Minor Prophets**

1. See "God Works through Kingdom Covenants," in Chapter 5 – "The Global Kingdom," in *The Secret of the Kingdom*, the first volume in this series.

2. September 1, 2014, Moody Publishers, moody.publishers@moody.edu

3. See Justice, Kindness, and Humility – **Kingdom Values** #65, #13 and #1 simultaneously, in *The Values of the Kingdom of God*, second volume in this series.

4. See Family Structure, **Kingdom Value #68**, in *The Values of the Kingdom*, the second volume in this series

**Chapter 6 – Matthew: The Gospel of the Kingdom**

1. *Thayer's Greek Lexicon*; from http://biblehub.com/greek/3097.htm; cited in September, 2014

2. See "Kingdom Access: How Do I Get in?," Chapter 3 of *The Secret of the Kingdom of God*, volume 1 in this series.

3. *The Expositor's Bible Commentary*; Frank E. Gaebelein, General Editor, J.D. Douglas, Associate Editor; on Matthew 4:3-4 and following; Zondervan Publishing House, 5300 Patterson Avenue SE, Grand Rapids, Michigan 49530; electronic version from CD.

4. Ibid.

5. Follow the Ribbi; Rabbi and Talmidim; from http://followtherabbi.com/guide/detail/rabbi-and-talmidim; cited on October 15, 2014.

6. See **Kingdom Values #1** through #8 in *The Values of the Kingdom of God*, second volume in this series.

7. https://www.lifesitenews.com/blogs/atheists-sound-the-alarm-decline-of-christianity-is-seriously-hurting-society.

8. Thayer's Greek Lexicon; http://biblehub.com/greek/4202.htm; cited October 18, 2014.

9. See "Seeking righteousness is priority number one" in Chapter 1 of *The Values of the Kingdom of God* – volume 2 of this series.

10. See more on this subject in "Kingdom Access: How Do I Get In?," Chapter 6 of The Secret of the Kingdom, volume 1 in this series.

11. *The Cost of Discipleship*; by Dietrich Bonhoeffer; from http://www.desiringgod.org/blog/posts/dietrich-bonhoeffer-was-hanged-today; cited November 3, 2014

12. *The New American Commentary*; Volume 22 - Matthew; By Craig L. Blomberg; © 1992 Broadman Press. Database ©2003 WORDsearch Corp.; online edition.

13. *The Feasts of the Lord, God's Prophetic Calendar from Calvary to the Kingdom*; Kevin Howard and Marvin Rosenthal; Thomas Nelson, Inc., 1997; Nashville, TN; p. 31.

14. Matthew 18:4 - HCSB; see "Faith like that of little children" in *The Secret of the Kingdom of God*, Chapter 3, "Kingdom Access: How Do I Get in?"

15. See "**Kingdom Value #43**: Prayer" in *The Values of the Kingdom of God*, volume 2 in this series.

16. See "**Kingdom Value #23**: Forgiving one another," in *The Values of the Kingdom of God*, volume 2 in this series.

17. For arguments on this position on the regeneration, see Chapter 6, "The Millennial Kingdom," under "The curse of nature will be lifted and there will be a renewal of all things on earth" in *The Secret of the Kingdom of God*, the first volume in this series.

18. "Service" and "Serving one Another" are **Kingdom Values**; see **Kingdom Values #22** and #30 in *The Values of the Kingdom of God*, volume 2 of this series.

19. *The Greatness of the Kingdom, An Inductive Study of the Kingdom of God*; by Alva J. McClain; BMH Books, Winona Lake, Indiana 46590; seventh printing, 1992; p. 345. Used by permission of the publisher.

20. *The New American Commentary*; Volume 22 - Matthew; By Craig L. Blomberg; © 1992 Broadman Press. Database ©2003 WORDsearch Corp.; online edition.

21. *The Bible Exposition Commentary*; New Testament, Volume 1; by Warren W. Wiersbe; © 2001 by Warren W. Wiersbe. Database © 2007 WORDsearch Corp. WORDsearch[CROSS].

### Chapter 7 – The Gospels of Mark, Luke and John

1. http://www.sharecare.com/health/healthy-hair-and-scalp/number-hair-head; cited December 23, 2019

2. See *www.worldometers.info/world-population* for a fascinating world population "clock," including births and deaths that occur during the day. Keeping tabs on all of those entering and exiting planet earth each second of the day—*that* is a lot to keep up with!

3. *God's War on Terror, Islam, Prophecy and the Bible*; by Walid Shoebat, with Joel Richardson; © 2008 Top Executive Media, 2012 version; e-book; pages 109, 110.

4. See *Kingdom Values* numbers **15, 21, 49, 55, 64** in *The Values of the Kingdom of God*, volume 2 in this series.

5. See "Kingdom Access: How Do I Get in?" which is Chapter 3 of *The Secret of the Kingdom of God*, volume 1 of this series.

6. See *Kingdom Value #1*, Humility, in Chapter 3 of *The Values of the Kingdom of God*, volume 2 of this series.

7. **HelpsBible.com**; © 1987, 2011 by Helps Ministries, Inc; http://biblehub.com/greek/2602.htm; cited March 18, 2014; in reference to Luke 16:16.

8. *The Greatness of the Kingdom*, *An Inductive Study of the Kingdom of God* by Alva J. McClain; © Copyright 1959. BMH Books, Winona Lake, Indiana 1992; p.p. 367-8. Used by permission of the publisher.

9. For more about the Kingdom in the Gospel of John, especially Chapters 5 through 17, see "The Son of God and the mirroring principle" in *The King of the Kingdom of God*, fourth and last volume in this series.

10. See Chapter 2, "What is the Kingdom of God?" and Chapter 3, "Kingdom Access: How Do I Get in?," in *The Secret of the Kingdom of God*, volume 1 in this series

11. Blaise Pascal, as quoted from powertochange.com/discover/faith/vacuum; cited December 29, 2019

12. https://blog.israelbiblicalstudies.com/jewish-studies/resurrection-lazarus-jewish-tradition-john-121-44/cited December 29, 2019.

13. *The Expositor's Bible Commentary*; The Gospel of John: Merrill C. Tenney; Th.B., Gordon College; A.M., Boston University; Ph.D. Harvard University; Zondervan Publishing House; electronic version from CD.

14. Ibid

15. See *Kingdom Value #30* in *The Values of the Kingdom of God*, volume 2 of this series.

16. A loose summary, based on *A Christian Love Story*; by Zola Levitt; 1978; Dallas, TX.

17. See *Kingdom Value #9* in *The Values of the Kingdom of God*, the second volume in this series.

18. *The Expositor's Bible Commentary*; The Gospel of John: Merrill C. Tenney; Th.B., Gordon College; A.M., Boston University; Ph.D. Harvard University; Zondervan Publishing House; electronic version from CD.

19. https://churchleaders.com/news/371359-what-does-the-bible-say-about-female-preachers.html. Cited February 26, 2020.

## Chapter 8 – History: Acts of the Apostles

1. *The Greatness of the Kingdom*, An Inductive Study of the Kingdom of God; by Alva J. McClain; BMH Books, Winona Lake, Indiana 46590; seventh printing, 1992; p. 405. Used by permission of the publisher.

2. See *The Values of the Kingdom of God*, volume 2 of this series.

3. See **Kingdom Value #8**, "Being Persecuted" and **Kingdom Value #57**, "Enduring Suffering," in *The Values of the Kingdom of God*, volume 2 in this series.

4. See **Kingdom Value #43** in *The Values of the Kingdom of God*, volume 2 of this series.

5. See **Kingdom Value #41** in *The Values of the Kingdom of God*, volume 2 in this series.

## Chapter 9 – The Letters of Paul

1. See "Kingdom Access: How Do I Get In?," which is Chapter 3 of *The Secret of the Kingdom of God*, volume 1 in this series.

2. https://www.christianity.com/church/church-history/timeline/1701-1800/william-careys-amazing-mission-11630319.html; cited January 16, 2020.

3. See "**Kingdom Values** – The Fruit of the Spirit" in Chapter 4 of *The Values of the Kingdom of God*, volume 2 in this series.

4. Strong's Greek 4776; https://biblehub.com/ephesians/2-6.htm.

5. A Commentary on Ephesians; Charles Hodge; Database © 2001 WORDsearch Corp.; electronic version; public domain.

6. *Heinrich August Wilhelm Meyer's NT Commentary*; Text Courtesy of BibleSupport.com; from the Bible Hub.

7. https://biblehub.com/greek/5251.htm; huperupsoó; cited January 16, 2020

8. *Holman Illustrated Bible Dictionary*; General Editor Trent C. Butler, PH.D.; Holman Bible Publishers, Nashville, Tennessee; 1991; RAPTURE; p. 1166. online version at www.mywsb.com.

9. Greek *harpagēsometha*; http://biblehub.com/greek/726.htm; HELPS Word-studies ; cited November 25, 2014.

## Chapter 10 – The General Letters

1. *The Expositor's Bible Commentary*; Frank E. Gaebelein, General Editor, J.D. Douglas, Associate Editor; Zondervan Publishing House; ISBN 0-310-2301-8; electronic version from CD.

2. Isaiah 65:17, Isaiah 66:2, and Revelation 21:1; see "The Eternal Kingdom" in Chapter 7, in *The Secret of the Kingdom of God*, first volume in this series.

## Chapter 11 – The Revelation of Jesus Christ

1. See *The Values of the Kingdom of God*, second volume in this series.

2. See **Kingdom Value #41** in *The Values of the Kingdom of God*, volume 2 of this series.

# About the Author

John Hatton has been a Bible teacher for over 40 years, teaching in English, Portuguese and Spanish, in the United States, Brazil and Chile. More recently, he taught at the *Instituto Bíblico Teológico* in Orlando, Florida, where he was the Director. He is presently one of the pastors at the *Primera Iglesia Bautista de Orlando*.

His parents, William Alvin and Lydia Catherine (Katie) Hatton, were missionaries to Brazil for 40 years, serving under the *International Mission Board* (*IMB*). They had four children: Lidia Dell, William (Bill), Sarah Janell and John.

John and his wife Monica joined the *IMB* and served for 23 years, living and ministering in El Paso, Texas; Hollywood, Florida; Santiago, Chile; and Rio de Janeiro, Brazil. For the last four years, John and Monica have served with *The Mailbox Club* as Area Coordinators for Brazil, where over 100,000 children are being reached, evangelized and discipled via weekly *Explorers* Bible Clubs.

John began writing *The Secret of the Kingdom of God* series over 20 years ago, first organizing relevant passages about the Kingdom, then commenting on them according to the pattern that emerged. The idea of categorizing the Kingdom under four distinct aspects naturally followed, being original with this author.

As a graphic designer and illustrator, John enjoys creating Bible charts and illustrating Bible characters, scenes and concepts. He has used his spiritual gift of teaching and natural talent of illustrating to better convey Bible truths.

John is the thankful husband of Monica, his wife of 42 years, the grateful father of Monique and Melissa, and the proud grandfather of Heidi Joy, Derek James and Asher Blue.

Photo by Melissa Hatton Smith

*The Highlights of the Kingdom of God*

# *The Secret of the Kingdom of God* Series

**The Secret of the Kingdom of God**
Volume 1 of this series.

Finally, a book about the Kingdom of God that brings all the different aspects together in one volume!

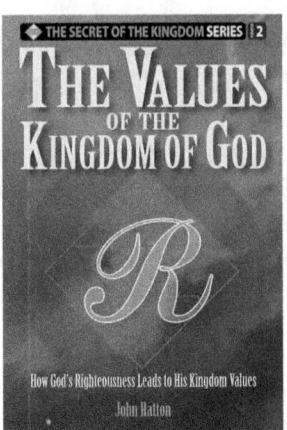

**The Values of the Kingdom of God**
Volume 2 of this series.

Discover why righteousness is so vital and study 70 **Kingdom Values** which reflect God's will for His people.

# COMING SOON!

Look for Volume 4 of *The Secret of the Kingdom* Series.

*The King of the Kingdom*
Volume 4 of this series.
This last volume of the series focuses on the identity, work and example of the Lord Jesus Christ as they relate to His Kingdom.

**www.kingdomsecret.org**

www.ingramcontent.com/pod-product-compliance
Lightning Source LLC
LaVergne TN
LVHW051041080426
835508LV00019B/1647